The
  Education of
Henry
  Adams

I

The Education of Henry Adams

An Autobiography

WITH A NEW INTRODUCTION
BY MARION L. STARKEY

TIME *Reading Program Special Edition*
TIME INCORPORATED, NEW YORK

TIME INC. BOOK DIVISION
EDITOR *Norman P. Ross*
COPY DIRECTOR *William Jay Gold*
ART DIRECTOR *Edward A. Hamilton*
CHIEF OF RESEARCH *Beatrice T. Dobie*
EDITOR, TIME READING PROGRAM *Max Gissen*
ASSISTANT EDITOR *Jerry Korn*
RESEARCHER *Ann S. Lang*
DESIGNER *Lore Levenberg*

PUBLISHER *Jerome S. Hardy*
GENERAL MANAGER *John A. Watters*

TIME MAGAZINE
EDITOR *Roy Alexander*
MANAGING EDITOR *Otto Fuerbringer*
PUBLISHER *Bernhard M. Auer*

COVER DESIGN *Hank Brennan*

Contents

Editors' Preface

Henry Adams in 1906, the year he devoted to writing *The Education of Henry Adams*, was a slight, bearded, solitary man of 68, possessing a fortune of a little less than a million dollars, living quietly in his home on Lafayette Square in Washington. He was on terms of good-natured raillery with his old friend Theodore Roosevelt, who lived in the White House across the Square. He rose early and spent much of the morning writing letters in a fine hand that resembled copperplate engraving. In the afternoon he walked briefly for exercise, wearing a top hat and a loose-fitting sack coat. Justice Oliver Wendell Holmes, another old friend, wrote that he enjoyed meeting Adams on his walks but did not like to visit him at home. The trouble with Adams at home was that he fancied himself as a power behind the scenes, formulating policy and advising statesmen. "When I happened to fall in with him on the street he could be delightful," Holmes wrote, "but when I called at his house and he was posing to himself as the old cardinal he would turn everything to dust and ashes."

During the summer he lived in a small apartment, up six flights of stairs, on the Bois de Boulogne in Paris. There too he wrote his letters, about the latest political gossip, or about the San Francisco earthquake, or about education in Russia. In all his many letters, with all their enormous range of subject, he never mentioned that he was writing *The Education of Henry Adams*. One biographer, Harold Dean Cater, has concluded that Adams never spoke of the book, or referred to it in any way, during the entire period that he worked on it. His older brother, Charles Francis Adams, first heard of *The Education of Henry Adams* in February 1907 when the author sent him one of the first copies: he had printed the book privately in an edition of only 40 copies and asked that Charles glance through it to note anything objectionable so that it could be corrected if a regularly published edition was ever prepared. Similar letters went to President Eliot of Harvard and to President Roosevelt and Senator Henry Cabot Lodge. The notes that he enclosed with the book were forbidding in their detachment. A typical one read: "The volume as it stands is merely a proof sent out for revision to persons interested. . . . Unless I attain my object—revision—I shall be at a great loss to know what next to do with the book—unless to throw it into the fire." Almost everyone kept his copy, and the reputation of the book spread so swiftly that Adams had to print more copies, a hundred in all, or risk offending old friends not included among the first 40. Roosevelt not only refused to make changes; he would not give back his copy on any terms.

The choppy arrangement of the last chapters of the book suggests that Adams indeed considered it a rough draft. He answered a letter of praise from William James by sending James a copy of his *Mont-Saint-Michel and Chartres*, calling attention to the quality of the last chapters of that book as compared with the unsatisfactory ending of the *Education*.

It is possible that the *Education* was preserved only because of the earlier book. Adams first printed *Mont-Saint-Michel and Chartres* in an edition of 150. As with the *Education*, he had sent copies only to experts whose advice he needed; he was venturing into a field of medieval architecture that was new to him, and he feared that advance criticism of authorities might blight his enthusiasm before he could state his case. But this small edition of *Mont-Saint-Michel and Chartres* became so celebrated that Adams was forced to copyright it and eventually to publish it. Its popularity softened his determination not to permit the *Education* to appear. Preparing a preface to be signed by Henry Cabot Lodge (he contrived with Lodge, somewhat to Lodge's bewilderment, to write the preface in Lodge's name), he arranged to have it published after his death. He died on March 27, 1918, and the *Education* appeared that fall. It was immediately recognized as one of the strangest and most truly original of American literary classics.

The Education of Henry Adams ranks among the great autobiographical works of all time. The *Education* was the more compelling because of the lack of a strong autobiographical tradition in American writing: the Adams book was not only the first American autobiography to belong with the major works of its kind in the literature of the Old World; it was also the first major American work to be written in the probing, introspective, intensely subjective spirit that has come to be considered representative of modern literature. As such its influence has been incalculable, and its publication marked a dividing line between two epochs in the intellectual life of the country.

Yet it remains a curious book. For example, Adams'
biographers have noted much that he left out of the
Education. He mentioned that a Professor Gurney was
responsible for his appointment to the history faculty at
Harvard, but he did not add that Gurney was married
to Ellen Hooper, his wife's sister. Adams barely touched
on the reports he sent to American newspapers from
London during the Civil War, implying that they were
no more than brief letters. In fact he published 23 articles
in *The New York Times* in 1861 alone. Most note-
worthy, as historian-author Marion L. Starkey points
out in her new introduction to this special edition,
Adams left out of the *Education* all references to his
own marriage.

His wedding to Marian Hooper took place in 1872
and lasted 13 years. "Clover," as he called her, was an
attractive woman, an unforgettable personality with a
gay common sense, a natural literary style and an easy
humor. It was while he was married to her that Adams
wrote most of the nine volumes of his great history of
the Administrations of Jefferson and Madison, his bi-
ographies of Albert Gallatin and John Randolph, and
the biography of Aaron Burr that he destroyed when
his publisher rejected it. It was then, also, that he wrote
his two novels, *Democracy*, published anonymously in
1880, and *Esther*, for which his wife served as the model.
There was no mistaking the happiness and the creative
energy of his married life; as he wrote to a friend in
1878, "It is like a dream of the golden age."

On December 7, 1885, a Washington newspaper reported that Adams had found his wife lying dead on the
floor of their house; the coroner's certificate said she had
come to her death through a self-administered dose of
potassium cyanide. Adams' life was shattered—and the

pattern of the *Education*, too, was shattered when Adams approached this part of his story. It is in the main a detailed autobiographical study, with a firmly identified cast of characters and a rambling but steady narrative. The chapters dealing with the diplomatic struggle in London during the Civil War are not only the standard account of that crucial episode in the history of the world; they are also a classic passage in the literature of diplomacy. The book carries the story of Adams' life forward as far as the year 1872, the year of his marriage. Then one turns the page and meets a new chapter heading: "Twenty Years After," followed by the date 1892.

For 30 years after her death, Adams never again spoke of his wife. For several years he traveled almost constantly. Whether traveling or at home he wrote his letters regularly, always keeping a good supply of fine note paper handy. Although the letters never mention the autobiography, they do touch frequently on a theme stated and restated in it: the catastrophe that seemed to threaten the modern world because power—steam power and electric power and power of every sort—had outrun human intelligence. "Our power is always running ahead of our mind," he wrote. He could not see that the modern world possessed any greater intellectual power than had been evident when he was a young antislavery idealist—"though it showed precious little then." But he was not without hope. It was possible that human society based on mechanical power could be made conscious of that power—of its complexity, of its hazards and even of its potential. "To me, the whole lesson lies in this experiment. Can our society double up its mind-capacity? It must do it or die; and I see no reason why it may not widen its consciousness of complex conditions far enough to escape wreck." That was written while

he was working on *The Education of Henry Adams*,
and his book became a major contribution in deepen-
ing the modern world's consciousness of its own complexity.

—THE EDITORS OF TIME

Introduction

From childhood Henry Adams knew that his family had already produced two Presidents. When the boy was taken on his first visit to the White House he inspected it with the proprietary eye of one who might be presently moving in. But the Adams lease on the White House had expired a decade before Henry was born. His father, Charles Francis—who started on the classic Adams route to the Presidency through diplomacy and whose work as American Minister to London in the desperate days of the Civil War was as influential as any diplomatic achievement of his grandfather, John, or his father, John Quincy—never made it. And Henry, who had ingested political knowledge with his porridge, who was all his life to be the intimate of statesmen, was never to hold office of any kind. "He never got to the point of playing the game at all," he says of himself in *The Education of Henry Adams*; "he lost himself in the study of it, watching the errors of the players." And this is remarkable in a man so richly endowed with the Adams genius.

What he seemed to lack was drive. The deficiency may have originated in an early attack of scarlet fever that stunted his growth. As a result he was "not good in a fight and his nerves were more delicate than boys' nerves ought to be." He may have been inhibited by the sheer eminence of his heritage. Or perhaps it was the quenching of one furious surge to action that he experienced after the Union disaster of Second Bull Run in the Civil War. His friends were dying in Virginia while he was in London copying documents. He paced the floor all one night and at breakfast told his parents that he was going to join the army in Virginia, "where he would have only bullets to wound him." He was then serving in his nearest approach to public office, as private secretary to his father. The latter, absorbed in the delicate task of preventing the British from recognizing the Confederacy, did not want him to leave, unofficial and "unattached" though his position was. It may have been the suppression of this honest instinct to act that later condemned Henry to the role of wry observer. As pressures subsided in London, he indulged in that dilettantism which was to characterize him in all fields but one.

Even so, when he went home in 1868 he still craved action. He made for Washington determined to become a political writer dedicated to reform. He soon found his way to the White House, as any Adams would, and one look at President Ulysses S. Grant stopped him in his tracks. "A great soldier might be a baby politician," he said; Grant as President "should have been extinct for ages" because his election "made evolution ludicrous."

Without a leader to follow, Adams drifted. He made the most of the capital's social life: "Adams found himself a young duke in Washington." He did some political pieces, eventually achieving the distinction of

being denounced by a senator as a "begonia," an epithet
he cherished for its oddity. Drift brought him back
to New England to serve seven reluctant years as assistant professor of history at Harvard; his performance
was superb, but it didn't satisfy. Even for an Adams-
without-portfolio, Washington was home. He went back
and completed among other works his nine-volume "scientific" history of the Administrations of Jefferson and
Madison. With mathematical precision and perhaps for
psychological reasons, it covers just those years when
the Adams family was least prominent. Historians consider it a masterpiece—and few but historians read it.

Not until old age did Henry Adams compose the two
works which would bring him enduring fame in the
popular sense. One, a kind of inspired guidebook to the
cathedrals of France, is *Mont-Saint-Michel and Chartres;*
the other was *The Education of Henry Adams.*

Librarians classify the *Education* as autobiography;
Adams would take umbrage at their doing so. Autobiographical it is, of course, but in Adams' mind he drew
on his personal experience only as an artist might insert
a self-portrait in a massive panorama. He composed it
in the third person, a mannerism that annoys a reader
unwilling to accept the author's austere purpose. And
though he reports much of his life with something like
total recall, he makes extraordinary omissions.

Any reader whose first acquaintance with Adams is
the *Education* is bound to be baffled by Chapter 21,
"Twenty Years After," and is entitled to an explanation.
Why has Adams elided two decades of middle life,
which were among his most productive? Why, just as
he has built himself a permanent Washington home, does
the man take to wandering the South Seas? Why on his
return does he spend contemplative hours before a
bronze statue in Rock Creek Cemetery which his friend

Augustus Saint-Gaudens had created for him in his absence?

Adams has veiled from the reader the central event of his life: his 13 years of happy marriage and the irremediable trauma of their ending, in the death of his wife Marian by her own hand. The hooded figure looking gravely into the infinite in his memorial to her. It bears no inscription.

A year before this tragedy Adams had written in his "heart's blood" and published, as privately as publication could be, his novel *Esther*, which was a fictionalized portrait of his wife. The *Education* does not even name her; one would suppose he had never married. Though he could write directly of his grief at the death of his sister, references to the loss of his wife are rare and oblique. In the *Education*: "He knew no tragedy so heartrending as introspection." In *Chartres*: "People who suffer beyond the formulas of expression—who are crushed into silence, and beyond pain—want no display of emotion—no bleeding heart—no weeping at the foot of the Cross—no hysterics—no phrases! They want to see God, and to know that He is watching over His own." The very dashes are eloquent.

Fortunately, Henry had the Adams toughness of fiber, and no Adams was suicide-prone. The later Adams, author of the *Education*, was like a gnarled old tree mutilated by storm, yet of such sound stock that it could achieve a late flowering, a ripe fruition. His lonely old age was fruitful—and sometimes happy.

During summers in Europe he often lived as within Proust's budding grove in the company of "nieces"— some blood relatives, some merely friends—who were the delight of his old age (he had no children). In his fifties he learned to ride a bicycle; in his sixties he mastered that alarming contraption, the automobile, to conduct the nieces on his incessant pilgrimages to the cathedrals of France. To them he dedicated a volume conceived in the sunniest of humors, his *Mont-Saint-Michel and Chartres*. And this led to the more somber work, the *Education*.

The chief quality of this book lies in its essential humanity, in what one may risk calling its underlying passion, the more powerful because it is always reined in, muted in irony. Little as Adams fancied himself as an autobiographer, his Boston-Quincy childhood is presented with irrepressible charm. So in its different way is his portrait of the perplexed young private secretary in London when all England seemed resolved to prevent an Adams from preserving the young republic which an Adams had helped create. All his young hatred of the British ruling class, from the dowdiness of its dowagers to the perfidy of its statesmen, surges into the record, though the "scientific" elder historian carefully qualifies its expression.

When *The Education of Henry Adams* became generally available to Americans, in 1918, they swiftly sent it to the top of the bestseller list. Would Adams have liked that? Better not to put impertinent questions to a shade of such gentlemanly reserve. Let us say that the man who relished being denounced as a "begonia"—and who was gratified when a recondite piece of his was pirated, as proof that he was being read—would have liked it very much indeed.

—MARION L. STARKEY

Editor's Preface to the 1918 Edition

This volume, written in 1905 as a sequel to the same author's "Mont-Saint-Michel and Chartres," was privately printed, to the number of one hundred copies, in 1906, and sent to the persons interested, for their assent, correction, or suggestion. The idea of the two books was thus explained at the end of Chapter 29:—

"Any schoolboy could see that man as a force must be measured by motion from a fixed point. Psychology helped here by suggesting a unit—the point of history when man held the highest idea of himself as a unit in a unified universe. Eight or ten years of study had led Adams to think he might use the century 1150–1250, expressed in Amiens Cathedral and the Works of Thomas Aquinas, as the unit from which he might measure motion down to his own time, without assuming anything as true or untrue, except relation. The movement might be studied at once in philosophy and mechanics. Setting himself to the task, he began a volume which he mentally knew as 'Mont-Saint-Michel and Chartres: A Study of Thirteenth-Century Unity.' From that point he proposed to fix a position for himself, which he could label: 'The Education of Henry Adams: A Study of Twentieth-Century Multiplicity.' With the help of these two points of relation, he hoped to project his lines forward and backward indefinitely, subject to correction from any one who should know better."

The "Chartres" was finished and privately printed in 1904. The "Education" proved to be more difficult. The point on which the author failed to please himself, and could get no light from readers or friends, was the usual one of literary form. Probably he saw it in advance, for he used to say, half in jest, that his great ambition was to complete St. Augustine's "Confessions," but that St. Augustine, like a great artist, had worked from multiplicity to unity, while he, like a small one, had to reverse the method and work back from unity to multiplicity. The scheme became unmanageable as he approached his end.

Probably he was, in fact, trying only to work into it his favorite theory of history, which now fills the last three or four chapters of the "Education," and he could not satisfy himself with his workmanship. At all events, he was still pondering over the problem in 1910, when he tried to deal with it in another way which might be more intelligible to students. He printed a small volume called "A Letter to American Teachers," which he sent to his associates in the American Historical Association, hoping to provoke some response. Before he could satisfy himself even on this minor point, a severe illness in the spring of 1912 put an end to his literary activity forever.

The matter soon passed beyond his control. In 1913 the Institute of Architects published the "Mont-Saint-Michel and Chartres." Already the "Education" had become almost as well known as the "Chartres," and was freely quoted by every book whose author requested it. The author could no longer withdraw either volume; he could no longer rewrite either, and he could not publish that which he thought unprepared and unfinished, although in his opinion the other was historically purposeless without its sequel. In the end, he preferred to leave the "Education" unpublished, avowedly incomplete, trusting that it might quietly fade from memory. According to his theory of history as explained in Chapters 33 and 34, the teacher was at best helpless, and, in the immediate future, silence next to good-temper was the mark of sense. After midsummer, 1914, the rule was made absolute.

The Massachusetts Historical Society now publishes the "Education" as it was printed in 1907, with only such marginal corrections as the author made, and it does this, not in opposition to the author's judgment, but only to put both volumes equally within reach of students who have occasion to consult them.

September, 1918   —HENRY CABOT LODGE

Author's Preface

Jean Jacques Rousseau began his famous "Confessions" by a vehement appeal to the Deity: "I have shown myself as I was; contemptible and vile when I was so; good, generous, sublime when I was so; I have unveiled my interior such as Thou thyself hast seen it, Eternal Father! Collect about me the innumerable swarm of my fellows; let them hear my confessions; let them groan at my unworthiness; let them blush at my meannesses! Let each of them discover his heart in his turn at the foot of Thy throne with the same sincerity; and then let any one of them tell Thee if he dares: 'I was a better man!' "

Jean Jacques was a very great educator in the manner of the eighteenth century, and has been commonly thought to have had more influence than any other teacher of his time; but his peculiar method of improving human nature has not been universally admired. Most educators of the nineteenth century have declined to show themselves before their scholars as objects more vile or contemptible than necessary, and even the humblest teacher hides, if possible, the faults with which nature has generously embellished us all, as it did Jean Jacques, thinking, as most religious minds are apt to do, that the Eternal Father himself may not feel unmixed pleasure at our thrusting under his eyes chiefly the least agreeable details of his creation.

As an infortunate result the twentieth century finds few recent guides to avoid, or to follow. American literature offers scarcely one working model for high education. The student must go back, beyond Jean Jacques, to Benjamin Franklin, to find a model even of self-teaching. Except in the abandoned sphere of the dead languages, no one has discussed what part of education has, in his personal experience, turned out to be useful, and what not. This volume attempts to discuss it.

As educator, Jean Jacques was, in one respect, easily first; he erected a monument of warning against the Ego. Since his time, and largely thanks to him, the Ego has steadily tended to efface itself, and, for purposes of model, to become a manikin on which the toilet of education is to be draped in order to show the fit or misfit of the clothes. The object of study is the garment, not the figure. The tailor adapts the manikin as well as the clothes to his patron's wants. The tailor's object, in this volume, is to fit young men, in universities or elsewhere, to be men of the world, equipped for any emergency; and the garment offered to them is meant to show the faults of the patchwork fitted on their fathers.

At the utmost, the active-minded young man should ask of his teacher only mastery of his tools. The young man himself, the subject of education, is a certain form of energy; the object to be gained is economy of his force; the training is partly the clearing away of obstacles, partly the direct application of effort. Once acquired, the tools and models may be thrown away.

The manikin, therefore, has the same value as any other

geometrical figure of three or more dimensions, which is used for the study of relation. For that purpose it cannot be spared; it is the only measure of motion, of proportion, of human condition; it must have the air of reality; must be taken for real; must be treated as though it had life. Who knows? Possibly it had!

February 16, 1907 —HENRY ADAMS

1

Quincy

(1838–1848)

Under the shadow of Boston State House, turning its back on the house of John Hancock, the little passage called Hancock Avenue runs, or ran, from Beacon Street, skirting the State House grounds, to Mount Vernon Street, on the summit of Beacon Hill; and there, in the third house below Mount Vernon Place, February 16, 1838, a child was born, and christened later by his uncle, the minister of the First Church after the tenets of Boston Unitarianism, as Henry Brooks Adams.

Had he been born in Jerusalem under the shadow of the Temple and circumcised in the Synagogue by his uncle the high priest, under the name of Israel Cohen, he would scarcely have been more distinctly branded, and not much more heavily handicapped in the races of the coming century, in running for such stakes as the century was to offer; but, on the other hand, the ordinary traveller, who does not enter the field of racing, finds advantage in being, so to speak, ticketed through life, with the safeguards of an old, established traffic. Safeguards are often irksome, but sometimes convenient, and if one needs them at all, one is apt to need them badly. A hundred years earlier, such safeguards as his would have secured any young man's success; and although in 1838 their value was not very great compared with what they would have had in 1738, yet the mere accident of starting a twentieth-century career from a nest of associations so colonial — so troglodytic — as the First Church, the Boston State House, Beacon Hill, John Hancock and John Adams, Mount Vernon Street and Quincy, all crowding on ten pounds of unconscious babyhood, was so queer as to offer a subject of curious speculation to the baby long after he had witnessed the solution. What could become of such a child of the seventeenth and eighteenth centuries, when he should wake up to find himself required to play the game of the twentieth? Had he been consulted, would he have cared to play the game at all, holding such cards as he held, and suspecting that the game was to be one of which neither he nor any one else back to the beginning of time knew the rules or the risks or the stakes? He was not consulted and was not responsible, but had he been taken into the confidence of his parents, he would certainly have told them to change nothing as far as concerned him. He would have been astounded by his own luck. Probably no child, born in the year, held better cards than he. Whether life was an honest game of chance, or whether the cards were marked and forced, he could not refuse to play his excellent hand. He could never make the usual plea of irresponsibility. He accepted the situation as though he had been a party to it, and under the same circumstances would do it again, the more readily for knowing the exact values. To his life as a whole he was a consenting, contracting party and partner from the moment he was born to the moment he died. Only with that understanding — as a consciously assenting member in full partnership with the society of his age — had his education an interest to himself or to others.

As it happened, he never got to the point of playing the game at all; he lost himself in the study of it, watching the errors of the players; but this is the only interest in the story, which otherwise has no moral and little incident. A story of education — seventy years of it — the practical value remains to the end in doubt, like other values about which men have disputed since the birth of Cain and Abel; but the practical value of the universe has never been stated in dollars. Although every one cannot be a Gargantua-Napoleon-Bismarck and walk off with the great bells of Notre Dame, every one must bear his own universe, and most persons are moderately interested in learning how their neighbors have managed to carry theirs.

This problem of education, started in 1838, went on for three years, while the baby grew, like other babies, unconsciously, as a vegetable, the outside world working as it never had worked before, to get his new universe ready for him. Often in old age he puzzled over the question whether, on the doctrine of chances, he was at liberty to accept himself or his world as an accident. No such accident had ever happened before in human experience. For him, alone, the old universe was thrown into the ash-heap and a new one created. He and his eighteenth-century, troglodytic Boston were suddenly cut apart — separated forever — in act if not in sentiment, by the opening of the Boston and Albany Railroad; the appearance of the first Cunard steamers in the bay; and the telegraphic messages which carried from Baltimore to Washington the news that Henry Clay and James K. Polk were nominated for the Presidency. This was in May, 1844; he was six years old; his new world was ready for use, and only fragments of the old met his eyes.

Of all this that was being done to complicate his education, he knew only the color of yellow. He first found himself sitting on a yellow kitchen floor in strong sunlight. He was three years old when he took this earliest step in education; a lesson of color. The second followed soon; a

lesson of taste. On December 3, 1841, he developed scarlet
fever. For several days he was as good as dead, reviving
only under the careful nursing of his family. When he
began to recover strength, about January 1, 1842, his
hunger must have been stronger than any other pleasure
or pain, for while in after life he retained not the faintest
recollection of his illness, he remembered quite clearly
his aunt entering the sick-room bearing in her hand a
saucer with a baked apple.

The order of impressions retained by memory might
naturally be that of color and taste, although one would
rather suppose that the sense of pain would be first to educate. In fact, the third recollection of the child was that
of discomfort. The moment he could be removed, he was
bundled up in blankets and carried from the little house
in Hancock Avenue to a larger one which his parents were
to occupy for the rest of their lives in the neighboring
Mount Vernon Street. The season was midwinter, January 10, 1842, and he never forgot his acute distress for
want of air under his blankets, or the noises of moving
furniture.

As a means of variation from a normal type, sickness
in childhood ought to have a certain value not to be
classed under any fitness or unfitness of natural selection;
and especially scarlet fever affected boys seriously, both
physically and in character, though they might through
life puzzle themselves to decide whether it had fitted or
unfitted them for success; but this fever of Henry Adams
took greater and greater importance in his eyes, from the
point of view of education, the longer he lived. At first,
the effect was physical. He fell behind his brothers two
or three inches in height, and proportionally in bone and
weight. His character and processes of mind seemed to
share in this fining-down process of scale. He was not
good in a fight, and his nerves were more delicate than

boys' nerves ought to be. He exaggerated these weaknesses as he grew older. The habit of doubt; of distrusting his own judgment and of totally rejecting the judgment of the world; the tendency to regard every question as open; the hesitation to act except as a choice of evils; the shirking of responsibility; the love of line, form, quality; the horror of ennui; the passion for companionship and the antipathy to society — all these are well-known qualities of New England character in no way peculiar to individuals but in this instance they seemed to be stimulated by the fever, and Henry Adams could never make up his mind whether, on the whole, the change of character was morbid or healthy, good or bad for his purpose. His brothers were the type; he was the variation.

As far as the boy knew, the sickness did not affect him at all, and he grew up in excellent health, bodily and mental, taking life as it was given; accepting its local standards without a difficulty, and enjoying much of it as keenly as any other boy of his age. He seemed to himself quite normal, and his companions seemed always to think him so. Whatever was peculiar about him was education, not character, and came to him, directly and indirectly, as the result of that eighteenth-century inheritance which he took with his name.

The atmosphere of education in which he lived was colonial, revolutionary, almost Cromwellian, as though he was steeped, from his greatest grandmother's birth, in the odor of political crime. Resistance to something was the law of New England nature; the boy looked out on the world with the instinct of resistance; for numberless generations his predecessors had viewed the world chiefly as a thing to be reformed, filled with evil forces to be abolished, and they saw no reason to suppose that they had wholly succeeded in the abolition; the duty was unchanged. That duty implied not only resistance to evil,

but hatred of it. Boys naturally look on all force as an
enemy, and generally find it so, but the New Englander,
whether boy or man, in his long struggle with a stingy or
hostile universe, had learned also to love the pleasure of
hating; his joys were few.

Politics, as a practice, whatever its professions, had always been the systematic organization of hatreds, and
Massachusetts politics had been as harsh as the climate.
The chief charm of New England was harshness of contrasts and extremes of sensibility — a cold that froze the
blood, and a heat that boiled it — so that the pleasure of
hating — one's self if no better victim offered — was not its
rarest amusement; but the charm was a true and natural
child of the soil, not a cultivated weed of the ancients.
The violence of the contrast was real and made the strongest motive of education. The double exterior nature gave
life its relative values. Winter and summer, cold and heat,
town and country, force and freedom, marked two modes
of life and thought, balanced like lobes of the brain. Town
was winter confinement, school, rule, discipline; straight,
gloomy streets, piled with six feet of snow in the middle;
frosts that made the snow sing under wheels or runners;
thaws when the streets became dangerous to cross; society of uncles, aunts, and cousins who expected children
to behave themselves, and who were not always gratified;
above all else, winter represented the desire to escape and
go free. Town was restraint, law, unity. Country, only
seven miles away, was liberty, diversity, outlawry, the
endless delight of mere sense impressions given by nature
for nothing, and breathed by boys without knowing it.

Boys are wild animals, rich in the treasures of sense, but
the New England boy had a wider range of emotions
than boys of more equable climates. He felt his nature
crudely, as it was meant. To the boy Henry Adams, summer was drunken. Among senses, smell was the strongest

— smell of hot pine-woods and sweet-fern in the scorching summer noon; of new-mown hay; of ploughed earth; of box hedges; of peaches, lilacs, syringas; of stables, barns, cow-yards; of salt water and low tide on the marshes; nothing came amiss. Next to smell came taste, and the children knew the taste of everything they saw or touched, from pennyroyal and flagroot to the shell of a pignut and the letters of a spelling-book — the taste of A-B, AB, suddenly revived on the boy's tongue sixty years afterwards. Light, line, and color as sensual pleasures, came later and were as crude as the rest. The New England light is glare, and the atmosphere harshens color. The boy was a full man before he ever knew what was meant by atmosphere; his idea of pleasure in light was the blaze of a New England sun. His idea of color was a peony, with the dew of early morning on its petals. The intense blue of the sea, as he saw it a mile or two away, from the Quincy hills; the cumuli in a June afternoon sky; the strong reds and greens and purples of colored prints and children's picture-books, as the American colors then ran; these were ideals. The opposites or antipathies, were the cold grays of November evenings, and the thick, muddy thaws of Boston winter. With such standards, the Bostonian could not but develop a double nature. Life was a double thing. After a January blizzard, the boy who could look with pleasure into the violent snow-glare of the cold white sunshine, with its intense light and shade, scarcely knew what was meant by tone. He could reach it only by education.

Winter and summer, then, were two hostile lives, and bred two separate natures. Winter was always the effort to live; summer was tropical license. Whether the children rolled in the grass, or waded in the brook, or swam in the salt ocean, or sailed in the bay, or fished for smelts in the creeks, or netted minnows in the salt-marshes, or took to the pine-woods and the granite quarries, or chased muskrats and hunted snapping-turtles in the swamps, or mushrooms or nuts on the autumn hills, summer and country were always sensual living, while winter was always compulsory learning. Summer was the multiplicity of nature; winter was school.

The bearing of the two seasons on the education of Henry Adams was no fancy; it was the most decisive force he ever knew; it ran through life, and made the division between its perplexing, warring, irreconcilable problems, irreducible opposites, with growing emphasis to the last year of study. From earliest childhood the boy was accustomed to feel that, for him, life was double. Winter and summer, town and country, law and liberty, were hostile, and the man who pretended they were not, was in his eyes a schoolmaster—that is, a man employed to tell lies to little boys. Though Quincy was but two hours' walk from Beacon Hill, it belonged in a different world. For two hundred years, every Adams, from father to son, had lived within sight of State Street, and sometimes had lived in it, yet none had ever taken kindly to the town, or been taken kindly by it. The boy inherited his double nature. He knew as yet nothing about his great-grandfather, who had died a dozen years before his own birth: he took for granted that any great-grandfather of his must have always been good, and his enemies wicked; but he divined his great-grandfather's character from his own. Never for a moment did he connect the two ideas of Boston and John Adams; they were separate and antagonistic; the idea of John Adams went with Quincy. He knew his grandfather John Quincy Adams only as an old man of seventy-five or eighty who was friendly and gentle with him, but except that he heard his grandfather always called "the President," and his grandmother "the Madam," he had no reason to suppose that his Adams

grandfather differed in character from his Brooks grandfather who was equally kind and benevolent. He liked
the Adams side best, but for no other reason than that it re-
minded him of the country, the summer, and the absence
of restraint. Yet he felt also that Quincy was in a way inferior to Boston, and that socially Boston looked down on
Quincy. The reason was clear enough even to a five-year-
old child. Quincy had no Boston style. Little enough
style had either; a simpler manner of life and thought
could hardly exist, short of cave-dwelling. The flint-and-
steel with which his grandfather Adams used to light his
own fires in the early morning was still on the mantelpiece of his study. The idea of a livery or even a dress
for servants, or of an evening toilette, was next to blas-
phemy. Bathrooms, water-supplies, lighting, heating, and
the whole array of domestic comforts, were unknown at
Quincy. Boston had already a bathroom, a water-supply,
a furnace, and gas. The superiority of Boston was evident,
but a child liked it no better for that.

The magnificence of his grandfather Brooks's house in
Pearl Street or South Street has long ago disappeared, but
perhaps his country house at Medford may still remain
to show what impressed the mind of a boy in 1845 with
the idea of city splendor. The President's place at Quincy
was the larger and older and far the more interesting of
the two; but a boy felt at once its inferiority in fashion.
It showed plainly enough its want of wealth. It smacked
of colonial age, but not of Boston style or plush curtains.
To the end of his life he never quite overcame the prejudice thus drawn in with his childish breath. He never
could compel himself to care for nineteenth-century style.
He was never able to adopt it, any more than his father
or grandfather or great-grandfather had done. Not that he
felt it as particularly hostile, for he reconciled himself
to much that was worse; but because, for some remote

reason, he was born an eighteenth-century child. The old house at Quincy was eighteenth century. What style it had was in its Queen Anne mahogany panels and its Louis Seize chairs and sofas. The panels belonged to an old colonial Vassall who built the house; the furniture had been brought back from Paris in 1789 or 1801 or 1817, along with porcelain and books and much else of old diplomatic remnants; and neither of the two eighteenth-century styles — neither English Queen Anne nor French Louis Seize — was comfortable for a boy, or for any one else. The dark mahogany had been painted white to suit daily life in winter gloom. Nothing seemed to favor, for a child's objects, the older forms. On the contrary, most boys, as well as grown-up people, preferred the new, with good reason, and the child felt himself distinctly at a disadvantage for the taste.

Nor had personal preference any share in his bias. The Brooks grandfather was as amiable and as sympathetic as the Adams grandfather. Both were born in 1767, and both died in 1848. Both were kind to children, and both belonged rather to the eighteenth than to the nineteenth centuries. The child knew no difference between them except that one was associated with winter and the other with summer; one with Boston, the other with Quincy. Even with Medford, the association was hardly easier. Once as a very young boy he was taken to pass a few days with his grandfather Brooks under charge of his aunt, but became so violently homesick that within twenty-four hours he was brought back in disgrace. Yet he could not remember ever being seriously homesick again.

The attachment to Quincy was not altogether sentimental or wholly sympathetic. Quincy was not a bed of thornless roses. Even there the curse of Cain set its mark. There as elsewhere a cruel universe combined to crush a child. As though three or four vigorous brothers and sisters, with the best will, were not enough to crush any child, every one else conspired towards an education which he hated. From cradle to grave this problem of running order through chaos, direction through space, discipline through freedom, unity through multiplicity, has always been, and must always be, the task of education, as it is the moral of religion, philosophy, science, art, politics, and economy; but a boy's will is his life, and he dies when it is broken, as the colt dies in harness, taking a new nature in becoming tame. Rarely has the boy felt kindly towards his tamers. Between him and his master has always been war. Henry Adams never knew a boy of his generation to like a master, and the task of remaining on friendly terms with one's own family, in such a relation, was never easy.

All the more singular it seemed afterwards to him that his first serious contact with the President should have been a struggle of will, in which the old man almost necessarily defeated the boy, but instead of leaving, as usual in such defeats, a lifelong sting, left rather an impression of as fair treatment as could be expected from a natural enemy. The boy met seldom with such restraint. He could not have been much more than six years old at the time — seven at the utmost — and his mother had taken him to Quincy for a long stay with the President during the summer. What became of the rest of the family he quite forgot; but he distinctly remembered standing at the house door one summer morning in a passionate outburst of rebellion against going to school. Naturally his mother was the immediate victim of his rage; that is what mothers are for, and boys also; but in this case the boy had his mother at unfair disadvantage, for she was a guest, and had no means of enforcing obedience. Henry showed a certain tactical ability by refusing to start, and he met all efforts at compulsion by successful, though too vehement protest. He was in fair way to win, and was holding his own, with sufficient energy, at the bottom of the long staircase which led up to the door of the President's library, when the door opened, and the old man slowly came down. Putting on his hat, he took the boy's hand without a word, and walked with him, paralyzed by awe, up the road to the town. After the first moments of consternation at this interference in a domestic dispute, the boy reflected that an old gentleman close on eighty would never trouble himself to walk near a mile on a hot summer morning over a shadeless road to take a boy to school, and that it would be strange if a lad imbued with the passion of freedom could not find a corner to dodge around, somewhere before reaching the school door. Then and always, the boy insisted that this reasoning justified his apparent submission; but the old man did not stop, and the boy saw all his strategical points turned, one after another, until he found himself seated inside the school, and obviously the centre of curious if not malevolent criticism. Not till then did the President release his hand and depart.

The point was that this act, contrary to the inalienable rights of boys, and nullifying the social compact, ought to have made him dislike his grandfather for life. He could not recall that it had this effect even for a moment. With a certain maturity of mind, the child must have recognized that the President, though a tool of tyranny, had done his disreputable work with a certain intelligence. He had shown no temper, no irritation, no personal feeling, and had made no display of force. Above all, he had held his tongue. During their long walk he had said nothing; he had uttered no syllable of revolting cant about the duty of obedience and the wickedness of resistance to law; he had shown no concern in the matter; hardly even a consciousness of the boy's existence. Probably his mind at that moment was actually troubling itself little about his grandson's iniquities, and much about the iniquities of President Polk, but the boy could scarcely at that age feel the whole satisfaction of thinking that President Polk was to be the vicarious victim of his own sins, and he gave his grandfather credit for intelligent silence. For this forbearance he felt instinctive respect. He admitted force as a form of right; he admitted even temper, under protest; but the seeds of a moral education would at that moment have fallen on the stoniest soil in Quincy, which is, as every one knows, the stoniest glacial and tidal drift known in any Puritan land.

Neither party to this momentary disagreement can have felt rancor, for during these three or four summers the old President's relations with the boy were friendly and almost intimate. Whether his older brothers and sisters were still more favored he failed to remember, but he was himself admitted to a sort of familiarity which, when in his turn he had reached old age, rather shocked him, for it must have sometimes tried the President's patience. He hung about the library; handled the books; deranged the papers; ransacked the drawers; searched the old purses and pocket-books for foreign coins; drew the sword-cane; snapped the travelling-pistols; upset everything in the corners, and penetrated the President's dressing-closet where a row of tumblers, inverted on the shelf, covered caterpillars which were supposed to become moths or butterflies, but never did. The Madam bore with fortitude the loss of the tumblers which her husband purloined for these hatcheries; but she made protest when he carried off her best cut-glass bowls to plant with acorns or peach-stones that he might see the roots grow, but which, she said, he commonly forgot like the caterpillars.

At that time the President rode the hobby of tree-culture, and some fine old trees should still remain to witness it, unless they have been improved off the ground; but his was a restless mind, and although he took his hobbies seriously and would have been annoyed had his grandchild asked whether he was bored like an English duke, he probably cared more for the processes than for the results, so that his grandson was saddened by the sight and smell of peaches and pears, the best of their kind, which he brought up from the garden to rot on his shelves for seed. With the inherited virtues of his Puritan ancestors, the little boy Henry conscientiously brought up to him in his study the finest peaches he found in the garden, and ate only the less perfect. Naturally he ate more by way of compensation, but the act showed that he bore no grudge. As for his grandfather, it is even possible that he may have felt a certain self-reproach for his temporary rôle of schoolmaster — seeing that his own career did not offer proof of the worldly advantages of docile obedience — for there still exists somewhere a little volume of critically edited Nursery Rhymes with the boy's name in full written in the President's trembling hand on the fly-leaf. Of course there was also the Bible, given to each child at birth, with the proper inscription in the President's hand on the fly-leaf; while their grandfather Brooks supplied the silver mugs.

So many Bibles and silver mugs had to be supplied, that a new house, or cottage, was built to hold them. It was "on the hill," five minutes' walk above "the old house," with a far view eastward over Quincy Bay, and northward over Boston. Till his twelfth year, the child passed his summers there, and his pleasures of childhood mostly centered in it. Of education he had as yet little to complain. Country schools were not very serious. Nothing stuck to the mind except home impressions, and the sharpest were those of kindred children; but as influences that warped a mind, none compared with the mere effect of the back of the President's bald head, as he sat in his pew on Sundays, in line with that of President Quincy, who, though some ten years younger, seemed to children about the same age. Before railways entered the New England town, every parish church showed half-a-dozen of these leading citizens, with gray hair, who sat on the main aisle in the best pews, and had sat there, or in some equivalent dignity, since the time of St. Augustine, if not since the glacial epoch. It was unusual for boys to sit behind a President grandfather, and to read over his head the tablet in memory of a President great-grandfather, who had "pledged his life, his fortune, and his sacred honor" to secure the independence of his country and so forth; but boys naturally supposed, without much reasoning, that other boys had the equivalent of President grandfathers, and that churches would always go on, with the bald-headed leading citizens on the main aisle, and Presidents or their equivalents on the walls. The Irish gardener once said to the child: "You'll be thinkin' you'll be President too!" The casualty of the remark made so strong an impression on his mind that he never forgot it. He could not remember ever to have thought on the subject; to him, that there should be a doubt of his being President was a new idea. What had been would continue to be. He doubted neither about Presidents nor about Churches, and no one suggested at that time a doubt whether a system of society which had lasted since Adam would outlast one Adams more.

The Madam was a little more remote than the President, but more decorative. She stayed much in her own room with the Dutch tiles, looking out on her garden with the box walks, and seemed a fragile creature to a boy who sometimes brought her a note or a message, and took distinct pleasure in looking at her delicate face under what seemed to him very becoming caps. He liked her refined figure; her gentle voice and manner; her vague effect of not belonging there, but to Washington or to Europe, like her furniture, and writing-desk with little glass doors above and little eighteenth-century volumes in old binding, labelled "Peregrine Pickle" or "Tom Jones" or "Hannah More." Try as she might, the Madam could never be Bostonian, and it was her cross in life, but to the boy it was her charm. Even at that age, he felt drawn to it. The Madam's life had been in truth far from Boston. She was born in London in 1775, daughter of Joshua Johnson, an American merchant, brother of Governor Thomas Johnson of Maryland; and Catherine Nuth, of an English family in London. Driven from England by the Revolutionary War, Joshua Johnson took his family to Nantes, where they remained till the peace. The girl Louisa Catherine was nearly ten years old when brought back to London, and her sense of nationality must have been confused; but the influence of the Johnsons and the services of Joshua obtained for him from President Washington the appointment of Consul in London on the organization of the Government in 1790. In 1794 President Washington appointed John Quincy Adams Minister to The Hague. He was twenty-seven years old when he returned to London, and found the Consul's house a very agreeable haunt. Louisa was then twenty.

At that time, and long afterwards, the Consul's house, far more than the Minister's, was the centre of contact for travelling Americans, either official or other. The Legation was a shifting point, between 1785 and 1815; but the Consulate, far down in the City, near the Tower, was convenient and inviting; so inviting that it proved fatal to young Adams. Louisa was charming, like a Romney portrait, but among her many charms that of being a New England woman was not one. The defect was serious. Her future mother-in-law, Abigail, a famous New England woman whose authority over her turbulent husband, the second President, was hardly so great as that which she exercised over her son, the sixth to be, was troubled by the fear that Louisa might not be made of stuff stern enough, or brought up in conditions severe enough, to suit a New England climate, or to make an efficient wife for her paragon son, and Abigail was right on that point, as on most others where sound judgment was involved; but sound judgment is sometimes a source of weakness rather than of force, and John Quincy already had reason to think that his mother held sound judgments on the subject of daughters-in-law which human nature, since the fall of Eve, made Adams helpless to realize. Being three thousand miles away from his mother, and equally far in love, he married Louisa in London, July 26, 1797, and took her to Berlin to be the head of the United States Legation. During three or four exciting years, the young bride lived in Berlin; whether she was happy or not, whether she was content or not, whether she was socially successful or not, her descendants did not surely know; but in any case she could by no chance have become educated there for a life in Quincy or Boston. In 1801 the overthrow of the Federalist Party drove her and her husband to America, and she became at last a member of the Quincy household, but by that time her children needed all her attention, and she remained there with occasional winters in Boston and Washington, till 1809. Her husband was made Senator in 1803, and in 1809 was appointed Minister to Russia. She went with him to St. Petersburg, taking her baby, Charles Francis, born in 1807; but broken-hearted at having to leave her two older boys behind. The life at St. Petersburg was hardly gay for her; they were far too poor to shine in that extravagant society; but she survived it, though her little girl baby did not, and in the winter of 1814–15, alone with the boy of seven years old, crossed Europe from St. Petersburg to

Paris, in her travelling-carriage, passing through the armies, and reaching Paris in the *Cent Jours* after Napoleon's return from Elba. Her husband next went to England as Minister, and she was for two years at the Court of the Regent. In 1817 her husband came home to be Secretary of State, and she lived for eight years in F Street, doing her work of entertainer for President Monroe's administration. Next she lived four miserable years in the White House. When that chapter was closed in 1829, she had earned the right to be tired and delicate, but she still had fifteen years to serve as wife of a Member of the House, after her husband went back to Congress in 1833. Then it was that the little Henry, her grandson, first remembered her, from 1843 to 1848, sitting in her panelled room, at breakfast, with her heavy silver teapot and sugar-bowl and cream-jug, which still exist somewhere as an heirloom of the modern safety-vault. By that time she was seventy years old or more, and thoroughly weary of being beaten about a stormy world. To the boy she seemed singularly peaceful, a vision of silver gray, presiding over her old President and her Queen Anne mahogany; an exotic, like her Sèvres china; an object of deference to every one, and of great affection to her son Charles; but hardly more Bostonian than she had been fifty years before, on her wedding-day, in the shadow of the Tower of London.

Such a figure was even less fitted than that of her old husband, the President, to impress on a boy's mind the standards of the coming century. She was Louis Seize, like the furniture. The boy knew nothing of her interior life, which had been, as the venerable Abigail, long since at peace, foresaw, one of severe stress and little pure satisfaction. He never dreamed that from her might come some of those doubts and self-questionings, those hesitations, those rebellions against law and discipline, which marked

more than one of her descendants; but he might even then
have felt some vague instinctive suspicion that he was to
inherit from her the seeds of the primal sin, the fall from
grace, the curse of Abel, that he was not of pure New
England stock, but half exotic. As a child of Quincy he
was not a true Bostonian, but even as a child of Quincy
he inherited a quarter taint of Maryland blood. Charles
Francis, half Marylander by birth, had hardly seen Boston till he was ten years old, when his parents left him
there at school in 1817, and he never forgot the experience. He was to be nearly as old as his mother had been
in 1845, before he quite accepted Boston, or Boston quite
accepted him.

A boy who began his education in these surroundings,
with physical strength inferior to that of his brothers, and
with a certain delicacy of mind and bone, ought rightly
to have felt at home in the eighteenth century and should,
in proper self-respect, have rebelled against the standards
of the nineteenth. The atmosphere of his first ten years
must have been very like that of his grandfather at the
same age, from 1767 till 1776, barring the battle of Bunker
Hill, and even as late as 1846, the battle of Bunker Hill
remained actual. The tone of Boston society was colonial.
The true Bostonian always knelt in self-abasement before
the majesty of English standards; far from concealing it
as a weakness, he was proud of it as his strength. The
eighteenth century ruled society long after 1850. Perhaps
the boy began to shake it off rather earlier than most of
his mates.

Indeed this prehistoric stage of education ended rather
abruptly with his tenth year. One winter morning he was
conscious of a certain confusion in the house in Mount
Vernon Street, and gathered, from such words as he could
catch, that the President, who happened to be then staying there, on his way to Washington, had fallen and hurt

himself. Then he heard the word paralysis. After that day he came to associate the word with the figure of his grandfather, in a tall-backed, invalid armchair, on one side of the spare bedroom fireplace, and one of his old friends, Dr. Parkman or P. P. F. Degrand, on the other side, both dozing.

The end of this first, or ancestral and Revolutionary, chapter came on February 21, 1848 — and the month of February brought life and death as a family habit — when the eighteenth century, as an actual and living companion, vanished. If the scene on the floor of the House, when the old President fell, struck the still simple-minded American public with a sensation unusually dramatic, its effect on a ten-year-old boy, whose boy-life was fading away with the life of his grandfather, could not be slight. One had to pay for Revolutionary patriots; grandfathers and grandmothers; Presidents; diplomats; Queen Anne mahogany and Louis Seize chairs, as well as for Stuart portraits. Such things warp young life. Americans commonly believed that they ruined it, and perhaps the practical common-sense of the American mind judged right. Many a boy might be ruined by much less than the emotions of the funeral service in the Quincy church, with its surroundings of national respect and family pride. By another dramatic chance it happened that the clergyman of the parish, Dr. Lunt, was an unusual pulpit orator, the ideal of a somewhat austere intellectual type, such as the school of Buckminster and Channing inherited from the old Congregational clergy. His extraordinarily refined appearance, his dignity of manner, his deeply cadenced voice, his remarkable English and his fine appreciation, gave to the funeral service a character that left an overwhelming impression on the boy's mind. He was to see many great functions — funerals and festivals — in after-life, till his only thought was to see no more, but he never again witnessed anything nearly so impressive to him as the last services at Quincy over the body of one President and the ashes of another.

The effect of the Quincy service was deepened by the official ceremony which afterwards took place in Faneuil Hall, when the boy was taken to hear his uncle, Edward Everett, deliver a Eulogy. Like all Mr. Everett's orations, it was an admirable piece of oratory, such as only an admirable orator and scholar could create; too good for a ten-year-old boy to appreciate at its value; but already the boy knew that the dead President could not be in it, and had even learned why he would have been out of place there; for knowledge was beginning to come fast. The shadow of the War of 1812 still hung over State Street; the shadow of the Civil War to come had already begun to darken Faneuil Hall. No rhetoric could have reconciled Mr. Everett's audience to his subject. How could he say there, to an assemblage of Bostonians in the heart of mercantile Boston, that the only distinctive mark of all the Adamses, since old Sam Adams's father a hundred and fifty years before, had been their inherited quarrel with State Street, which had again and again broken out into riot, bloodshed, personal feuds, foreign and civil war, wholesale banishments and confiscations, until the history of Florence was hardly more turbulent than that of Boston? How could he whisper the word Hartford Convention before the men who had made it? What would have been said had he suggested the chance of Secession and Civil War?

Thus already, at ten years old, the boy found himself standing face to face with a dilemma that might have puzzled an early Christian. What was he? — where was he going? Even then he felt that something was wrong, but he concluded that it must be Boston. Quincy had always been right, for Quincy represented a moral principle — the principle of resistance to Boston. His Adams ancestors must have been right, since they were always hostile to State Street. If State Street was wrong, Quincy must be right! Turn the dilemma as he pleased, he still came back on the eighteenth century and the law of Resistance; of Truth; of Duty, and of Freedom. He was a ten-year-old priest and politician. He could under no circumstances have guessed what the next fifty years had in store, and no one could teach him; but sometimes, in his old age, he wondered — and could never decide — whether the most clear and certain knowledge would have helped him. Supposing he had seen a New York stock-list of 1900, and had studied the statistics of railways, telegraphs, coal, and steel — would he have quitted his eighteenth-century, his ancestral prejudices, his abstract ideals, his semi-clerical training, and the rest, in order to perform an expiatory pilgrimage to State Street, and ask for the fatted calf of his grandfather Brooks and a clerkship in the Suffolk Bank?

Sixty years afterwards he was still unable to make up his mind. Each course had its advantages, but the material advantages, looking back, seemed to lie wholly in State Street.

2

Boston

(1848–1854)

Peter Chardon Brooks, the other grandfather, died January 1, 1849, bequeathing what was supposed to be the largest estate in Boston, about two million dollars, to his seven surviving children: four sons — Edward, Peter Chardon, Gorham, and Sydney; three daughters — Charlotte, married to Edward Everett; Ann, married to Nathaniel Frothingham, minister of the First Church; and Abigail Brown, born April 25, 1808, married September 3, 1829, to Charles Francis Adams, hardly a year older than herself. Their first child, born in 1830, was a daughter, named Louisa Catherine, after her Johnson grandmother; the second was a son, named John Quincy, after his President grandfather; the third took his father's name, Charles Francis; while the fourth, being of less account, was in a way given to his mother, who named him Henry Brooks, after a favorite brother just lost. More followed, but these, being younger, had nothing to do with the arduous process of educating.

The Adams connection was singularly small in Boston, but the family of Brooks was singularly large and even brilliant, and almost wholly of clerical New England stock. One might have sought long in much larger and

older societies for three brothers-in-law more distinguished or more scholarly than Edward Everett, Dr.
Frothingham, and Mr. Adams. One might have sought
equally long for seven brothers-in-law more unlike. No
doubt they all bore more or less the stamp of Boston, or at
least of Massachusetts Bay, but the shades of difference
amounted to contrasts. Mr. Everett belonged to Boston
hardly more than Mr. Adams. One of the most ambitious of
Bostonians, he had broken bounds early in life by leaving
the Unitarian pulpit to take a seat in Congress where he
had given valuable support to J. Q. Adams's administration; support which, as a social consequence, led to the
marriage of the President's son, Charles Francis, with Mr.
Everett's youngest sister-in-law, Abigail Brooks. The
wreck of parties which marked the reign of Andrew Jackson had interfered with many promising careers, that of
Edward Everett among the rest, but he had risen with the
Whig Party to power, had gone as Minister to England,
and had returned to America with the halo of a European
reputation, and undisputed rank second only to Daniel
Webster as the orator and representative figure of Boston.
The other brother-in-law, Dr. Frothingham, belonged to
the same clerical school, though in manner rather the less
clerical of the two. Neither of them had much in common
with Mr. Adams, who was a younger man, greatly biassed
by his father, and by the inherited feud between Quincy
and State Street; but personal relations were friendly as
far as a boy could see, and the innumerable cousins went
regularly to the First Church every Sunday in winter, and
slept through their uncle's sermons, without once thinking
to ask what the sermons were supposed to mean for them.
For two hundred years the First Church had seen the same
little boys, sleeping more or less soundly under the same or
similar conditions, and dimly conscious of the same
feuds; but the feuds had never ceased, and the boys had

always grown up to inherit them. Those of the generation of 1812 had mostly disappeared in 1850; death had cleared that score; the quarrels of John Adams, and those of John Quincy Adams were no longer acutely personal; the game was considered as drawn; and Charles Francis Adams might then have taken his inherited rights of political leadership in succession to Mr. Webster and Mr. Everett, his seniors. Between him and State Street the relation was more natural than between Edward Everett and State Street; but instead of doing so, Charles Francis Adams drew himself aloof and renewed the old war which had already lasted since 1700. He could not help it. With the record of J. Q. Adams fresh in the popular memory, his son and his only representative could not make terms with the slave-power, and the slave-power overshadowed all the great Boston interests. No doubt Mr. Adams had principles of his own, as well as inherited, but even his children, who as yet had no principles, could equally little follow the lead of Mr. Webster or even of Mr. Seward. They would have lost in consideration more than they would have gained in patronage. They were anti-slavery by birth, as their name was Adams and their home was Quincy. No matter how much they had wished to enter State Street, they felt that State Street never would trust them, or they it. Had State Street been Paradise, they must hunger for it in vain, and it hardly needed Daniel Webster to act as archangel with the flaming sword, to order them away from the door.

Time and experience, which alter all perspectives, altered this among the rest, and taught the boy gentler judgment, but even when only ten years old, his face was already fixed, and his heart was stone, against State Street; his education was warped beyond recovery in the direction of Puritan politics. Between him and his patriot grandfather at the same age, the conditions had changed little.

The year 1848 was like enough to the year 1776 to make a fair parallel. The parallel, as concerned bias of education, was complete when, a few months after the death of John Quincy Adams, a convention of anti-slavery delegates met at Buffalo to organize a new party and named candidates for the general election in November: for President, Martin Van Buren; for Vice-President, Charles Francis Adams.

For any American boy the fact that his father was running for office would have dwarfed for the time every other excitement, but even apart from personal bias, the year 1848, for a boy's road through life, was decisive for twenty years to come. There was never a side-path of escape. The stamp of 1848 was almost as indelible as the stamp of 1776, but in the eighteenth or any earlier century, the stamp mattered less because it was standard, and every one bore it; while men whose lives were to fall in the generation between 1865 and 1900 had, first of all, to get rid of it, and take the stamp that belonged to their time. This was their education. To outsiders, immigrants, adventurers, it was easy, but the old Puritan nature rebelled against change. The reason it gave was forcible. The Puritan thought his thought higher and his moral standards better than those of his successors. So they were. He could not be convinced that moral standards had nothing to do with it, and that utilitarian morality was good enough for him, as it was for the graceless. Nature had given to the boy Henry a character that, in any previous century, would have led him into the Church; he inherited dogma and *a priori* thought from the beginning of time; and he scarcely needed a violent reaction like anti-slavery politics to sweep him back into Puritanism with a violence as great as that of a religious war.

Thus far he had nothing to do with it; his education was chiefly inheritance, and during the next five or six years, his father alone counted for much. If he were to worry successfully through life's quicksands, he must depend chiefly on his father's pilotage; but, for his father, the channel lay clear, while for himself an unknown ocean lay beyond. His father's business in life was to get past the dangers of the slave-power, or to fix its bounds at least. The task done, he might be content to let his sons pay for the pilotage; and it mattered little to his success whether they paid it with their lives wasted on battle-fields or in misdirected energies and lost opportunity. The generation that lived from 1840 to 1870 could do very well with the old forms of education; that which had its work to do between 1870 and 1900 needed something quite new.

His father's character was therefore the larger part of his education, as far as any single person affected it, and for that reason, if for no other, the son was always a much interested critic of his father's mind and temper. Long after his death as an old man of eighty, his sons continued to discuss this subject with a good deal of difference in their points of view. To his son Henry, the quality that distinguished his father from all the other figures in the family group, was that, in his opinion, Charles Francis Adams possessed the only perfectly balanced mind that ever existed in the name. For a hundred years, every newspaper scribbler had, with more or less obvious excuse, derided or abused the older Adamses for want of judgment. They abused Charles Francis for his judgment. Naturally they never attempted to assign values to either; that was the children's affair; but the traits were real. Charles Francis Adams was singular for mental poise — absence of self-assertion or self-consciousness — the faculty of standing apart without seeming aware that he was alone — a balance of mind and temper that neither challenged nor avoided notice, nor admitted question of superiority or inferiority, of jealousy, of personal motives, from any source, even under great pressure. This unusual poise of judgment and temper, ripened by age, became the more striking to his son Henry as he learned to measure the mental faculties themselves, which were in no way exceptional either for depth or range. Charles Francis Adams's memory was hardly above the average; his mind was not bold like his grandfather's or restless like his father's, or imaginative or oratorical — still less mathematical; but it worked with singular perfection, admirable self-restraint, and instinctive mastery of form. Within its range it was a model.

The standards of Boston were high, much affected by the old clerical self-respect which gave the Unitarian clergy unusual social charm. Dr. Channing, Mr. Everett, Dr. Frothingham, Dr. Palfrey, President Walker, R. W. Emerson, and other Boston ministers of the same school, would have commanded distinction in any society; but the Adamses had little or no affinity with the pulpit, and still less with its eccentric offshoots, like Theodore Parker, or Brook Farm, or the philosophy of Concord. Besides its clergy, Boston showed a literary group, led by Ticknor, Prescott, Longfellow, Motley, O. W. Holmes; but Mr. Adams was not one of them; as a rule they were much too Websterian. Even in science Boston could claim a certain eminence, especially in medicine, but Mr. Adams cared very little for science. He stood alone. He had no master — hardly even his father. He had no scholars — hardly even his sons.

Almost alone among his Boston contemporaries, he was not English in feeling or in sympathies. Perhaps a hundred years of acute hostility to England had something to do with this family trait; but in his case it went further and became indifference to social distinction. Never once in forty years of intimacy did his son notice in him a trace of snobbishness. He was one of the exceedingly small number of Americans to whom an English duke or duchess seemed to be indifferent, and royalty itself nothing more than a slightly inconvenient presence. This was, it is true, rather the tone of English society in his time, but Americans were largely responsible for changing it, and Mr. Adams had every possible reason for affecting the manner of a courtier even if he did not feel the sentiment. Never did his son see him flatter or vilify, or show a sign of envy or jealousy; never a shade of vanity or self-conceit. Never a tone of arrogance! Never a gesture of pride!

The same thing might perhaps have been said of John Quincy Adams, but in him his associates averred that it was accompanied by mental restlessness and often by lamentable want of judgment. No one ever charged Charles Francis Adams with this fault. The critics charged him with just the opposite defect. They called him cold. No doubt, such perfect poise — such intuitive self-adjustment — was not maintained by nature without a sacrifice of the qualities which would have upset it. No doubt, too, that even his restless-minded, introspective, self-conscious children who knew him best were much too ignorant of the world and of human nature to suspect how rare and complete was the model before their eyes. A coarser instrument would have impressed them more. Average human nature is very coarse, and its ideals must necessarily be average. The world never loved perfect poise. What the world does love is commonly absence of poise, for it has to be amused. Napoleons and Andrew Jacksons amuse it, but it is not amused by perfect balance. Had Mr. Adams's nature been cold, he would have followed Mr. Webster, Mr. Everett, Mr. Seward, and Mr. Winthrop in the lines of party discipline and self-interest. Had it been less balanced than it was, he would have gone with Mr. Garrison, Mr. Wendell Phillips, Mr. Edmund

Quincy, and Theodore Parker, into secession. Between the two paths he found an intermediate one, distinctive and characteristic — he set up a party of his own.

This political party became a chief influence in the education of the boy Henry in the six years 1848 to 1854, and violently affected his character at the moment when character is plastic. The group of men with whom Mr. Adams associated himself, and whose social centre was the house in Mount Vernon Street, numbered only three: Dr. John G. Palfrey, Richard H. Dana, and Charles Sumner. Dr. Palfrey was the oldest, and in spite of his clerical education, was to a boy often the most agreeable, for his talk was lighter and his range wider than that of the others; he had wit, or humor, and the give-and-take of dinner-table exchange. Born to be a man of the world, he forced himself to be clergyman, professor, or statesman, while, like every other true Bostonian, he yearned for the ease of the Athenæum Club in Pall Mall or the Combination Room at Trinity. Dana at first suggested the opposite; he affected to be still before the mast, a direct, rather bluff, vigorous seaman, and only as one got to know him better one found the man of rather excessive refinement trying with success to work like a day-laborer, deliberately hardening his skin to the burden, as though he were still carrying hides at Monterey. Undoubtedly he succeeded, for his mind and will were robust, but he might have said what his lifelong friend William M. Evarts used to say: "I pride myself on my success in doing not the things I like to do, but the things I don't like to do." Dana's ideal of life was to be a great Englishman, with a seat on the front benches of the House of Commons until he should be promoted to the woolsack; beyond all, with a social status that should place him above the scuffle of provincial and unprofessional annoyances; but he forced himself to take life as it came, and he suffocated his longings with grim self-discipline, by mere force of will. Of the four men, Dana was the most marked. Without dogmatism or self-assertion, he seemed always to be fully in sight, a figure that completely filled a well-defined space. He, too, talked well, and his mind worked close to its subject, as a lawyer's should; but disguise and silence it as he liked, it was aristocratic to the tenth generation.

In that respect, and in that only, Charles Sumner was like him, but Sumner, in almost every other quality, was quite different from his three associates — altogether out of line. He, too, adored English standards, but his ambition led him to rival the career of Edmund Burke. No young Bostonian of his time had made so brilliant a start, but rather in the steps of Edward Everett than of Daniel Webster. As an orator he had achieved a triumph by his oration against war; but Boston admired him chiefly for his social success in England and on the Continent; success that gave to every Bostonian who enjoyed it a halo never acquired by domestic sanctity. Mr. Sumner, both by interest and instinct, felt the value of his English connection, and cultivated it the more as he became socially an outcast from Boston society by the passions of politics. He was rarely without a pocket-full of letters from duchesses or noblemen in England. Having sacrificed to principle his social position in America, he clung the more closely to his foreign attachments. The Free Soil Party fared ill in Beacon Street. The social arbiters of Boston — George Ticknor and the rest — had to admit, however unwillingly, that the Free Soil leaders could not mingle with the friends and followers of Mr. Webster. Sumner was socially ostracized, and so, for that matter, were Palfrey, Dana, Russell, Adams, and all the other avowed anti-slavery leaders, but for them it mattered less, because they had houses and families of their own; while Sumner had neither wife nor household, and, though the most socially ambitious of all,

and the most hungry for what used to be called polite society, he could enter hardly half-a-dozen houses in Boston.
Longfellow stood by him in Cambridge, and even in Beacon Street he could always take refuge in the house of
Mr. Lodge, but few days passed when he did not pass
some time in Mount Vernon Street. Even with that, his
solitude was glacial, and reacted on his character. He had
nothing but himself to think about. His superiority was,
indeed, real and incontestable; he was the classical ornament of the anti-slavery party; their pride in him was unbounded, and their admiration outspoken.

The boy Henry worshipped him, and if he ever regarded any older man as a personal friend, it was Mr.
Sumner. The relation of Mr. Sumner in the household was
far closer than any relation of blood. None of the uncles
approached such intimacy. Sumner was the boy's ideal of
greatness; the highest product of nature and art. The only
fault of such a model was its superiority which defied imi-
tation. To the twelve-year-old boy, his father, Dr. Palfrey, Mr. Dana, were men, more or less like what he
himself might become; but Mr. Sumner was a different
order — heroic.

As the boy grew up to be ten or twelve years old, his
father gave him a writing-table in one of the alcoves of his
Boston library, and there, winter after winter, Henry
worked over his Latin Grammar and listened to these four
gentlemen discussing the course of anti-slavery politics.
The discussions were always serious; the Free Soil Party
took itself quite seriously; and they were habitual because
Mr. Adams had undertaken to edit a newspaper as the
organ of these gentlemen, who came to discuss its policy
and expression. At the same time Mr. Adams was editing
the "Works" of his grandfather John Adams, and made
the boy read texts for proof-correction. In after years his
father sometimes complained that, as a reader of *Novan-*

glus and Massachusettensis, Henry had shown very little consciousness of punctuation; but the boy regarded this part of school life only as a warning, if he ever grew up to write dull discussions in the newspapers, to try to be dull in some different way from that of his great-grandfather. Yet the discussions in the *Boston Whig* were carried on in much the same style as those of John Adams and his opponent, and appealed to much the same society and the same habit of mind. The boy got as little education, fitting him for his own time, from the one as from the other, and he got no more from his contact with the gentlemen themselves who were all types of the past.

Down to 1850, and even later, New England society was still directed by the professions. Lawyers, physicians, professors, merchants were classes, and acted not as individuals, but as though they were clergymen and each profession were a church. In politics the system required competent expression; it was the old Ciceronian idea of government by *the best* that produced the long line of New England statesmen. They chose men to represent them because they wanted to be well represented, and they chose the best they had. Thus Boston chose Daniel Webster, and Webster took, not as pay, but as *honorarium,* the cheques raised for him by Peter Harvey from the Appletons, Perkinses, Amorys, Searses, Brookses, Lawrences, and so on, who begged him to represent them. Edward Everett held the rank in regular succession to Webster. Robert C. Winthrop claimed succession to Everett. Charles Sumner aspired to break the succession, but not the system. The Adamses had never been, for any length of time, a part of this State succession; they had preferred the national service, and had won all their distinction outside the State, but they too had required State support and had commonly received it. The little group of men in Mount Vernon Street were an offshoot of this system;

they were statesmen, not politicians; they guided public opinion, but were little guided by it.

The boy naturally learned only one lesson from his saturation in such air. He took for granted that this sort of world, more or less the same that had always existed in Boston and Massachusetts Bay, was the world which he was to fit. Had he known Europe he would have learned no better. The Paris of Louis Philippe, Guizot, and de Tocqueville, as well as the London of Robert Peel, Macaulay, and John Stuart Mill, were but varieties of the same upper-class *bourgeoisie* that felt instinctive cousinship with the Boston of Ticknor, Prescott, and Motley. Even the typical grumbler Carlyle, who cast doubts on the real capacity of the middle class, and who at times thought himself eccentric, found friendship and alliances in Boston — still more in Concord. The system had proved so successful that even Germany wanted to try it, and Italy yearned for it. England's middle-class government was the ideal of human progress.

Even the violent reaction after 1848, and the return of all Europe to military practices, never for a moment shook the true faith. No one, except Karl Marx, foresaw radical change. What announced it? The world was producing sixty or seventy million tons of coal, and might be using nearly a million steam-horse-power, just beginning to make itself felt. All experience since the creation of man, all divine revelation or human science, conspired to deceive and betray a twelve-year-old boy who took for granted that his ideas, which were alone respectable, would be alone respected.

Viewed from Mount Vernon Street, the problem of life was as simple as it was classic. Politics offered no difficulties, for there the moral law was a sure guide. Social perfection was also sure, because human nature worked for Good, and three instruments were all she asked — Suffrage, Common Schools, and Press. On these points doubt was forbidden. Education was divine, and man needed only a correct knowledge of facts to reach perfection:

> "Were half the power that fills the world with terror,
>   Were half the wealth bestowed on camps and courts,
> Given to redeem the human mind from error,
>   There were no need of arsenals nor forts."

Nothing quieted doubt so completely as the mental calm of the Unitarian clergy. In uniform excellence of life and character, moral and intellectual, the score of Unitarian clergymen about Boston, who controlled society and Harvard College, were never excelled. They proclaimed as their merit that they insisted on no doctrine, but taught, or tried to teach, the means of leading a virtuous, useful, unselfish life, which they held to be sufficient for salvation. For them, difficulties might be ignored; doubts were waste of thought; nothing exacted solution. Boston had solved the universe; or had offered and realized the best solution yet tried. The problem was worked out.

Of all the conditions of his youth which afterwards puzzled the grown-up man, this disappearance of religion puzzled him most. The boy went to church twice every Sunday; he was taught to read his Bible, and he learned religious poetry by heart; he believed in a mild deism; he prayed; he went through all the forms; but neither to him nor to his brothers or sisters was religion real. Even the mild discipline of the Unitarian Church was so irksome that they all threw it off at the first possible moment, and never afterwards entered a church. The religious instinct had vanished, and could not be revived, although one made in later life many efforts to recover it. That the most powerful emotion of man, next to the sexual, should disappear, might be a personal defect of his own; but that the most intelligent society, led by the most intelligent clergy, in the most moral conditions he ever knew, should have solved all the problems of the universe so thoroughly as to have quite ceased making itself anxious about past or future, and should have persuaded itself that all the problems which had convulsed human thought from earliest recorded time, were not worth discussing, seemed to him the most curious social phenomenon he had to account for in a long life. The faculty of turning away one's eyes as one approaches a chasm is not unusual, and Boston showed, under the lead of Mr. Webster, how successfully it could be done in politics; but in politics a certain number of men did at least protest. In religion and philosophy no one protested. Such protest as was made took forms more simple than the silence, like the deism of Theodore Parker, and of the boy's own cousin Octavius Frothingham, who distressed his father and scandalized Beacon Street by avowing scepticism that seemed to solve no old problems, and to raise many new ones. The less aggressive protest of Ralph Waldo Emerson, was, from an old-world point of view, less serious. It was *naïf*.

The children reached manhood without knowing religion, and with the certainty that dogma, metaphysics, and abstract philosophy were not worth knowing. So one-sided an education could have been possible in no other country or time, but it became, almost of necessity, the more literary and political. As the children grew up, they exaggerated the literary and the political interests. They joined in the dinner-table discussions and from childhood the boys were accustomed to hear, almost every day, table-talk as good as they were ever likely to hear again. The eldest child, Louisa, was one of the most sparkling creatures her brother met in a long and varied experience of bright women. The oldest son, John, was afterwards re-

garded as one of the best talkers in Boston society, and
perhaps the most popular man in the State, though apt to be
on the unpopular side. Palfrey and Dana could be entertaining when they pleased, and though Charles Sumner
could hardly be called light in hand, he was willing to be
amused, and smiled grandly from time to time; while Mr.
Adams, who talked relatively little, was always a good
listener, and laughed over a witticism till he choked.

By way of educating and amusing the children, Mr.
Adams read much aloud, and was sure to read political
literature, especially when it was satirical, like the speeches
of Horace Mann and the "Epistles" of "Hosea Biglow,"
with great delight to the youth. So he read Longfellow
and Tennyson as their poems appeared, but the children
took possession of Dickens and Thackeray for themselves.
Both were too modern for tastes founded on Pope and
Dr. Johnson. The boy Henry soon became a desultory
reader of every book he found readable, but these were
commonly eighteenth-century historians because his
father's library was full of them. In the want of positive
instincts, he drifted into the mental indolence of history.
So, too, he read shelves of eighteenth-century poetry,
but when his father offered his own set of Wordsworth as
a gift on condition of reading it through, he declined.
Pope and Gray called for no mental effort; they were easy
reading; but the boy was thirty years old before his education reached Wordsworth.

This is the story of an education, and the person or persons who figure in it are supposed to have values only as
educators or educated. The surroundings concern it only
so far as they affect education. Sumner, Dana, Palfrey, had
values of their own, like Hume, Pope, and Wordsworth,
which any one may study in their works; here all appear
only as influences on the mind of a boy very nearly the

average of most boys in physical and mental stature. The influence was wholly political and literary. His father made no effort to force his mind, but left him free play, and this was perhaps best. Only in one way his father rendered him a great service by trying to teach him French and giving him some idea of a French accent. Otherwise the family was rather an atmosphere than an influence. The boy had a large and overpowering set of brothers and sisters, who were modes or replicas of the same type, getting the same education, struggling with the same problems, and solving the question, or leaving it unsolved much in the same way. They knew no more than he what they wanted or what to do for it, but all were conscious that they would like to control power in some form; and the same thing could be said of an ant or an elephant. Their form was tied to politics or literature. They amounted to one individual with half-a-dozen sides or facets; their temperaments reacted on each other and made each child more like the other. This was also education, but in the type, and the Boston or New England type was well enough known. What no one knew was whether the individual who thought himself a representative of this type, was fit to deal with life.

As far as outward bearing went, such a family of turbulent children, given free rein by their parents, or indifferent to check, should have come to more or less grief. Certainly no one was strong enough to control them, least of all their mother, the queen-bee of the hive, on whom nine-tenths of the burden fell, on whose strength they all depended, but whose children were much too self-willed and self-confident to take guidance from her, or from any one else, unless in the direction they fancied. Father and mother were about equally helpless. Almost every large family in those days produced at least one black sheep, and if this generation of Adamses escaped, it was as much a matter of surprise to them as to their neighbors. By some happy chance they grew up to be decent citizens, but Henry Adams, as a brand escaped from the burning, always looked back with astonishment at their luck. The fact seemed to prove that they were born, like birds, with a certain innate balance. Home influences alone never saved the New England boy from ruin, though sometimes they may have helped to ruin him; and the influences outside of home were negative. If school helped, it was only by reaction. The dislike of school was so strong as to be a positive gain. The passionate hatred of school methods was almost a method in itself. Yet the day-school of that time was respectable, and the boy had nothing to complain of. In fact, he never complained. He hated it because he was here with a crowd of other boys and compelled to learn by memory a quantity of things that did not amuse him. His memory was slow, and the effort painful. For him to conceive that his memory could compete for school prizes with machines of two or three times its power, was to prove himself wanting not only in memory, but flagrantly in mind. He thought his mind a good enough machine, if it were given time to act, but it acted wrong if hurried. Schoolmasters never gave time.

In any and all its forms, the boy detested school, and the prejudice became deeper with years. He always reckoned his school days, from ten to sixteen years old, as time thrown away. Perhaps his needs turned out to be exceptional, but his existence was exceptional. Between 1850 and 1900 nearly every one's existence was exceptional. For success in the life imposed on him he needed, as afterwards appeared, the facile use of only four tools: Mathematics, French, German, and Spanish. With these, he could master in very short time any special branch of inquiry, and feel at home in any society. Latin and Greek, he could, with the help of the modern languages, learn more completely by the intelligent work of six weeks than in the six years he spent on them at school. These four tools were necessary to his success in life, but he never controlled any one of them.

Thus, at the outset, he was condemned to failure more or less complete in the life awaiting him, but not more so than his companions. Indeed, had his father kept the boy at home, and given him half an hour's direction every day, he would have done more for him than school ever could do for them. Of course, school-taught men and boys looked down on home-bred boys, and rather prided themselves on their own ignorance, but the man of sixty can generally see what he needed in life, and in Henry Adams's opinion it was not school.

Most school experience was bad. Boy associations at fifteen were worse than none. Boston at that time offered few healthy resources for boys or men. The bar-room and billiard-room were more familiar than parents knew. As a rule boys could skate and swim and were sent to dancing-school; they played a rudimentary game of baseball, football, and hockey; a few could sail a boat; still fewer had been out with a gun to shoot yellow-legs or a stray wild duck; one or two may have learned something of natural history if they came from the neighborhood of Concord; none could ride across country, or knew what shooting with dogs meant. Sport as a pursuit was unknown. Boat-racing came after 1850. For horse-racing, only the trotting-course existed. Of all pleasures, winter sleighing was still the gayest and most popular. From none of these amusements could the boy learn anything likely to be of use to him in the world. Books remained as in the eighteenth century, the source of life, and as they came out — Thackeray, Dickens, Bulwer, Tennyson, Macaulay, Carlyle, and the rest — they were devoured; but as far as happiness went, the happiest hours of the boy's education were passed in summer lying on a musty heap of Congressional Documents in the old farmhouse at Quincy, reading "Quentin Durward," "Ivanhoe," and "The Talisman," and raiding the garden at intervals for peaches and pears. On the whole he learned most then.

3

Washington

(1850–1854)

Except for politics, Mount Vernon Street had the merit of leaving the boy-mind supple, free to turn with the world, and if one learned next to nothing, the little one did learn needed not to be unlearned. The surface was ready to take any form that education should cut into it, though Boston, with singular foresight, rejected the old designs. What sort of education was stamped elsewhere, a Bostonian had no idea, but he escaped the evils of other standards by having no standard at all; and what was true of school was true of society. Boston offered none that could help outside. Every one now smiles at the bad taste of Queen Victoria aₗd Louis Philippe — the society of the forties — but the taste was only a reflection of the social slack-water between a tide passed, and a tide to come. Boston belonged to neither, and hardly even to America. Neither aristocratic nor industrial nor social, Boston girls and boys were not nearly as unformed as English boys and girls, but had less means of acquiring form as they grew older. Women counted for little as models. Every boy, from the age of seven, fell in love at frequent intervals with some girl — always more or less the same little girl — who had nothing to teach him, or he to teach her, except rather familiar and provincial manners, until they married and bore children to repeat the habit. The idea of attaching one's self to a married woman, or of polishing one's manners to suit the standards of women of thirty, could hardly have entered the mind of a young Bostonian, and would have scandalized his parents. From women the boy got the domestic virtues and nothing else. He might not even catch the idea that women had more to give. The garden of Eden was hardly more primitive.

To balance this virtue, the Puritan city had always hidden a darker side. Blackguard Boston was only too educational, and to most boys much the more interesting. A successful blackguard must enjoy great physical advantages besides a true vocation, and Henry Adams had neither; but no boy escaped some contact with vice of a very low form. Blackguardism came constantly under boys' eyes, and had the charm of force and freedom and superiority to culture or decency. One might fear it, but no one honestly despised it. Now and then it asserted itself as education more roughly than school ever did. One of the commonest boy-games of winter, inherited directly from the eighteenth century, was a game of war on Boston Common. In old days the two hostile forces were called North-Enders and South-Enders. In 1850 the North-Enders still survived as a legend, but in practice it was a battle of the Latin School against all comers, and the Latin School, for snowball, included all the boys of the West End. Whenever, on a half-holiday, the weather was soft enough to soften the snow, the Common was apt to be the scene of a fight, which began in daylight with the Latin School in force, rushing their opponents down to Tremont Street, and which generally ended at dark by the Latin School dwindling in numbers and disappearing. As the Latin School grew weak, the roughs and young blackguards grew strong. As long as snowballs were the only weapon, no one was much hurt, but a stone may be put in a snowball, and in the dark a stick or a slungshot in the hands of a boy is as effective as a knife. One afternoon the fight had been long and exhausting. The boy Henry, following, as his habit was, his bigger brother Charles, had taken part in the battle, and had felt his courage much depressed by seeing one of his trustiest leaders, Henry Higginson — "Bully Hig," his school name — struck by a stone over the eye, and led off the field bleeding in rather a ghastly manner. As night came on, the Latin School was steadily forced back to the Beacon Street Mall where they could retreat no further without disbanding, and by that time only a small band was left, headed by two heroes, Savage and Marvin. A dark mass of figures could be seen below, making ready for the last rush, and rumor said that a swarm of blackguards from the slums, led by a grisly terror called Conky Daniels, with a club and a hideous reputation, was going to put an end to the Beacon Street cowards forever. Henry wanted to run away with the others, but his brother was too big to run away, so they stood still and waited immolation. The dark mass set up a shout, and rushed forward. The Beacon Street boys turned and fled up the steps, except Savage and Marvin and the few champions who would not run. The terrible Conky Daniels swaggered up, stopped a moment with his bodyguard to swear a few oaths at Marvin, and then swept on and chased the flyers, leaving the few boys untouched who stood their ground. The obvious moral taught that blackguards were not so black as they were painted; but the boy Henry had passed through as much terror as though he were Turenne or Henri IV, and ten or twelve years afterwards when these same boys were fighting and falling on all the battle-fields of Virginia and Maryland, he wondered whether their education on Boston Common had taught Savage and Marvin how to die.

If violence were a part of complete education, Boston was not incomplete. The idea of violence was familiar to the anti-slavery leaders as well as to their followers. Most of them suffered from it. Mobs were always possible. Henry never happened to be actually concerned in a mob, but he, like every other boy, was sure to be on hand wherever a mob was expected, and whenever he heard Garrison or Wendell Phillips speak, he looked for trouble. Wendell Phillips on a platform was a model dangerous for youth. Theodore Parker in his pulpit was not much safer. Worst of all, the execution of the Fugitive Slave Law in Boston — the sight of Court Square packed with bayonets, and his own friends obliged to line the streets under arms as State militia, in order to return a negro to slavery — wrought frenzy in the brain of a fifteen-year-old, eighteenth-century boy from Quincy, who wanted to miss no reasonable chance of mischief.

One lived in the atmosphere of the Stamp Act, the Tea Tax, and the Boston Massacre. Within Boston, a boy was first an eighteenth-century politician, and afterwards only a possibility; beyond Boston the first step led only further into politics. After February, 1848, but one slight tie remained of all those that, since 1776, had connected Quincy with the outer world. The Madam stayed in Washington, after her husband's death, and in her turn was struck by paralysis and bedridden. From time to time her son Charles, whose affection and sympathy for his mother in her many tribulations were always pronounced, went on to see her, and in May, 1850, he took with him his twelve-year-old son. The journey was meant as education, and as education it served the purpose of fixing in memory the stage of a boy's thought in 1850. He could not remember taking special interest in the railroad journey or in New York; with railways and cities he was familiar enough. His first impression was the novelty of crossing New York

Bay and finding an English railway carriage on the Camden and Amboy Railroad. This was a new world; a suggestion of corruption in the simple habits of American life; a step to exclusiveness never approached in Boston; but it was amusing. The boy rather liked it. At Trenton the train set him on board a steamer which took him to Philadelphia where he smelt other varieties of town life; then again by boat to Chester, and by train to Havre de Grace; by boat to Baltimore and thence by rail to Washington. This was the journey he remembered. The actual journey may have been quite different, but the actual journey has no interest for education. The memory was all that mattered; and what struck him most, to remain fresh in his mind all his lifetime, was the sudden change that came over the world on entering a slave State. He took education politically. The mere raggedness of outline could not have seemed wholly new, for even Boston had its ragged edges, and the town of Quincy was far from being a vision of neatness or good-repair; in truth, he had never seen a finished landscape; but Maryland was raggedness of a new kind. The railway, about the size and character of a modern tram, rambled through unfenced fields and woods, or through village streets, among a haphazard variety of pigs, cows, and negro babies, who might all have used the cabins for pens and styes, had the Southern pig required styes, but who never showed a sign of care. This was the boy's impression of what slavery caused, and, for him, was all it taught. Coming down in the early morning from his bedroom in his grandmother's house — still called the Adams Building — in F Street and venturing outside into the air reeking with the thick odor of the catalpa trees, he found himself on an earth-road, or village street, with wheel-tracks meandering from the colonnade of the Treasury hard by, to the white marble columns and fronts of the Post Office and Patent Office which faced each other in the distance, like white Greek temples in the abandoned gravel-pits of a deserted Syrian city. Here and there low wooden houses were scattered along the streets, as in other Southern villages, but he was chiefly attracted by an unfinished square marble shaft, half-a-mile below, and he walked down to inspect it before breakfast. His aunt drily remarked that, at this rate, he would soon get through all the sights; but she could not guess — having lived always in Washington — how little the sights of Washington had to do with its interest.

The boy could not have told her; he was nowhere near an understanding of himself. The more he was educated, the less he understood. Slavery struck him in the face; it was a nightmare; a horror; a crime; the sum of all wickedness! Contact made it only more repulsive. He wanted to escape, like the negroes, to free soil. Slave States were dirty, unkempt, poverty-stricken, ignorant, vicious! He had not a thought but repulsion for it; and yet the picture had another side. The May sunshine and shadow had something to do with it; the thickness of foliage and the heavy smells had more; the sense of atmosphere, almost new, had perhaps as much again; and the brooding indolence of a warm climate and a negro population hung in the atmosphere heavier than the catalpas. The impression was not simple, but the boy liked it: distinctly it remained on his mind as an attraction, almost obscuring Quincy itself. The want of barriers, of pavements, of forms; the looseness, the laziness; the indolent Southern drawl; the pigs in the streets; the negro babies and their mothers with bandanas; the freedom, openness, swagger, of nature and man, soothed his Johnson blood. Most boys would have felt it in the same way, but with him the feeling caught on to an inheritance. The softness of his gentle old grandmother as she lay in bed and chatted with him, did not come from Boston. His aunt was anything rather than Bostonian. He did not wholly come from Boston himself. Though Washington belonged to a different world, and the two worlds could not live together, he was not sure that he enjoyed the Boston world most. Even at twelve years old he could see his own nature no more clearly than he would at twelve hundred, if by accident he should happen to live so long.

His father took him to the Capitol and on the floor of the Senate, which then, and long afterwards, until the era of tourists, was freely open to visitors. The old Senate Chamber resembled a pleasant political club. Standing behind the Vice-President's chair, which is now the Chief Justice's, the boy was presented to some of the men whose names were great in their day, and as familiar to him as his own. Clay and Webster and Calhoun were there still, but with them a Free Soil candidate for the Vice-Presidency had little to do; what struck boys most was their type. Senators were a species; they all wore an air, as they wore a blue dress coat or brass buttons; they were Romans. The type of Senator in 1850 was rather charming at its best, and the Senate, when in good temper, was an agreeable body, numbering only some sixty members, and affecting the airs of courtesy. Its vice was not so much a vice of manners or temper as of attitude. The statesman of all periods was apt to be pompous, but even pomposity was less offensive than familiarity — on the platform as in the pulpit — and Southern pomposity, when not arrogant, was genial and sympathetic, almost quaint and childlike in its simple-mindedness; quite a different thing from the Websterian or Conklinian pomposity of the North. The boy felt at ease there, more at home than he had ever felt in Boston State House, though his acquaintance with the codfish in the House of Representatives went back beyond distinct recollection. Senators spoke kindly to him, and seemed to feel so, for they had known his family socially;

and, in spite of slavery, even J. Q. Adams in his later years, after he ceased to stand in the way of rivals, had few personal enemies. Decidedly the Senate, pro-slavery though it were, seemed a friendly world.

This first step in national politics was a little like the walk before breakfast; an easy, careless, genial, enlarging stride into a fresh and amusing world, where nothing was finished, but where even the weeds grew rank. The second step was like the first, except that it led to the White House. He was taken to see President Taylor. Outside, in a paddock in front, "Old Whitey," the President's charger, was grazing, as they entered; and inside, the President was receiving callers as simply as if he were in the paddock too. The President was friendly, and the boy felt no sense of strangeness that he could ever recall. In fact, what strangeness should he feel? The families were intimate; so intimate that their friendliness outlived generations, civil war, and all sorts of rupture. President Taylor owed his election to Martin Van Buren and the Free Soil Party. To him, the Adamses might still be of use. As for the White House, all the boy's family had lived there, and, barring the eight years of Andrew Jackson's reign, had been more or less at home there ever since it was built. The boy half thought he owned it, and took for granted that he should some day live in it. He felt no sensation whatever before Presidents. A President was a matter of course in every respectable family; he had two in his own; three, if he counted old Nathaniel Gorham, who was the oldest and first in distinction. Revolutionary patriots, or perhaps a Colonial Governor, might be worth talking about, but any one could be President, and some very shady characters were likely to be. Presidents, Senators, Congressmen, and such things were swarming in every street.

Every one thought alike whether they had ancestors or not. No sort of glory hedged Presidents as such, and, in the whole country, one could hardly have met with an admission of respect for any office or name, unless it were George Washington. That was — to all appearance sincerely — respected. People made pilgrimages to Mount Vernon and made even an effort to build Washington a monument. The effort had failed, but one still went to Mount Vernon, although it was no easy trip. Mr. Adams took the boy there in a carriage and pair, over a road that gave him a complete Virginia education for use ten years afterwards. To the New England mind, roads, schools, clothes, and a clean face were connected as part of the law of order or divine system. Bad roads meant bad morals. The morals of this Virginia road was clear, and the boy fully learned it. Slavery was wicked, and slavery was the cause of this road's badness which amounted to social crime — and yet, at the end of the road and product of the crime stood Mount Vernon and George Washington.

Luckily boys accept contradictions as readily as their elders do, or this boy might have become prematurely wise. He had only to repeat what he was told — that George Washington stood alone. Otherwise this third step in his Washington education would have been his last. On that line, the problem of progress was not soluble, whatever the optimists and orators might say— or, for that matter, whatever they might think. George Washington could not be reached on Boston lines. George Washington was a primary, or, if Virginians liked it better, an ultimate relation, like the Pole Star, and amid the endless restless motion of every other visible point in space, he alone remained steady, in the mind of Henry Adams, to the end. All the other points shifted their bearings; John Adams, Jefferson, Madison, Franklin, even John Marshall, took varied lights, and assumed new relations, but Mount Vernon always remained where it was, with no practicable road to reach it; and yet, when he got there, Mount Vernon was only Quincy in a Southern setting. No doubt it was much more charming, but it was the same eighteenth century, the same old furniture, the same old patriot, and the same old President.

The boy took to it distinctively. The broad Potomac and the coons in the trees, the bandanas and the box-hedges, the bedrooms upstairs and the porch outside, even Martha Washington herself in memory, were as natural as the tides and the May sunshine; he had only enlarged his horizon a little; but he never thought to ask himself or his father how to deal with the moral problem that deduced George Washington from the sum of all wickedness. In practice, such trifles as contradictions in principle are easily set aside; the faculty of ignoring them makes the practical man; but any attempt to deal with them seriously as education is fatal. Luckily Charles Francis Adams never preached and was singularly free from cant. He may have had views of his own, but he let his son Henry satisfy himself with the simple elementary fact that George Washington stood alone.

Life was not yet complicated. Every problem had a solution, even the negro. The boy went back to Boston more political than ever, and his politics were no longer so modern as the eighteenth century, but took a strong tone of the seventeenth. Slavery drove the whole Puritan community back on its Puritanism. The boy thought as dogmatically as though he were one of his own ancestors. The Slave power took the place of Stuart kings and Roman popes. Education could go no further in that course, and ran off into emotion; but, as the boy gradually found his surroundings change, and felt himself no longer an isolated atom in a hostile universe, but a sort of herring-fry in a shoal of moving fish, he began to learn the first and easier lessons of practical politics. Thus far he had seen nothing but eighteenth-century statesmanship. America and he began, at the same time, to become aware of a new force under the innocent surface of party machinery. Even at that early moment, a rather slow boy felt dimly conscious that he might meet some personal difficulties in trying to reconcile sixteenth-century principles and eighteenth-century statesmanship with late nineteenth-century party organization. The first vague sense of feeling an unknown living obstacle in the dark came in 1851.

The Free Soil conclave in Mount Vernon Street belonged, as already said, to the statesman class, and, like Daniel Webster, had nothing to do with machinery. Websters or Sewards depended on others for machine work and money — on Peter Harveys and Thurlow Weeds, who spent their lives in it, took most of the abuse, and asked no reward. Almost without knowing it, the subordinates ousted their employers and created a machine which no one but themselves could run. In 1850 things had not quite reached that point. The men who ran the small Free Soil machine were still modest, though they became famous enough in their own right. Henry Wilson, John B. Alley, Anson Burlingame, and the other managers, negotiated a bargain with the Massachusetts Democrats giving the State to the Democrats and a seat in the Senate to the Free Soilers. With this bargain Mr. Adams and his statesman friends would have nothing to do, for such a coalition was in their eyes much like jockeys selling a race. They did not care to take office as pay for votes sold to pro-slavery Democrats. Theirs was a correct, not to say noble, position; but, as a matter of fact, they took the benefit of the sale, for the coalition chose Charles Sumner as its candidate for the Senate, while George S. Boutwell was made Governor for the Democrats. This was the boy's first lesson in practical politics, and a sharp one; not that he troubled himself with moral doubts, but that he learned the nature of a flagrantly corrupt political bargain in which he was too good to take part, but not too good to take profit. Charles Sumner happened to be the partner to receive these stolen goods, but between his friend and his father the boy felt no distinction, and, for him, there was none. He entered into no casuistry on the matter. His friend was right because his friend, and the boy shared the glory. The question of education did not rise while the conflict lasted. Yet every one saw as clearly then as afterwards that a lesson of some sort must be learned and understood, once for all. The boy might ignore, as a mere historical puzzle, the question how to deduce George Washington from the sum of all wickedness, but he had himself helped to deduce Charles Sumner from the sum of political corruption. On that line, too, education could go no further. Tammany Hall stood at the end of the vista.

Mr. Alley, one of the strictest of moralists, held that his object in making the bargain was to convert the Democratic Party to anti-slavery principles, and that he did it. Henry Adams could rise to no such moral elevation. He was only a boy, and his object in supporting the coalition was that of making his friend a Senator. It was as personal as though he had helped to make his friend a millionaire. He could never find a way of escaping immoral conclusions, except by admitting that he and his father and Sumner were wrong, and this he was never willing to do, for the consequences of this admission were worse than those of the other. Thus, before he was fifteen years old, he had managed to get himself into a state of moral confusion from which he never escaped. As a politician, he was already corrupt, and he never could see how any practical politician could be less corrupt than himself.

Apology, as he understood himself, was cant or cowardice. At the time he never even dreamed that he needed to apologize, though the press shouted it at him from every corner, and though the Mount Vernon Street conclave agreed with the press; yet he could not plead ignorance, and even in the heat of the conflict, he never cared to defend the coalition. Boy as he was, he knew enough to know that something was wrong, but his only interest was the election. Day after day, the General Court balloted; and the boy haunted the gallery, following the roll-call, and wondered what Caleb Cushing meant by calling Mr. Sumner a "one-eyed abolitionist." Truly the difference in meaning with the phrase "one-ideaed abolitionist," which was Mr. Cushing's actual expression, is not very great, but neither the one nor the other seemed to describe Mr. Sumner to the boy, who never could have made the error of classing Garrison and Sumner together, or mistaking Caleb Cushing's relation to either. Temper ran high at that moment, while Sumner every day missed his election by only one or two votes. At last, April 24, 1851, standing among the silent crowd in the gallery, Henry heard the vote announced which gave Sumner the needed number. Slipping under the arms of the bystanders, he ran home as hard as he could, and burst into the dining-room where Mr. Sumner was seated at table with the family. He enjoyed the glory of telling Sumner that he was elected; it was probably the proudest moment in the life of either.

The next day, when the boy went to school, he noticed numbers of boys and men in the streets wearing black crape on their arm. He knew few Free Soil boys in Boston; his acquaintances were what he called proslavery; so he thought proper to tie a bit of white silk ribbon round his own arm by way of showing that his friend Mr. Sumner was not wholly alone. This little piece of bravado passed unnoticed; no one even cuffed his ears;

but in later life he was a little puzzled to decide which symbol was the more correct. No one then dreamed of four years' war, but every one dreamed of secession. The symbol for either might well be matter of doubt.

This triumph of the Mount Vernon Street conclave capped the political climax. The boy, like a million other American boys, was a politician, and what was worse, fit as yet to be nothing else. He should have been, like his grandfather, a protégé of George Washington, a statesman designated by destiny, with nothing to do but look directly ahead, follow orders, and march. On the contrary, he was not even a Bostonian; he felt himself shut out of Boston as though he were an exile; he never thought of himself as a Bostonian; he never looked about him in Boston, as boys commonly do wherever they are, to select the street they like best, the house they want to live in, the profession they mean to practise. Always he felt himself somewhere else; perhaps in Washington with its social ease; perhaps in Europe; and he watched with vague unrest from the Quincy hills the smoke of the Cunard steamers stretching in a long line to the horizon, and disappearing every other Saturday or whatever the day might be, as though the steamers were offering to take him away, which was precisely what they were doing.

Had these ideas been unreasonable, influences enough were at hand to correct them; but the point of the whole story, when Henry Adams came to look back on it, seemed to be that the ideas were more than reasonable; they were the logical, necessary, mathematical result of conditions old as history and fixed as fate — invariable sequence in man's experience. The only idea which would have been quite unreasonable scarcely entered his mind. This was the thought of going westward and growing up with the country. That he was not in the least fitted for going West made no objection whatever, since he was much better fitted than most of the persons that went. The convincing reason for staying in the East was that he had there every advantage over the West. He could not go wrong. The West must inevitably pay an enormous tribute to Boston and New York. One's position in the East was the best in the world for every purpose that could offer an object for going westward. If ever in history men had been able to calculate on a certainty for a lifetime in advance, the citizens of the great Eastern seaports could do it in 1850 when their railway systems were already laid out. Neither to a politician nor to a businessman nor to any of the learned professions did the West promise any certain advantage, while it offered uncertainties in plenty.

At any other moment in human history, this education, including its political and literary bias, would have been not only good, but quite the best. Society had always welcomed and flattered men so endowed. Henry Adams had every reason to be well pleased with it, and not ill-pleased with himself. He had all he wanted. He saw no reason for thinking that any one else had more. He finished with school, not very brilliantly, but without finding fault with the sum of his knowledge. Probably he knew more than his father, or his grandfather, or his great-grandfather had known at sixteen years old. Only on looking back, fifty years later, at his own figure in 1854, and pondering on the needs of the twentieth century, he wondered whether, on the whole, the boy of 1854 stood nearer to the thought of 1904, or to that of the year 1. He found himself unable to give a sure answer. The calculation was clouded by the undetermined values of twentieth-century thought, but the story will show his reasons for thinking that, in essentials like religion, ethics, philosophy; in history, literature, art; in the concepts of all science, except perhaps mathematics, the American boy of 1854 stood nearer the year 1 than to the year 1900. The education he had received bore little relation to the education he needed. Speaking as an American of 1900, he had as yet no education at all. He knew not even where or how to begin.

4

Harvard College

(1854–1858)

One day in June, 1854, young Adams walked for the last time down the steps of Mr. Dixwell's school in Boylston Place, and felt no sensation but one of unqualified joy that this experience was ended. Never before or afterwards in his life did he close a period so long as four years without some sensation of loss — some sentiment of habit — but school was what in after life he commonly heard his friends denounce as an intolerable bore. He was born too old for it. The same thing could be said of most New England boys. Mentally they never were boys. Their education as men should have begun at ten years old. They were fully five years more mature than the English or European boy for whom schools were made. For the purposes of future advancement, as afterwards appeared, these first six years of a possible education were wasted in doing imperfectly what might have been done perfectly in one, and in any case would have had small value. The next regular step was Harvard College. He was more than glad to go. For generation after generation, Adamses and Brookses and Boylstons and Gorhams had gone to

Harvard College, and although none of them, as far as known, had ever done any good there, or thought himself the better for it, custom, social ties, convenience, and, above all, economy, kept each generation in the track. Any other education would have required a serious effort, but no one took Harvard College seriously. All went there because their friends went there, and the College was their ideal of social self-respect.

Harvard College, as far as it educated at all, was a mild and liberal school, which sent young men into the world with all they needed to make respectable citizens, and something of what they wanted to make useful ones. Leaders of men it never tried to make. Its ideals were altogether different. The Unitarian clergy had given to the College a character of moderation, balance, judgment, restraint, what the French called *mesure;* excellent traits, which the College attained with singular success, so that its graduates could commonly be recognized by the stamp, but such a type of character rarely lent itself to autobiography. In effect, the school created a type but not a will. Four years of Harvard College, if successful, resulted in an autobiographical blank, a mind on which only a water-mark had been stamped.

The stamp, as such things went, was a good one. The chief wonder of education is that it does not ruin everybody concerned in it, teachers and taught. Sometimes in after life, Adams debated whether in fact it had not ruined him and most of his companions, but, disappointment apart, Harvard College was probably less hurtful than any other university then in existence. It taught little, and and that little ill, but it left the mind open, free from bias, ignorant of facts, but docile. The graduate had few strong prejudices. He knew little, but his mind remained supple, ready to receive knowledge.

What caused the boy most disappointment was the

little he got from his mates. Speaking exactly, he got less than nothing, a result common enough in education. Yet the College Catalogue for the years 1854 to 1861 shows a list of names rather distinguished in their time. Alexander Agassiz and Phillips Brooks led it; H. H. Richardson and O. W. Holmes helped to close it. As a rule the most promising of all die early, and never get their names into a Dictionary of Contemporaries, which seems to be the only popular standard of success. Many died in the war. Adams knew them all, more or less; he felt as much regard, and quite as much respect for them then, as he did after they won great names and were objects of a vastly wider respect; but, as help towards education, he got nothing whatever from them or they from him until long after they had left college. Possibly the fault was his, but one would like to know how many others shared it. Accident counts for much in companionship as in marriage. Life offers perhaps only a score of possible companions, and it is mere chance whether they meet as early as school or college, but it is more than a chance that boys brought up together under like conditions have nothing to give each other. The Class of 1858, to which Henry Adams belonged, was a typical collection of young New Englanders, quietly penetrating and aggressively commonplace; free from meannesses, jealousies, intrigues, enthusiasms, and passions; not exceptionally quick; not consciously sceptical; singularly indifferent to display, artifice, florid expression, but not hostile to it when it amused them; distrustful of themselves, but little disposed to trust any one else; with not much humor of their own, but full of readiness to enjoy the humor of others; negative to a degree that in the long run became positive and triumphant. Not harsh in manners or judgment, rather liberal and open-minded, they were still as a body the most formidable critics one would care to meet, in a long life exposed to criticism. They never flattered, seldom praised; free from vanity, they were not intolerant of it; but they were objectiveness itself; their attitude was a law of nature; their judgment beyond appeal, not an act either of intellect or emotion or of will, but a sort of gravitation.

This was Harvard College incarnate, but even for Harvard College, the Class of 1858 was somewhat extreme. Of unity this band of nearly one hundred young men had no keen sense, but they had equally little energy of repulsion. They were pleasant to live with, and above the average of students — German, French, English, or what not — but chiefly because each individual appeared satisfied to stand alone. It seemed a sign of force; yet to stand alone is quite natural when one has no passions; still easier when one has no pains.

Into this unusually dissolvent medium, chance insisted on enlarging Henry Adams's education by tossing a trio of Virginians as little fitted for it as Sioux Indians to a treadmill. By some further affinity, these three outsiders fell into relation with the Bostonians among whom Adams as a schoolboy belonged, and in the end with Adams himself, although they and he knew well how thin an edge of friendship separated them in 1856 from mortal enmity. One of the Virginians was the son of Colonel Robert E. Lee, of the Second United States Cavalry; the two others who seemed instinctively to form a staff for Lee, were town-Virginians from Petersburg. A fourth outsider came from Cincinnati and was half Kentuckian, N. L. Anderson, Longworth on the mother's side. For the first time Adams's education brought him in contact with new types and taught him their values. He saw the New England type measure itself with another, and he was part of the process.

Lee, known through life as "Roony," was a Virginian of the eighteenth century, much as Henry Adams was a

Bostonian of the same age. Roony Lee had changed little from the type of his grandfather, Light Horse Harry. Tall, largely built, handsome, genial, with liberal Virginian openness towards all he liked, he had also the Virginian habit of command and took leadership as his natural habit. No one cared to contest it. None of the New Englanders wanted command. For a year, at least, Lee was the most popular and prominent young man in his class, but then seemed slowly to drop into the background. The habit of command was not enough, and the Virginian had little else. He was simple beyond analysis; so simple that even the simple New England student could not realize him. No one knew enough to know how ignorant he was; how childlike; how helpless before the relative complexity of a school. As an animal, the Southerner seemed to have every advantage, but even as an animal he steadily lost ground.

The lesson in education was vital to these young men, who, within ten years, killed each other by scores in the act of testing their college conclusions. Strictly, the Southerner had no mind; he had temperament. He was not a scholar; he had no intellectual training; he could not analyze an idea, and he could not even conceive of admitting two; but in life one could get along very well without ideas, if one had only the social instinct. Dozens of eminent statesmen were men of Lee's type, and maintained themselves well enough in the legislature, but college was a sharper test. The Virginian was weak in vice itself, though the Bostonian was hardly a master of crime. The habits of neither were good; both were apt to drink hard and to live low lives; but the Bostonian suffered less than the Virginian. Commonly the Bostonian would take some care of himself even in his worst stages, while the Virginian became quarrelsome and dangerous. When a Virginian had brooded a few days over an imaginary grief and substantial whiskey, none of his Northern friends could be sure that he might not be waiting, round the corner, with a knife or pistol, to revenge insult by the dry light of *delirium tremens;* and when things reached this condition, Lee had to exhaust his authority over his own staff. Lee was a gentleman of the old school, and, as every one knows, gentlemen of the old school drank almost as much as gentlemen of the new school; but this was not his trouble. He was sober even in the excessive violence of political feeling in those years; he kept his temper and his friends under control.

Adams liked the Virginians. No one was more obnoxious to them, by name and prejudice; yet their friendship was unbroken and even warm. At a moment when the immediate future posed no problem in education so vital as the relative energy and endurance of North and South, this momentary contact with Southern character was a sort of education for its own sake; but this was not all. No doubt the self-esteem of the Yankee, which tended naturally to self-distrust, was flattered by gaining the slow conviction that the Southerner, with his slave-owning limitations, was as little fit to succeed in the struggle of modern life as though he were still a maker of stone axes, living in caves, and hunting the *bos primigenius*, and that every quality in which he was strong, made him weaker; but Adams had begun to fear that even in this respect one eighteenth-century type might not differ deeply from another. Roony Lee had changed little from the Virginian of a century before; but Adams was himself a good deal nearer the type of his great-grandfather than to that of a railway superintendent. He was little more fit than the Virginians to deal with a future America which showed no fancy for the past. Already Northern society betrayed a preference for economists over diplomats or soldiers — one might even call it a jealousy — against which two eighteenth-century types had little chance to live, and which they had in common to fear.

Nothing short of this curious sympathy could have brought into close relations two young men so hostile as Roony Lee and Henry Adams, but the chief difference between them as collegians consisted only in their difference of scholarship: Lee was a total failure; Adams a partial one. Both failed, but Lee felt his failure more sensibly, so that he gladly seized the chance of escape by accepting a commission offered him by General Winfield Scott in the force then being organized against the Mormons. He asked Adams to write his letter of acceptance, which flattered Adams's vanity more than any Northern compliment could do, because, in days of violent political bitterness, it showed a certain amount of good temper. The diplomat felt his profession.

If the student got little from his mates, he got little more from his masters. The four years passed at college were, for his purposes, wasted. Harvard College was a good school, but at bottom what the boy disliked most was any school at all. He did not want to be one in a hundred — one per cent of an education. He regarded himself as the only person for whom his education had value, and he wanted the whole of it. He got barely half of an average. Long afterwards, when the devious path of life led him back to teach in his turn what no student naturally cared or needed to know, he diverted some dreary hours of faculty-meetings by looking up his record in the class-lists, and found himself graded precisely in the middle. In the one branch he most needed — mathematics — barring the few first scholars, failure was so nearly universal that no attempt at grading could have had value, and whether he stood fortieth or ninetieth must have been an accident or the personal favor of the professor. Here his education failed lamentably. At best he could never have been a mathematician; at worst he would never have cared to be one; but he needed to read mathematics, like any other universal language, and he never reached the alphabet.

Beyond two or three Greek plays, the student got nothing from the ancient languages. Beyond some incoherent theories of free-trade and protection, he got little from Political Economy. He could not afterwards remember to have heard the name of Karl Marx mentioned, or the title of "Capital." He was equally ignorant of Auguste Comte. These were the two writers of his time who most influenced its thought. The bit of practical teaching he afterwards reviewed with most curiosity was the course in Chemistry, which taught him a number of theories that befogged his mind for a lifetime. The only teaching that appealed to his imagination was a course of lectures by Louis Agassiz on the Glacial Period and Palæontology, which had more influence on his curiosity than the rest of the college instruction altogether. The entire work of the four years could have been easily put into the work of any four months in after life.

Harvard College was a negative force, and negative forces have value. Slowly it weakened the violent political bias of childhood, not by putting interests in its place, but by mental habits which had no bias at all. It would also have weakened the literary bias, if Adams had been capable of finding other amusement, but the climate kept him steady to desultory and useless reading, till he had run through libraries of volumes which he forgot even to their title-pages. Rather by instinct than by guidance, he turned to writing, and his professors or tutors occasionally gave his English composition a hesitating approval; but in that branch, as in all the rest, even when he made a long struggle for recognition, he never convinced his teachers that his abilities, at their best, warranted placing him on the rank-list, among the first third of his class. Instructors generally reach a fairly accurate gauge of their scholars' powers. Henry Adams himself held the opinion that his instructors were very nearly right, and when he became a professor in his turn, and made mortifying mistakes in ranking his scholars, he still obstinately insisted that on the whole, he was not far wrong. Student or professor, he accepted the negative standard because it was the standard of the school.

He never knew what other students thought of it, or what they thought they gained from it; nor would their opinion have much affected his. From the first, he wanted to be done with it, and stood watching vaguely for a path and a direction. The world outside seemed large, but the paths that led into it were not many and lay mostly through Boston, where he did not want to go. As it happened, by pure chance, the first door of escape that seemed to offer a hope led into Germany, and James Russell Lowell opened it.

Lowell, on succeeding Longfellow as Professor of Belles-Lettres, had duly gone to Germany, and had brought back whatever he found to bring. The literary world then agreed that truth survived in Germany alone, and Carlyle, Matthew Arnold, Renan, Emerson, with scores of popular followers, taught the German faith. The literary world had revolted against the yoke of coming capitalism — its money-lenders, its bank directors, and its railway magnates. Thackeray and Dickens followed Balzac in scratching and biting the unfortunate middle class with savage ill-temper, much as the middle class had scratched and bitten the Church and Court for a hundred years before. The middle class had the power, and held its coal and iron well in hand, but the satirists and idealists seized the press, and as they were agreed that the Second Empire was a disgrace to France and a danger to England, they turned to Germany because at that moment

Germany was neither economical nor military, and a hundred years behind western Europe in the simplicity of its standard. German thought, method, honesty, and even taste, became the standards of scholarship. Goethe was raised to the rank of Shakespeare — Kant ranked as a law-giver above Plato. All serious scholars were obliged to become German, for German thought was revolutionizing criticism. Lowell had followed the rest, not very enthusiastically, but with sufficient conviction, and invited his scholars to join him. Adams was glad to accept the invitation, rather for the sake of cultivating Lowell than Germany, but still in perfect good faith. It was the first serious attempt he had made to direct his own education, and he was sure of getting some education out of it; not perhaps anything that he expected, but at least a path.

Singularly circuitous and excessively wasteful of energy the path proved to be, but the student could never see what other was open to him. He could have done no better had he foreseen every stage of his coming life, and he would probably have done worse. The preliminary step was pure gain. James Russell Lowell had brought back from Germany the only new and valuable part of its universities, the habit of allowing students to read with him privately in his study. Adams asked the privilege, and used it to read a little, and to talk a great deal, for the personal contact pleased and flattered him, as that of older men ought to flatter and please the young even when they altogether exaggerate its value. Lowell was a new element in the boy's life. As practical a New Englander as any, he leaned towards the Concord faith rather than towards Boston where he properly belonged; for Concord, in the dark days of 1856, glowed with pure light. Adams approached it in much the same spirit as he would have entered a Gothic Cathedral, for he well knew that the priests regarded him as only a worm. To the

Concord Church all Adamses were minds of dust and emptiness, devoid of feeling, poetry or imagination; little higher than the common scourings of State Street; politicians of doubtful honesty; natures of narrow scope; and already, at eighteen years old, Henry had begun to feel uncertainty about so many matters more important than Adamses that his mind rebelled against no discipline merely personal, and he was ready to admit his unworthiness if only he might penetrate the shrine. The influence of Harvard College was beginning to have its effect. He was slipping away from fixed principles; from Mount Vernon Street; from Quincy; from the eighteenth century; and his first steps led toward Concord.

He never reached Concord, and to Concord Church he, like the rest of mankind who accepted a material universe, remained always an insect, or something much lower — a man. It was surely no fault of his that the universe seemed to him real; perhaps — as Mr. Emerson justly said — it was so; in spite of the long-continued effort of a lifetime, he perpetually fell back into the heresy that if anything universal was unreal, it was himself and not the appearances; it was the poet and not the banker; it was his own thought, not the thing that moved it. He did not lack the wish to be transcendental. Concord seemed to him, at one time, more real than Quincy; yet in truth Russell Lowell was as little transcendental as Beacon Street. From him the boy got no revolutionary thought whatever — objective or subjective as they used to call it — but he got good-humored encouragement to do what amused him, which consisted in passing two years in Europe after finishing the four years of Cambridge.

The result seemed small in proportion to the effort, but it was the only positive result he could ever trace to the influence of Harvard College, and he had grave doubts whether Harvard College influenced even that. Negative results in plenty he could trace, but he tended towards negation on his own account, as one side of the New England mind had always done, and even there he could never feel sure that Harvard College had more than reflected a weakness. In his opinion the education was not serious, but in truth hardly any Boston student took it seriously, and none of them seemed sure that President Walker himself, or President Felton after him, took it more seriously than the students. For them all, the college offered chiefly advantages vulgarly called social, rather than mental.

Unluckily for this particular boy, social advantages were his only capital in life. Of money he had not much, of mind not more, but he could be quite certain that, barring his own faults, his social position would never be questioned. What he needed was a career in which social position had value. Never in his life would he have to explain who he was; never would he have need of acquaintance to strengthen his social standing; but he needed greatly some one to show him how to use the acquaintance he cared to make. He made no acquaintance in college which proved to have the smallest use in after life. All his Boston friends he knew before, or would have known in any case, and contact of Bostonian with Bostonian was the last education these young men needed. Cordial and intimate as their college relations were, they all flew off in different directions the moment they took their degrees. Harvard College remained a tie, indeed, but a tie little stronger than Beacon Street and not so strong as State Street. Strangers might perhaps gain something from the college if they were hard pressed for social connections. A student like H. H. Richardson, who came from far away New Orleans, and had his career before him to chase rather than to guide, might make valuable friendships at college. Certainly Adams made no acquaintance there that he valued in after life so much as Richardson, but still more certainly the college relation had little to do with the later friendship. Life is a narrow valley, and the roads run close together. Adams would have attached himself to Richardson in any case, as he attached himself to John La Farge or Augustus St. Gaudens or Clarence King or John Hay, none of whom were at Harvard College. The valley of life grew more and more narrow with years, and certain men with common tastes were bound to come together. Adams knew only that he would have felt himself on a more equal footing with them had he been less ignorant, and had he not thrown away ten years of early life in acquiring what he might have acquired in one.

Socially or intellectually, the college was for him negative and in some ways mischievous. The most tolerant man of the world could not see good in the lower habits of the students, but the vices were less harmful than the virtues. The habit of drinking — though the mere recollection of it made him doubt his own veracity, so fantastic it seemed in later life — may have done no great or permanent harm; but the habit of looking at life as a social relation — an affair of society — did no good. It cultivated a weakness which needed no cultivation. If it had helped to make men of the world, or give the manners and instincts of any profession — such as temper, patience, courtesy, or a faculty of profiting by the social defects of opponents — it would have been education better worth having than mathematics or languages; but so far as it helped to make anything, it helped only to make the college standard permanent through life. The Bostonian educated at Harvard College remained a collegian, if he stuck only to what the college gave him. If parents went on, generation after generation, sending their children to Harvard College for the sake of its social advantages, they perpetuated an inferior social type, quite as ill-fitted as the Oxford type for success in the next generation.

Luckily the old social standard of the college, as President Walker or James Russell Lowell still showed it, was admirable, and if it had little practical value or personal influence on the mass of students, at least it preserved the tradition for those who liked it. The Harvard graduate was neither American nor European, nor even wholly Yankee; his admirers were few, and his critics many; perhaps his worst weakness was his self-criticism and self-consciousness; but his ambitions, social or intellectual, were not necessarily cheap even though they might be negative. Afraid of serious risks, and still more afraid of personal ridicule, he seldom made a great failure of life, and nearly always led a life more or less worth living. So Henry Adams, well aware that he could not succeed as a scholar, and finding his social position beyond improvement or need of effort, betook himself to the single ambition which otherwise would scarcely have seemed a true outcome of the college, though it was the last remnant of the old Unitarian supremacy. He took to the pen. He wrote.

The College Magazine printed his work, and the College Societies listened to his addresses. Lavish of praise the readers were not; the audiences, too, listened in silence; but this was all the encouragement any Harvard collegian had a reasonable hope to receive; grave silence was a form of patience that meant possible future acceptance; and Henry Adams went on writing. No one cared enough to criticise, except himself who soon began to suffer from reaching his own limits. He found that he could not be this — or that — or the other; always precisely the things he wanted to be. He had not wit or scope or force. Judges always ranked him beneath a rival, if he had any; and he believed the judges were right. His work seemed to him thin, commonplace, feeble. At times he felt his own weakness so fatally that he could not go on; when he had nothing to say, he could not say it, and he found that he had very little to say at best. Much that he then wrote must be still in existence in print or manuscript, though he never cared to see it again, for he felt no doubt that it was in reality just what he thought it. At best it showed only a feeling for form; an instinct of exclusion. Nothing shocked — not even its weakness.

Inevitably an effort leads to an ambition — creates it — and at that time the ambition of the literary student, which almost took place of the regular prizes of scholarship, was that of being chosen as the representative of his class — the Class Orator — at the close of their course. This was political as well as literary success, and precisely the sort of eighteenth-century combination that fascinated an eighteenth-century boy. The idea lurked in his mind, at first as a dream, in no way serious or even possible, for he stood outside the number of what were known as popular men. Year by year, his position seemed to improve, or perhaps his rivals disappeared, until at last, to his own great astonishment, he found himself a candidate. The habits of the college permitted no active candidacy; he and his rivals had not a word to say for or against themselves, and he was never even consulted on the subject; he was not present at any of the proceedings, and how it happened he never could quite divine, but it did happen, that one evening on returning from Boston he received notice of his election, after a very close contest, as Class Orator over the head of the first scholar, who was undoubtedly a better orator and a more popular man. In politics the success of the poorer candidate is common enough, and Henry Adams was a fairly trained politician, but he never understood how he managed to defeat not only a more capable but a more popular rival.

To him the election seemed a miracle. This was no mock-modesty; his head was as clear as ever it was in an indifferent canvass, and he knew his rivals and their following as well as he knew himself. What he did not know, even after four years of education, was Harvard College. What he could never measure was the bewildering impersonality of the men, who, at twenty years old, seemed to set no value either on official or personal standards. Here were nearly a hundred young men who had lived together intimately during four of the most impressionable years of life, and who, not only once but again and again, in different ways, deliberately, seriously, dispassionately, chose as their representatives precisely those of their companions who seemed least to represent them. As far as these Orators and Marshals had any position at all in a collegiate sense, it was that of indifference to the college. Henry Adams never professed the smallest faith in universities of any kind, either as boy or man, nor had he the faintest admiration for the university graduate, either in Europe or in America; as a collegian he was only known apart from his fellows by his habit of standing outside the college; and yet the singular fact remained that this commonplace body of young men chose him repeatedly to express his and their commonplaces. Secretly, of course, the successful candidate flattered himself — and them — with the hope that they might perhaps not be so commonplace as they thought themselves; but this was only another proof that all were identical. They saw in him a representative — the kind of representative they wanted — and he saw in them the most formidable array of judges he could ever meet, like so many mirrors of himself, an infinite reflection of his own shortcomings.

All the same, the choice was flattering; so flattering that it actually shocked his vanity; and would have shocked it more, if possible, had he known that it was to be the only flattery of the sort he was ever to receive. The function of Class Day was, in the eyes of nine-tenths of the students, altogether the most important of the college, and the figure of the Orator was the most conspicuous in the function. Unlike the Orators at regular Commencements, the Class Day Orator stood alone, or had only the Poet for rival. Crowded into the large church, the students, their families, friends, aunts, uncles and chaperones, attended all the girls of sixteen or twenty who wanted to show their summer dresses or fresh complexions, and there, for an hour or two, in a heat that might have melted bronze, they listened to an Orator and a Poet in clergyman's gowns, reciting such platitudes as their own experience and their mild censors permitted them to utter. What Henry Adams said in his Class Oration of 1858 he soon forgot to the last word, nor had it the least value for education; but he naturally remembered what was said of it. He remembered especially one of his eminent uncles or relations remarking that, as the work of so young a man, the oration was singularly wanting in enthusiasm. The young man — always in search of education — asked himself whether, setting rhetoric aside, this absence of enthusiasm was a defect or a merit, since, in either case, it was all that Harvard College taught, and all that the hundred young men, whom he was trying to represent, expressed. Another comment threw more light on the effect of the college education. One of the elderly gentlemen noticed the orator's "perfect self-possession." Self-possession indeed! If Harvard College gave nothing else, it gave calm. For four years each student had been obliged to figure daily before dozens of young men who knew each other to the last fibre. One had done little but read papers to Societies, or act comedy in the Hasty Pudding, not to speak of all sorts of regular exercises, and no audience in future life would ever be so intimately and terribly intelligent as these. Three-fourths of the graduates would rather have addressed the Council of Trent or the British Parliament than have acted Sir Anthony Absolute or Dr. Ollapod before a gala audience of the Hasty Pudding. Self-possession was the strongest part of Harvard College, which certainly taught them to stand alone, so that nothing seemed stranger to its graduates than the paroxysms of terror before the public which often overcame the graduates of European universities. Whether this was, or was not, education, Henry Adams never knew. He was ready to stand up before any audience in America or Europe, with nerves rather steadier for the excitement, but whether he should ever have anything to say, remained to be proved. As yet he knew nothing. Education had not begun.

5

Berlin

(1858–1859)

A fourth child has the strength of his weakness. Being of no great value, he may throw himself away if he likes, and never be missed. Charles Francis Adams, the father, felt no love for Europe, which, as he and all the world agreed, unfitted Americans for America. A captious critic might have replied that all the success he or his father or his grandfather achieved was chiefly due to the field that Europe gave them, and it was more than likely that without the help of Europe they would have all remained local politicians or lawyers, like their neighbors, to the end. Strictly followed, the rule would have obliged them never to quit Quincy; and, in fact, so much more timid are parents for their children than for themselves, that Mr. and Mrs. Adams would have been content to see their children remain forever in Mount Vernon Street, unexposed to the temptations of Europe, could they have relied on the moral influences of Boston itself. Although the parents little knew what took place under their eyes, even the mothers saw enough to make them uneasy. Perhaps their dread of vice, haunting past and present, worried them less than their dread of daughters-in-law or sons-in-law who might not fit into the somewhat narrow quarters of home. On all sides were risks. Every year some young person alarmed the parental heart even in Boston, and although the temptations of Europe were irresistible, removal from the temptations of Boston might be imperative. The boy Henry wanted to go to Europe; he seemed well behaved, when any one was looking at him; he observed conventions, when he could not escape them; he was never quarrelsome, towards a superior; his morals were apparently good, and his moral principles, if he had any, were not known to be bad. Above all, he was timid and showed a certain sense of self-respect, when in public view. What he was at heart, no one could say; least of all himself; but he was probably human, and no worse than some others. Therefore, when he presented to an exceedingly indulgent father and mother his request to begin at a German university the study of the Civil Law — although neither he nor they knew what the Civil Law was, or any reason for his studying it — the parents dutifully consented, and walked with him down to the railway-station at Quincy to bid him good-bye, with a smile which he almost thought a tear.

Whether the boy deserved such indulgence, or was worth it, he knew no more than they, or than a professor at Harvard College; but whether worthy or not, he began his third or fourth attempt at education in November, 1858, by sailing on the steamer Persia, the pride of Captain Judkins and the Cunard Line; the newest, largest and fastest steamship afloat. He was not alone. Several of his college companions sailed with him, and the world looked cheerful enough until, on the third day, the world — as far as concerned the young man — ran into a heavy storm. He learned then a lesson that stood by him better than any university teaching ever did — the meaning of a November gale on the mid-Atlantic — which, for mere physical misery, passed endurance. The subject offered him material for none but serious treatment; he could never see the humor of sea-sickness; but it united itself with a great variety of other impressions which made the first month of travel altogether the rapidest school of education he had yet found. The stride in knowledge seemed gigantic. One began at last to see that a great many impressions were needed to make a very little education, but how many could be crowded into one day without making any education at all, became the *pons asinorum* of tourist mathematics. How many would turn out to be wrong, or whether any could turn out right, was ultimate wisdom.

The ocean, the Persia, Captain Judkins, and Mr. G. P. R. James, the most distinguished passenger, vanished one Sunday morning in a furious gale in the Mersey, to make place for the drearier picture of a Liverpool street as seen from the Adelphi coffee-room in November murk, followed instantly by the passionate delights of Chester and the romance of red-sandstone architecture. Millions of Americans have felt this succession of emotions. Possibly very young and ingenuous tourists feel them still, but in days before tourists, when the romance was a reality, not a picture, they were overwhelming. When the boys went out to Eaton Hall, they were awed, as Thackeray or Dickens would have felt in the presence of a Duke. The very name of Grosvenor struck a note of grandeur. The long suite of lofty, gilded rooms with their gilded furniture; the portraits; the terraces; the gardens, the landscape; the sense of superiority in the England of the fifties, actually set the rich nobleman apart, above Americans and shopkeepers. Aristocracy was real. So was the England of Dickens. Oliver Twist and Little Nell lurked in every churchyard shadow, not as shadow but alive. Even Charles the First was not very shadowy, standing on the tower to see his army defeated. Nothing thereabouts had very much changed since he lost his battle and his head. An eighteenth-century American boy fresh from Boston naturally took it all for education, and was amused at this sort of lesson. At least he thought he felt it.

Then came the journey up to London through Birmingham and the Black District, another lesson, which needed much more to be rightly felt. The plunge into darkness lurid with flames; the sense of unknown horror in this weird gloom which then existed nowhere else, and never had existed before, except in volcanic craters; the violent contrast between this dense, smoky, impenetrable darkness, and the soft green charm that one glided into, as one emerged — the revelation of an unknown society of the pit — made a boy uncomfortable, though he had no idea that Karl Marx was standing there waiting for him, and that sooner or later the process of education would have to deal with Karl Marx much more than with Professor Bowen of Harvard College or his Satanic free-trade majesty John Stuart Mill. The Black District was a practical education, but it was infinitely far in the distance. The boy ran away from it, as he ran away from everything he disliked.

Had he known enough to know where to begin he would have seen something to study, more vital than the Civil Law, in the long, muddy, dirty, sordid, gas-lit dreariness of Oxford Street as his dingy four-wheeler dragged its weary way to Charing Cross. He did notice one peculiarity about it worth remembering. London was still London. A certain style dignified its grime; heavy, clumsy, arrogant, purse-proud, but not cheap; insular but large; barely tolerant of an outside world, and absolutely self-confident. The boys in the streets made such free comments on the American clothes and figures, that the travellers hurried to put on tall hats and long overcoats to escape criticism. No stranger had rights even in the Strand.

The eighteenth century held its own. History muttered down Fleet Street, like Dr. Johnson, in Adams's ear; Vanity Fair was alive on Piccadilly in yellow chariots with coachmen in wigs, on hammer-cloths; footmen with canes, on the footboard, and a shrivelled old woman inside; half the great houses, black with London smoke, bore large funereal hatchments; every one seemed insolent, and the most insolent structures in the world were the Royal Exchange and the Bank of England. In November, 1858, London was still vast, but it was the London of the eighteenth century that an American felt and hated.

Education went backward. Adams, still a boy, could not guess how intensely intimate this London grime was to become to him as a man, but he could still less conceive himself returning to it fifty years afterwards, noting at each turn how the great city grew smaller as it doubled in size; cheaper as it quadrupled its wealth; less imperial as its empire widened; less dignified as it tried to be civil. He liked it best when he hated it. Education began at the end, or perhaps would end at the beginning. Thus far it had remained in the eighteenth century, and the next step took it back to the sixteenth. He crossed to Antwerp. As the Baron Osy steamed up the Scheldt in the morning mists, a travelling band on deck began to play, and groups of peasants, working along the fields, dropped their tools to join in dancing. Ostade and Teniers were as much alive as they ever were, and even the Duke of Alva was still at home. The thirteenth-century cathedral towered above a sixteenth-century mass of tiled roofs, ending abruptly in walls and a landscape that had not changed. The taste of the town was thick, rich, ripe, like a sweet wine; it was mediæval, so that Rubens seemed modern; it was one of the strongest and fullest flavors that ever touched the young man's palate; but he might as well have drunk out his excitement in old Malmsey, for all the education he got from it. Even in art, one can hardly begin with Antwerp Cathedral and the Descent from the Cross. He merely got drunk on his emotions, and had then to get sober as he best could. He was terribly sober when he saw Antwerp half a century afterwards. One lesson he did learn without suspecting that he must immediately lose it. He felt his middle ages and the sixteenth century alive. He was young enough, and the towns were dirty enough — unimproved, unrestored, untouristed — to retain the sense of reality. As a taste or a smell, it was education, especially because it lasted barely ten years longer; but it was education only sensual. He never dreamed of trying to educate himself to the Descent from the Cross. He was only too happy to feel himself kneeling at the foot of the Cross; he learned only to loathe the sordid necessity of getting up again, and going about his stupid business.

This was one of the foreseen dangers of Europe, but it vanished rapidly enough to reassure the most anxious of parents. Dropped into Berlin one morning without guide or direction, the young man in search of education floundered in a mere mess of misunderstandings. He could never recall what he expected to find, but whatever he expected, it had no relation with what it turned out to be. A student at twenty takes easily to anything, even to Berlin, and he would have accepted the thirteenth century pure and simple since his guides assured him that this was his right path; but a week's experience left him dazed and dull. Faith held out, but the paths grew dim. Berlin astonished him, but he had no lack of friends to show him all the amusement it had to offer. Within a day or two he was running about with the rest to beer-cellars and music-halls and dance-rooms, smoking bad tobacco, drinking poor beer, and eating sauerkraut and sausages as though he knew no better. This was easy. One can always descend the social ladder. The trouble came when he asked for the education he was promised. His friends took him to be registered as a student of the university; they selected his professors and courses; they showed him where to buy the Institutes of Gaius and several German works on the Civil Law in numerous volumes; and they led him to his first lecture.

His first lecture was his last. The young man was not very quick, and he had almost religious respect for his guides and advisers; but he needed no more than one hour to satisfy him that he had made another failure in education, and this time a fatal one. That the language would require at least three months' hard work before he could touch the Law was an annoying discovery; but the shock that upset him was the discovery of the university itself. He had thought Harvard College a torpid school, but it was instinct with life compared with all that he could see of the University of Berlin. The German students were strange animals, but their professors were beyond pay. The mental attitude of the university was not of an American world. What sort of instruction prevailed in other branches, or in science, Adams had no occasion to ask, but in the Civil Law he found only the lecture system in its deadliest form as it flourished in the thirteenth century. The professor mumbled his comments; the students made, or seemed to make, notes; they could have learned from books or discussion in a day more than they could learn from him in a month, but they must pay his fees, follow his course, and be his scholars, if they wanted a degree. To an American the result was worthless. He could make no use of the Civil Law without some previous notion of the Common Law; but the student who knew enough of the Common Law to understand what he wanted, had only to read the Pandects or the commentators at his ease in America, and be his own professor.

Neither the method nor the matter nor the manner could profit an American education.

This discovery seemed to shock none of the students. They went to the lectures, made notes, and read textbooks, but never pretended to take their professor seriously. They were much more serious in reading Heine. They knew no more than Heine what good they were getting, beyond the Berlin accent — which was bad; and the beer — which was not to compare with Munich; and the dancing — which was better at Vienna. They enjoyed the beer and music, but they refused to be responsible for the education. Anyway, as they defended themselves, they were learning the language.

So the young man fell back on the language, and being slow at languages, he found himself falling behind all his friends, which depressed his spirits, the more because the gloom of a Berlin winter and of Berlin architecture seemed to him a particular sort of gloom never attained elsewhere. One day on the Linden he caught sight of Charles Sumner in a cab, and ran after him. Sumner was then recovering from the blows of the South Carolinian cane or club, and he was pleased to find a young worshipper in the remote Prussian wilderness. They dined together and went to hear "William Tell" at the Opera. Sumner tried to encourage his friend about his difficulties of language: "I came to Berlin," or Rome, or whatever place it was, as he said with his grand air of mastery, "I came to Berlin, unable to say a word in the language; and three months later when I went away, I talked it to my cabman." Adams felt himself quite unable to attain in so short a time such social advantages, and one day complained of his trials to Mr. Robert Apthorp, of Boston, who was passing the winter in Berlin for the sake of its music. Mr. Apthorp told of his own similar struggle, and how he had entered a public school and sat for months with ten-year-old boys,

reciting their lessons and catching their phrases. The idea
suited Adams's desperate frame of mind. At least it ridded
him of the university and the Civil Law and American
associations in beer-cellars. Mr. Apthorp took the trouble
to negotiate with the head-master of the Friedrichs-
Wilhelm-Werdersches Gymnasium for permission to
Henry Adams to attend the school as a member of the
Ober-tertia, a class of boys twelve or thirteen years old,
and there Adams went for three months as though he had
not always avoided high schools with singular antipathy.
He never did anything else so foolish, but he was given a
bit of education which served him some purpose in life.

It was not merely the language, though three months
passed in such fashion would teach a poodle enough to
talk with a cabman, and this was all that foreign students
could expect to do, for they never by any chance would
come in contact with German society, if German society
existed, about which they knew nothing. Adams never
learned to talk German well, but the same might be said
of his English, if he could believe Englishmen. He learned
not to annoy himself on this account. His difficulties with
the language gradually ceased. He thought himself quite
Germanized in 1859. He even deluded himself with the
idea that he read it as though it were English, which proved
that he knew little about it; but whatever success he had
in his own experiment interested him less than his contact
with German education.

He had revolted at the American school and university; he had instantly rejected the German university;
and as his last experience of education he tried the German high school. The experiment was hazardous. In 1858
Berlin was a poor, keen-witted, provincial town, simple,
dirty, uncivilized, and in most respects disgusting. Life
was primitive beyond what an American boy could have
imagined. Overridden by military methods and bureau-

cratic pettiness, Prussia was only beginning to free her hands from internal bonds. Apart from discipline, activity scarcely existed. The future Kaiser Wilhelm I, regent for his insane brother King Friedrich Wilhelm IV, seemed to pass his time looking at the passers-by from the window of his modest palace on the Linden. German manners, even at Court, were sometimes brutal, and German thoroughness at school was apt to be routine. Bismarck himself was then struggling to begin a career against the inertia of the German system. The condition of Germany was a scandal and nuisance to every earnest German, all whose energies were turned to reforming it from top to bottom; and Adams walked into a great public school to get educated, at precisely the time when the Germans wanted most to get rid of the education they were forced to follow. As an episode in the search for education, this adventure smacked of Heine.

The school system has doubtless changed, and at all events the schoolmasters are probably long ago dead; the story has no longer a practical value, and had very little even at the time; one could at least say in defence of the German school that it was neither very brutal nor very immoral. The head-master was excellent in his Prussian way, and the other instructors were not worse than in other schools; it was their system that struck the systemless American with horror. The arbitrary training given to the memory was stupefying; the strain that the memory endured was a form of torture; and the feats that the boys performed, without complaint, were pitiable. No other faculty than the memory seemed to be recognized. Least of all was any use made of reason, either analytic, synthetic, or dogmatic. The German government did not encourage reasoning.

All State education is a sort of dynamo machine for polarizing the popular mind; for turning and holding its

lines of force in the direction supposed to be most effective for State purposes. The German machine was terribly efficient. Its effect on the children was pathetic. The
Friedrichs-Wilhelm-Wedersches Gymnasium was an old
building in the heart of Berlin which served the educational needs of the small tradesmen or *bourgeoisie* of the
neighborhood; the children were Berliner-kinder if ever
there were such, and of a class suspected of sympathy and
concern in the troubles of 1848. None was noble or
connected with good society. Personally they were rather
sympathetic than not, but as the objects of education they
were proofs of nearly all the evils that a bad system could
give. Apparently Adams, in his rigidly illogical pursuit,
had at last reached his ideal of a viciously logical education. The boys' physique showed it first, but their physique could not be wholly charged to the school. German
food was bad at best, and a diet of sauerkraut, sausage,
and beer could never be good; but it was not the food
alone that made their faces white and their flesh flabby.
They never breathed fresh air; they had never heard of
a playground; in all Berlin not a cubic inch of oxygen
was admitted in winter into an inhabited building; in the
school every room was tightly closed and had no ventila-
tion; the air was foul beyond all decency; but when the
American opened a window in the five minutes between
hours, he violated the rules and was invariably rebuked.
As long as cold weather lasted, the windows were shut.
If the boys had a holiday, they were apt to be taken on
long tramps in the Thiergarten or elsewhere, always ending in over-fatigue, tobacco-smoke, sausages, and beer.
With this, they were required to prepare daily lessons
that would have quickly broken down strong men of a
healthy habit, and which they could learn only because
their minds were morbid. The German university had

seemed a failure, but the German high school was something very near an indictable nuisance.

Before the month of April arrived, the experiment of German education had reached this point. Nothing was left of it except the ghost of the Civil Law shut up in the darkest of closets, never to gibber again before any one who could repeat the story. The derisive Jew laughter of Heine ran through the university and everything else in Berlin. Of course, when one is twenty years old, life is bound to be full, if only of Berlin beer, although German student life was on the whole the thinnest of beer, as an American looked on it, but though nothing except small fragments remained of the education that had been so promising — or promised — this is only what most often happens in life, when by-products turn out to be more valuable than staples. The German university and German law were failures; German society, in an American sense, did not exist, or if it existed, never showed itself to an American; the German theatre, on the other hand, was excellent, and German opera, with the ballet, was almost worth a journey to Berlin; but the curious and perplexing result of the total failure of German education was that the student's only clear gain — his single step to a higher life — came from time wasted; studies neglected; vices indulged; education reversed — it came from the despised beer-garden and music-hall; and it was accidental, unintended, unforeseen.

When his companions insisted on passing two or three afternoons in the week at music-halls, drinking beer, smoking German tobacco, and looking at fat German women knitting, while an orchestra played dull music, Adams went with them for the sake of the company, but with no pretence of enjoyment; and when Mr. Apthorp gently protested that he exaggerated his indifference, for of course he enjoyed Beethoven, Adams replied simply that he loathed Beethoven; and felt a slight surprise when Mr. Apthorp and the others laughed as though they thought it humor. He saw no humor in it. He supposed that, except musicians, every one thought Beethoven a bore, as every one except mathematicians thought mathematics a bore. Sitting thus at his beer-table, mentally impassive, he was one day surprised to notice that his mind followed the movement of a Sinfonie. He could not have been more astonished had he suddenly read a new language. Among the marvels of education, this was the most marvellous. A prison-wall that barred his senses on one great side of life, suddenly fell, of its own accord, without so much as his knowing when it happened. Amid the fumes of coarse tobacco and poor beer, surrounded by the commonest of German Haus-frauen, a new sense burst out like a flower in his life, so superior to the old senses, so bewildering, so astonished at its own existence, that he could not credit it, and watched it as something apart, accidental, and not to be trusted. He slowly came to admit that Beethoven had partly become intelligible to him, but he was the more inclined to think that Beethoven must be much overrated as a musician, to be so easily followed. This could not be called education, for he had never so much as listened to the music. He had been thinking of other things. Mere mechanical repetition of certain sounds had stuck to his unconscious mind. Beethoven might have this power, but not Wagner, or at all events not the Wagner later than "Tannhäuser." Near forty years passed before he reached the "Götterdämmerung."

One might talk of the revival of an atrophied sense — the mechanical reaction of a sleeping consciousness — but no other sense awoke. His sense of line and color remained as dull as ever, and as far as ever below the level of an artist. His metaphysical sense did not spring into life, so that his mind could leap the bars of German expression into sympathy with the idealities of Kant and Hegel. Although he insisted that his faith in German thought and literature was exalted, he failed to approach German thought, and he shed never a tear of emotion over the pages of Goethe and Schiller. When his father rashly ventured from time to time to write him a word of common sense, the young man would listen to no sense at all, but insisted that Berlin was the best of educations in the best of Germanies; yet, when, at last, April came, and some genius suggested a tramp in Thüringen, his heart sang like a bird; he realized what a nightmare he had suffered, and he made up his mind that, wherever else he might, in the infinities of space and time, seek for education, it should not be again in Berlin.

6

Rome

(1859–1860)

The tramp in Thüringen lasted four-and-twenty hours.
By the end of the first walk, his three companions — John
Bancroft, James J. Higginson, and B. W. Crowninshield,
all Boston and Harvard College like himself — were satisfied with what they had seen, and when they sat down to
rest on the spot where Goethe had written —

> "Warte nur! balde
> Ruhest du auch!" —

the profoundness of the thought and the wisdom of the
advice affected them so strongly that they hired a wagon
and drove to Weimar the same night. They were all quite
happy and lighthearted in the first fresh breath of leafless
spring, and the beer was better than at Berlin, but they
were all equally in doubt why they had come to Germany,
and not one of them could say why they stayed. Adams
stayed because he did not want to go home, and he had
fears that his father's patience might be exhausted if he
asked to waste time elsewhere.

They could not think that their education required a
return to Berlin. A few days at Dresden in the spring

weather satisfied them that Dresden was a better spot for general education than Berlin, and equally good for reading Civil Law. They were possibly right. There was nothing to study in Dresden, and no education to be gained, but the Sistine Madonna and the Correggios were famous; the theatre and opera were sometimes excellent, and the Elbe was prettier than the Spree. They could always fall back on the language. So he took a room in the household of the usual small government clerk with the usual plain daughters, and continued the study of the language. Possibly one might learn something more by accident, as one had learned something of Beethoven. For the next eighteen months the young man pursued accidental education, since he could pursue no other; and by great good fortune, Europe and America were too busy with their own affairs to give much attention to his. Accidental education had every chance in its favor, especially because nothing came amiss.

Perhaps the chief obstacle to the youth's education, now that he had come of age, was his honesty; his simpleminded faith in his intentions. Even after Berlin had become a nightmare, he still persuaded himself that his German education was a success. He loved, or thought he loved the people, but the Germany he loved was the eighteenth-century which the Germans were ashamed of, and were destroying as fast as they could. Of the Germany to come, he knew nothing. Military Germany was his abhorrence. What he liked was the simple character; the good-natured sentiment; the musical and metaphysical abstraction; the blundering incapacity of the German for practical affairs. At that time every one looked on Germany as incapable of competing with France, England or America in any sort of organized energy. Germany had no confidence in herself, and no reason to feel it. She had no unity, and no reason to want it. She never had unity.

Her religious and social history, her economical interests, her military geography, her political convenience, had always tended to eccentric rather than concentric motion. Until coal-power and railways were created, she was mediæval by nature and geography, and this was what Adams, under the teachings of Carlyle and Lowell, liked.

He was in a fair way to do himself lasting harm, floundering between worlds passed and worlds coming, which had a habit of crushing men who stayed too long at the points of contact. Suddenly the Emperor Napoleon declared war on Austria and raised a confused point of morals in the mind of Europe. France was the nightmare of Germany, and even at Dresden one looked on the return of Napoleon to Leipsic as the most likely thing in the world. One morning the government clerk, in whose family Adams was staying, rushed into his room to consult a map in order that he might measure the distance from Milan to Dresden. The third Napoleon had reached Lombardy, and only fifty or sixty years had passed since the first Napoleon had begun his military successes from an Italian base.

An enlightened young American, with eighteenth-century tastes capped by fragments of a German education and the most excellent intentions, had to make up his mind about the moral value of these conflicting forces. France was the wicked spirit of moral politics, and whatever helped France must be so far evil. At that time Austria was another evil spirit. Italy was the prize they disputed, and for at least fifteen hundred years had been the chief object of their greed. The question of sympathy had disturbed a number of persons during that period. The question of morals had been put in a number of cross-lights. Should one be Guelph or Ghibelline? No doubt, one was wiser than one's neighbors who had found no way of settling this question since the days of the cave-dwellers, but ignorance did better to discard the attempt to be wise, for wisdom had been singularly baffled by the problem. Better take sides first, and reason about it for the rest of life.

Not that Adams felt any real doubt about his sympathies or wishes. He had not been German long enough for befogging his mind to that point, but the moment was decisive for much to come, especially for political morals. His morals were the highest, and he clung to them to preserve his self-respect; but steam and electricity had brought about new political and social concentrations, or were making them necessary in the line of his moral principles — freedom, education, economic development and so forth — which required association with allies as doubtful as Napoleon III, and robberies with violence on a very extensive scale. As long as he could argue that his opponents were wicked, he could join in robbing and killing them without a qualm; but it might happen that the good were robbed. Education insisted on finding a moral foundation for robbery. He could hope to begin life in the character of no animal more moral than a monkey unless he could satisfy himself when and why robbery and murder were a virtue and duty. Education founded on mere self-interest was merely Guelph and Ghibelline over again — Machiavelli translated into American.

Luckily for him he had a sister much brighter than he ever was — though he thought himself a rather superior person — who after marrying Charles Kuhn, of Philadelphia, had come to Italy, and, like all good Americans and English, was hotly Italian. In July, 1859, she was at Thun in Switzerland, and there Henry Adams joined them. Women have, commonly, a very positive moral sense; that which they will, is right; that which they reject, is wrong; and their will, in most cases, ends by settling the moral. Mrs. Kuhn had a double superiority. She not only adored Italy, but she cordially disliked Germany in all its varieties. She saw no gain in helping her brother to be Germanized, and she wanted him much to be civilized. She was the first young woman he was ever intimate with — quick, sensitive, wilful, or full of will, energetic, sympathetic and intelligent enough to supply a score of men with ideas — and he was delighted to give her the reins — to let her drive him where she would. It was his first experiment in giving the reins to a woman, and he was so much pleased with the results that he never wanted to take them back. In after life he made a general law of experience — no woman had ever driven him wrong; no man had ever driven him right.

Nothing would satisfy Mrs. Kuhn but to go to the seat of war as soon as the armistice was declared. Wild as the idea seemed, nothing was easier. The party crossed the St. Gothard and reached Milan, picturesque with every sort of uniform and every sign of war. To young Adams this first plunge into Italy passed Beethoven as a piece of accidental education. Like music, it differed from other education in being, not a means of pursuing life, but one of the ends attained. Further, on these lines, one could not go. It had but one defect — that of attainment. Life had no richer impression to give; it offers barely half-a-dozen such, and the intervals seem long. Exactly what they teach would puzzle a Berlin jurist; yet they seem to have an economic value, since most people would decline to part with even their faded memories except at a valuation ridiculously extravagant. They were also what men pay most for; but one's ideas become hopelessly mixed in trying to reduce such forms of education to a standard of exchangeable value, and, as in political economy, one had best disregard altogether what cannot be stated in equivalents.

The proper equivalent of pleasure is pain, which is also a form of education.

Not satisfied with Milan, Mrs. Kuhn insisted on invading the enemy's country, and the carriage was chartered for Innsbruck by way of the Stelvio Pass. The Valtellina, as the carriage drove up it, showed war. Garibaldi's Cacciatori were the only visible inhabitants. No one could say whether the pass was open, but in any case no carriage had yet crossed. At the inns the handsome young officers in command of the detachments were delighted to accept invitations to dinner and to talk all the evening of their battles to the charming patriot who sparkled with interest and flattery, but not one of them knew whether their enemies, the abhorred Austrian Jägers, would let the travellers through their lines. As a rule, gaiety was not the character failing in any party that Mrs. Kuhn belonged to, but when at last, after climbing what was said to be the finest carriage-pass in Europe, the carriage turned the last shoulder, where the glacier of the Ortler Spitze tumbled its huge mass down upon the road, even Mrs. Kuhn gasped when she was driven directly up to the barricade and stopped by the double line of sentries stretching on either side up the mountains, till the flash of the gun barrels was lost in the flash of the snow. For accidental education the picture had its value. The earliest of these pictures count for most, as first impressions must, and Adams never afterwards cared much for landscape education, except perhaps in the tropics for the sake of the contrast. As education, that chapter, too, was read, and set aside.

The handsome blond officers of the Jägers were not to be beaten in courtesy by the handsome young olive-toned officers of the Cacciatori. The eternal woman as usual, when she is young, pretty, and engaging, had her way, and the barricade offered no resistance. In fifteen minutes the carriage was rolling down to Mals, swarming with German soldiers and German fleas, worse than the Italian; and German language, thought, and atmosphere, of which young Adams, thanks to his glimpse of Italy, never again felt quite the old confident charm.

Yet he could talk to his cabman and conscientiously did his cathedrals, his Rhine, and whatever his companions suggested. Faithful to his self-contracted scheme of passing two winters in study of the Civil Law, he went back to Dresden with a letter to the Frau Hofräthin von Reichenbach, in whose house Lowell and other Americans had pursued studies more or less serious. In those days, "The Initials" was a new book. The charm which its clever author had laboriously woven over Munich gave also a certain reflected light to Dresden. Young Adams had nothing to do but take fencing-lessons, visit the galleries and go to the theatre; but his social failure in the line of "The Initials," was humiliating and he succumbed to it. The Frau Hofräthin herself was sometimes roused to huge laughter at the total discomfiture and helplessness of the young American in the face of her society. Possibly an education may be the wider and the richer for a large experience of the world; Raphael Pumpelly and Clarence King, at about the same time, were enriching their education by a picturesque intimacy with the manners of the Apaches and Digger Indians. All experience is an arch, to build upon. Yet Adams admitted himself unable to guess what use his second winter in Germany was to him, or what he expected it to be. Even the doctrine of accidental education broke down. There were no accidents in Dresden. As soon as the winter was over, he closed and locked the German door with a long breath of relief, and took the road to Italy. He had then pursued his education, as it pleased him, for eighteen months, and in spite of the infinite variety of new impressions which had packed themselves into his mind, he knew no more, for his practical purposes, than the day he graduated. He had made no step towards a profession. He was as ignorant as a schoolboy of society. He was unfit for any career in Europe, and unfitted for any career in America, and he had not natural intelligence enough to see what a mess he had thus far made of his education.

By twisting life to follow accidental and devious paths, one might perhaps find some use for accidental and devious knowledge, but this had been no part of Henry Adams's plan when he chose the path most admired by the best judges, and followed it till he found it led nowhere. Nothing had been further from his mind when he started in November, 1858, than to become a tourist, but a mere tourist, and nothing else, he had become in April, 1860, when he joined his sister in Florence. His father had been in the right. The young man felt a little sore about it. Supposing his father asked him, on his return, what equivalent he had brought back for the time and money put into his experiment! The only possible answer would be: "Sir, I am a tourist!"

The answer was not what he had meant it to be, and he was not likely to better it by asking his father, in turn, what equivalent his brothers or cousins or friends at home had got out of the same time and money spent in Boston. All they had put into the law was certainly thrown away, but were they happier in science? In theory one might say, with some show of proof, that a pure, scientific education was alone correct; yet many of his friends who took it, found reason to complain that it was anything but a pure, scientific world in which they lived.

Meanwhile his father had quite enough perplexities of his own, without seeking more in his son's errors. His Quincy district had sent him to Congress, and in the spring of 1860 he was in the full confusion of nominating candidates for the Presidential election in November. He supported Mr. Seward. The Republican Party was an unknown force, and the Democratic Party was torn to pieces. No one could see far into the future. Fathers could blunder as well as sons, and, in 1860, every one was conscious of being dragged along paths much less secure than those of the European tourist. For the time, the young man was safe from interference, and went on his way with a light heart to take whatever chance fragments of education God or the devil was pleased to give him, for he knew no longer the good from the bad.

He had of both sorts more than he knew how to use. Perhaps the most useful purpose he set himself to serve was that of his pen, for he wrote long letters, during the next three months, to his brother Charles, which his brother caused to be printed in the *Boston Courier;* and the exercise was good for him. He had little to say, and said it not very well, but that mattered less. The habit of expression leads to the search for something to express. Something remains as a residuum of the commonplace itself, if one strikes out every commonplace in the expression. Young men as a rule saw little in Italy, or anywhere else, and in after life, when Adams began to learn what some men could see, he shrank into corners of shame at the thought that he should have betrayed his own inferiority as though it were his pride, while he invited his neighbors to measure and admire; but it was still the nearest approach he had yet made to an intelligent act.

For the rest, Italy was mostly an emotion and the emotion naturally centred in Rome. The American parent, curiously enough, while bitterly hostile to Paris, seemed rather disposed to accept Rome as legitimate education, though abused; but to young men seeking education in a serious spirit, taking for granted that everything had a

cause, and that nature tended to an end, Rome was altogether the most violent vice in the world, and Rome
before 1870 was seductive beyond resistance. The month
of May, 1860, was divine. No doubt other young men, and
occasionally young women, have passed the month of
May in Rome since then, and conceive that the charm
continues to exist. Possibly it does — in them — but in 1860
the lights and shadows were still mediæval, and mediæval
Rome was alive; the shadows breathed and glowed, full of
soft forms felt by lost senses. No sand-blast of science had
yet skinned off the epidermis of history, thought, and feeling. The pictures were uncleaned, the churches unrestored, the ruins unexcavated. Mediæval Rome was
sorcery. Rome was the worst spot on earth to teach
nineteenth-century youth what to do with a twentieth-
century world. One's emotions in Rome were one's private affair, like one's glass of absinthe before dinner in
the Palais Royal; they must be hurtful, else they could not
have been so intense; and they were surely immoral, for
no one, priest or politician, could honestly read in the ruins
of Rome any other certain lesson than that they were evidence of the just judgments of an outraged God against
all the doings of man. This moral unfitted young men for
every sort of useful activity; it made Rome a gospel of
anarchy and vice; the last place under the sun for educating the young; yet it was, by common consent, the only
spot that the young — of either sex and every race — pas-
sionately, perversely, wickedly loved.

Boys never see a conclusion; only on the edge of the
grave can man conclude anything; but the first impulse
given to the boy is apt to lead or drive him for the rest of
his life into conclusion after conclusion that he never
dreamed of reaching. One looked idly enough at the
Forum or at St. Peter's, but one never forgot the look,
and it never ceased reacting. To a young Bostonian, fresh

from Germany, Rome seemed a pure emotion, quite free
from economic or actual values, and he could not in reason
or common sense foresee that it was mechanically piling
up conundrum after conundrum in his educational path,
which seemed unconnected but that he had got to connect; that seemed insoluble but had got to be somehow
solved. Rome was not a beetle to be dissected and
dropped; not a bad French novel to be read in a railway
train and thrown out of the window after other bad
French novels, the morals of which could never approach
the immorality of Roman history. Rome was actual; it was
England; it was going to be America. Rome could not be
fitted into an orderly, middle-class, Bostonian, systematic
scheme of evolution. No law of progress applied to it. Not
even time-sequences — the last refuge of helpless historians
— had value for it. The Forum no more led to the Vatican
than the Vatican to the Forum. Rienzi, Garibaldi, Tiberius
Gracchus, Aurelian might be mixed up in any relation of
time, along with a thousand more, and never lead to a
sequence. The great word Evolution had not yet, in 1860,
made a new religion of history, but the old religion had
preached the same doctrine for a thousand years without
finding in the entire history of Rome anything but flat
contradiction.

Of course both priests and evolutionists bitterly denied
this heresy, but what they affirmed or denied in 1860 had
very little importance indeed for 1960. Anarchy lost no
ground meanwhile. The problem became only the more
fascinating. Probably it was more vital in May, 1860, than
it had been in October, 1764, when the idea of writing the
Decline and Fall of the city first started to the mind of
Gibbon, "in the close of the evening, as I sat musing in the
Church of the Zoccolanti or Franciscan Friars, while they
were singing Vespers in the Temple of Jupiter, on the
ruins of the Capitol." Murray's Handbook had the grace

to quote this passage from Gibbon's "Autobiography," which led Adams more than once to sit at sunset on the steps of the Church of Santa Maria di Ara Cœli, curiously wondering that not an inch had been gained by Gibbon — or all the historians since — towards explaining the Fall. The mystery remained unsolved; the charm remained intact. Two great experiments of Western civilization had left there the chief monuments of their failure, and nothing proved that the city might not still survive to express the failure of a third.

The young man had no idea what he was doing. The thought of posing for a Gibbon never entered his mind. He was a tourist, even to the depths of his subconsciousness, and it was well for him that he should be nothing else, for even the greatest of men cannot sit with dignity, "in the close of evening, among the ruins of the Capitol," unless they have something quite original to say about it. Tacitus could do it; so could Michael Angelo; and so, at a pinch, could Gibbon, though in figure hardly heroic; but, in sum, none of them could say very much more than the tourist, who went on repeating to himself the eternal question: — Why! Why!! Why!!! — as his neighbor, the blind beggar, might do, sitting next him, on the church steps. No one ever had answered the question to the satisfaction of any one else; yet every one who had either head or heart, felt that sooner or later he must make up his mind what answer to accept. Substitute the word America for the word Rome, and the question became personal.

Perhaps Henry learned something in Rome, though he never knew it, and never sought it. Rome dwarfs teachers. The greatest men of the age scarcely bore the test of posing with Rome for a background. Perhaps Garibaldi — possibly even Cavour — could have sat "in the close of the evening, among the ruins of the Capitol," but one hardly saw Napoleon III there, or Palmerston or Tennyson or Longfellow. One morning, Adams happened to be chatting in the studio of Hamilton Wilde, when a middle-aged Englishman came in, evidently excited, and told of the shock he had just received, when riding near the Circus Maximus, at coming unexpectedly on the guillotine, where some criminal had been put to death an hour or two before. The sudden surprise had quite overcome him; and Adams, who seldom saw the point of a story till time had blunted it, listened sympathetically to learn what new form of grim horror had for the moment wiped out the memory of two thousand years of Roman bloodshed, or the consolation, derived from history and statistics, that most citizens of Rome seemed to be the better for guillotining. Only by slow degrees, he grappled the conviction that the victim of the shock was Robert Browning; and, on the background of the Circus Maximus, the Christian martyrs flaming as torches, and the morning's murderer on the block, Browning seemed rather in place, as a middle-aged gentlemanly English Pippa Passes; while afterwards, in the light of Belgravia dinner-tables, he never made part of his background except by effacement. Browning might have sat with Gibbon, among the ruins, and few Romans would have smiled.

Yet Browning never revealed the poetic depths of Saint Francis; William Story could not touch the secret of Michael Angelo; and Mommsen hardly said all that one felt by instinct in the lives of Cicero and Cæsar. They taught what, as a rule, needed no teaching, the lessons of a rather cheap imagination and cheaper politics. Rome was a bewildering complex of ideas, experiments, ambitions, energies; without her, the Western world was pointless and fragmentary; she gave heart and unity to it all; yet Gibbon might have gone on for the whole century, sitting among the ruins of the Capitol, and no one would have passed, capable of telling him what it meant. Perhaps it meant nothing.

So it ended; the happiest month of May that life had yet offered, fading behind the present, and probably beyond the past, somewhere into abstract time, grotesquely out of place with the Berlin scheme or a Boston future. Adams explained to himself that he was absorbing knowledge. He would have put it better had he said that knowledge was absorbing him. He was passive. In spite of swarming impressions he knew no more when he left Rome than he did when he entered it. As a marketable object, his value was less. His next step went far to convince him that accidental education, whatever its economical return might be, was prodigiously successful as an object in itself. Everything conspired to ruin his sound scheme of life, to make him a vagrant as well as pauper. He went on to Naples, and there, in the hot June, heard rumors that Garibaldi and his thousand were about to attack Palermo. Calling on the American Minister, Chandler of Pennsylvania, he was kindly treated, not for his merit, but for his name, and Mr. Chandler amiably consented to send him to the seat of war as bearer of despatches to Captain Palmer of the American sloop of war Iroquois. Young Adams seized the chance, and went to Palermo in a government transport filled with fleas, commanded by a charming Prince Caracciolo.

He told all about it to the *Boston Courier*, where the narrative probably exists to this day, unless the files of the *Courier* have wholly perished; but of its bearing on education the *Courier* did not speak. He himself would have much liked to know whether it had any bearing whatever, and what was its value as a post-graduate course. Quite apart from its value as life attained, realized, capitalized, it had also a certain value as a lesson in something, though Adams could never classify the branch of study.

Loosely, the tourist called it knowledge of men, but it was just the reverse; it was knowledge of one's ignorance of men. Captain Palmer of the Iroquois, who was a friend of the young man's uncle, Sydney Brooks, took him with the officers of the ship to make an evening call on Garibaldi, whom they found in the Senate House towards sunset, at supper with his picturesque and piratic staff, in the full noise and color of the Palermo revolution. As a spectacle, it belonged to Rossini and the Italian opera, or to Alexandre Dumas at the least, but the spectacle was not its educational side. Garibaldi left the table, and, sitting down at the window, had a few words of talk with Captain Palmer and young Adams. At that moment, in the summer of 1860, Garibaldi was certainly the most serious of the doubtful energies in the world; the most essential to gauge rightly. Even then society was dividing between banker and anarchist. One or the other, Garibaldi must serve. Himself a typical anarchist, sure to overshadow Europe and alarm empires bigger than Naples, his success depended on his mind; his energy was beyond doubt.

Adams had the chance to look this sphinx in the eyes, and, for five minutes, to watch him like a wild animal, at the moment of his greatest achievement and most splendid action. One saw a quiet-featured, quiet-voiced man in a red flannel shirt; absolutely impervious; a type of which Adams knew nothing. Sympathetic it was, and one felt that it was simple; one suspected even that it might be childlike, but could form no guess of its intelligence. In his own eyes Garibaldi might be a Napoleon or a Spartacus; in the hands of Cavour he might become a Condottiere; in the eyes of history he might, like the rest of the world, be only the vigorous player in the game he did not understand. The student was none the wiser.

This compound nature of patriot and pirate had illumined Italian history from the beginning, and was no more intelligible to itself than to a young American who had no experience in double natures. In the end, if the "Autobiography" tells truth, Garibaldi saw and said that he had not understood his own acts; that he had been an instrument; that he had served the purposes of the class he least wanted to help; yet in 1860 he thought himself the revolution anarchic, Napoleonic, and his ambition was unbounded. What should a young Bostonian have made of a character like this, internally alive with childlike fancies, and externally quiet, simple, almost innocent; uttering with apparent conviction the usual commonplaces of popular politics that all politicians use as the small change of their intercourse with the public; but never betraying a thought?

Precisely this class of mind was to be the toughest problem of Adams's practical life, but he could never make anything of it. The lesson of Garibaldi, as education, seemed to teach the extreme complexity of extreme simplicity; but one could have learned this from a glow-worm. One did not need the vivid recollection of the low-voiced, simple-mannered, seafaring captain of Genoese adventurers and Sicilian brigands, supping in the July heat and Sicilian dirt and revolutionary clamor, among the barricaded streets of insurgent Palermo, merely in order to remember that simplicity is complex.

Adams left the problem as he found it, and came north to stumble over others, less picturesque but nearer. He squandered two or three months on Paris. From the first he had avoided Paris, and had wanted no French influence in his education. He disapproved of France in the lump. A certain knowledge of the language one must have; enough to order dinner and buy a theatre ticket; but more he did not seek. He disliked the Empire and the Emperor particularly, but this was a trifle; he disliked most the French mind. To save himself the trouble of drawing up a long list of all that he disliked, he disapproved of the whole, once for all, and shut them figuratively out of his life. France was not serious, and he was not serious in going there.

He did this in good faith, obeying the lessons his teachers had taught him; but the curious result followed that, being in no way responsible for the French and sincerely disapproving them, he felt quite at liberty to enjoy to the full everything he disapproved. Stated thus crudely, the idea sounds derisive; but, as a matter of fact, several thousand Americans passed much of their time there on this understanding. They sought to take share in every function that was open to approach, as they sought tickets to the opera, because they were not a part of it. Adams did like the rest. All thought of serious education had long vanished. He tried to acquire a few French idioms, without even aspiring to master a subjunctive, but he succeeded better in acquiring a modest taste for Bordeaux and Burgundy and one or two sauces; for the Trois Frères Provençaux and Voisin's and Philippe's and the Café Anglais; for the Palais Royal Theatre, and the Variétés and the Gymnase; for the Brohans and Bressant, Rose Chéri and Gil Perez, and other lights of the stage. His friends were good to him. Life was amusing. Paris rapidly became familiar. In a month or six weeks he forgot even to disapprove of it; but he studied nothing, entered no society, and made no acquaintance. Accidental education went far in Paris, and one picked up a deal of knowledge that might become useful; perhaps, after all, the three months passed there might serve better purpose than the twenty-one months passed elsewhere; but he did not intend it — did not think it — and looked at it as a momentary and frivolous vacation before going home to fit himself for life. Therewith, after staying as long as he could and spending all the money he dared, he started with mixed emotions but no education, for home.

7

Treason

(1860–1861)

When, forty years afterwards, Henry Adams looked back over his adventures in search of knowledge, he asked himself whether fortune or fate had ever dealt its cards quite so wildly to any of his known antecessors as when it led him to begin the study of law and to vote for Abraham Lincoln on the same day.

He dropped back on Quincy like a lump of lead; he rebounded like a football, tossed into space by an unknown energy which played with all his generation as a cat plays with mice. The simile is none too strong. Not one man in America wanted the Civil War, or expected or intended it. A small minority wanted secession. The vast majority wanted to go on with their occupations in peace. Not one, however clever or learned, guessed what happened. Possibly a few Southern loyalists in despair might dream it as an impossible chance; but none planned it.

As for Henry Adams, fresh from Europe and chaos of another sort, he plunged at once into a lurid atmosphere of politics, quite heedless of any education or forethought. His past melted away. The prodigal was welcomed home, but not even his father asked a malicious question about the Pandects. At the utmost, he hinted at some shade of prodigality by quietly inviting his son to act as private secretary during the winter in Washington, as though any young man who could afford to throw away two winters on the Civil Law could afford to read Blackstone for another winter without a master. The young man was beyond satire, and asked only a pretext for throwing all education to the east wind. November at best is sad, and November at Quincy had been from earliest childhood the least gay of seasons. Nowhere else does the uncharitable autumn wreak its spite so harshly on the frail wreck of the grasshopper summer; yet even a Quincy November seemed temperate before the chill of a Boston January.

This was saying much, for the November of 1860 at Quincy stood apart from other memories as lurid beyond description. Although no one believed in civil war, the air reeked of it, and the Republicans organized their clubs and parades as Wide-Awakes in a form military in all things except weapons. Henry reached home in time to see the last of these processions, stretching in ranks of torches along the hillside, file down through the November night to the Old House, where Mr. Adams, their Member of Congress, received them, and, let them pretend what they liked, their air was not that of innocence.

Profoundly ignorant, anxious, and curious, the young man packed his modest trunk again, which had not yet time to be unpacked, and started for Washington with his family. Ten years had passed since his last visit, but very little had changed. As in 1800 and 1850, so in 1860, the same rude colony was camped in the same forest, with the same unfinished Greek temples for workrooms, and sloughs for roads. The Government had an air of social instability and incompleteness that went far to support the right of secession in theory as in fact; but right or wrong, secession was likely to be easy where there was so little to secede from. The Union was a sentiment, but not much more, and in December, 1860, the sentiment about the Capitol was chiefly hostile, so far as it made itself felt. John Adams was better off in Philadelphia in 1776 than his great-grandson Henry in 1860 in Washington.

Patriotism ended by throwing a halo over the Continental Congress, but over the close of the Thirty-sixth Congress in 1860–61, no halo could be thrown by any one who saw it. Of all the crowd swarming in Washington that winter, young Adams was surely among the most ignorant and helpless, but he saw plainly that the knowledge possessed by everybody about him was hardly greater than his own. Never in a long life did he seek to master a lesson so obscure. Mr. Sumner was given to saying after Oxenstiern: "Quantula sapientia mundus regitur!" Oxenstiern talked of a world that wanted wisdom; but Adams found himself seeking education in a world that seemed to him both unwise and ignorant. The Southern secessionists were certainly unbalanced in mind – fit for medical treatment, like other victims of hallucination – haunted by suspicion, by *idées fixes*, by violent morbid excitement; but this was not all. They were stupendously ignorant of the world. As a class, the cotton-planters were mentally one-sided, ill-balanced, and provincial to a degree rarely known. They were a close society on whom the new fountains of power had poured a stream of wealth and slaves that acted like oil on flame. They showed a young student his first object-lesson of the way in which excess of power worked when held by inadequate hands.

This might be a commonplace of 1900, but in 1860 it was paradox. The Southern statesmen were regarded as standards of statesmanship, and such standards barred education. Charles Sumner's chief offence was his insistence on Southern ignorance, and he stood a living proof of it. To this school, Henry Adams had come for a new education, and the school was seriously, honestly, taken by most of the world, including Europe, as proper for the purpose, although the Sioux Indians would have taught less mischief. From such contradictions among intelligent people, what was a young man to learn?

He could learn nothing but cross-purpose. The old and typical Southern gentleman developed as cotton-planter had nothing to teach or to give, except warning. Even as example to be avoided, he was too glaring in his defiance of reason, to help the education of a reasonable being. No one learned a useful lesson from the Confederate school except to keep away from it. Thus, at one sweep, the whole field of instruction south of the Potomac was shut off; it was overshadowed by the cotton-planters, from whom one could learn nothing but bad temper, bad manners, poker, and treason.

Perforce, the student was thrown back on Northern precept and example; first of all, on his New England surroundings. Republican houses were few in Washington, and Mr. and Mrs. Adams aimed to create a social centre for New Englanders. They took a house on I Street, looking over Pennsylvania Avenue, well out towards Georgetown — the Markoe house — and there the private secretary began to learn his social duties, for the political were confined to committee-rooms and lobbies of the Capitol. He had little to do, and knew not how to do it rightly, but he knew of no one who knew more.

The Southern type was one to be avoided; the New England type was one's self. It had nothing to show except one's own features. Setting aside Charles Sumner, who stood quite alone and was the boy's oldest friend, all the New Englanders were sane and steady men, well-balanced, educated, and free from meanness or intrigue — men whom one liked to act with, and who, whether graduates or not, bore the stamp of Harvard College. Anson

Burlingame was one exception, and perhaps Israel Washburn another; but as a rule the New Englander's strength was his poise which almost amounted to a defeat. He offered no more target for love than for hate; he attracted as little as he repelled; even as a machine, his motion seemed never accelerated. The character, with its force or feebleness, was familiar: one knew it to the core; one was it — had been run in the same mould.

There remained the Central and Western States, but there the choice of teachers was not large and in the end narrowed itself to Preston King, Henry Winter Davis, Owen Lovejoy, and a few other men born with social faculty. Adams took most kindly to Henry J. Raymond, who came to view the field for the *New York Times*, and who was a man of the world. The average Congressman was civil enough, but had nothing to ask except offices, and nothing to offer but the views of his district. The average Senator was more reserved, but had not much more to say, being always, excepting one or two genial natures, handicapped by his own importance.

Study it as one might, the hope of education, till the arrival of the President-elect, narrowed itself to the possible influence of only two men — Sumner and Seward.

Sumner was then fifty years old. Since his election as Senator in 1851 he had passed beyond the reach of his boy friend, and, after his Brooks injuries, his nervous system never quite recovered its tone; but perhaps eight or ten years of solitary existence as Senator had most to do with his development. No man, however strong, can serve ten years as schoolmaster, priest, or Senator, and remain fit for anything else. All the dogmatic stations in life have the effect of fixing a certain stiffness of attitude forever, as though they mesmerized the subject. Yet even among Senators there were degrees in dogmatism, from the frank

South Carolinian brutality, to that of Webster, Benton, Clay, or Sumner himself, until in extreme cases, like Conkling, it became Shakespearian and *bouffe* — as Godkin used to call it — like Malvolio. Sumner had become dogmatic like the rest, but he had at least the merit of qualities that warranted dogmatism. He justly thought, as Webster had thought before him, that his great services and sacrifices, his superiority in education, his oratorical power, his political experience, his representative character at the head of the whole New England contingent, and, above all, his knowledge of the world, made him the most important member of the Senate; and no Senator had ever saturated himself more thoroughly with the spirit and temper of the body.

Although the Senate is much given to admiring in its members a superiority less obvious or quite invisible to outsiders, one Senator seldom proclaims his own inferiority to another, and still more seldom likes to be told of it. Even the greatest Senators seemed to inspire little personal affection in each other, and betrayed none at all. Sumner had a number of rivals who held his judgment in no high esteem, and one of these was Senator Seward. The two men would have disliked each other by instinct had they lived in different planets. Each was created only for exasperating the other; the virtues of one were the faults of his rival, until no good quality seemed to remain of either. That the public service must suffer was certain, but what were the sufferings of the public service compared with the risks run by a young mosquito — a private secretary — trying to buzz admiration in the ears of each, and unaware that each would impatiently slap at him for belonging to the other? Innocent and unsuspicious beyond what was permitted even in a nursery, the private secretary courted both.

Private secretaries are servants of a rather low order,

whose business is to serve sources of power. The first news of a professional kind, imparted to private secretary Adams on reaching Washington, was that the President-elect, Abraham Lincoln, had selected Mr. Seward for his Secretary of State, and that Seward was to be the medium for communicating his wishes to his followers. Every young man naturally accepted the wishes of Mr. Lincoln as orders, the more because he could see that the new President was likely to need all the help that several million young men would be able to give, if they counted on having any President at all to serve. Naturally one waited impatiently for the first meeting with the new Secretary of State.

Governor Seward was an old friend of the family. He professed to be a disciple and follower of John Quincy Adams. He had been Senator since 1849, when his responsibilities as leader had separated him from the Free Soil contingent, for, in the dry light of the first Free Soil faith, the ways of New York politics and of Thurlow Weed had not won favor; but the fierce heat which welded the Republican Party in 1856 melted many such barriers, and when Mr. Adams came to Congress in December, 1859, Governor Seward instantly renewed his attitude of family friend, became a daily intimate in the household, and lost no chance of forcing his fresh ally to the front.

A few days after their arrival in December, 1860, the Governor, as he was always called, came to dinner, alone, as one of the family, and the private secretary had the chance he wanted to watch him as carefully as one generally watches men who dispose of one's future. A slouching, slender figure; a head like a wise macaw; a beaked nose; shaggy eyebrows; unorderly hair and clothes; hoarse voice; offhand manner; free talk, and perpetual cigar, offered a new type — of western New York — to fathom; a type in one way simple because it was only double —

political and personal; but complex because the political
had become nature, and no one could tell which was the
mask and which the features. At table, among friends, Mr.
Seward threw off restraint, or seemed to throw it off, in
reality, while in the world he threw it off, like a politician,
for effect. In both cases he chose to appear as a free talker,
who loathed pomposity and enjoyed a joke; but how
much was nature and how much was mask, he was himself
too simple a nature to know. Underneath the surface he
was conventional after the conventions of western New
York and Albany. Politicians thought it unconventional-
ity. Bostonians thought it provincial. Henry Adams
thought it charming. From the first sight, he loved the
Governor, who, though sixty years old, had the youth
of his sympathies. He noticed that Mr. Seward was never
petty or personal; his talk was large; he generalized; he
never seemed to pose for statesmanship; he did not require
an attitude of prayer. What was more unusual — almost
singular and quite eccentric — he had some means, unknown to other Senators, of producing the effect of
unselfishness.

Superficially Mr. Seward and Mr. Adams were contrasts; essentially they were much alike. Mr. Adams was
taken to be rigid, but the Puritan character in all its forms
could be supple enough when it chose; and in Massachusetts all the Adamses had been attacked in succession as no
better than political mercenaries. Mr. Hildreth, in his
standard history, went so far as to echo with approval the
charge that treachery was hereditary in the family. Any
Adams had at least to be thick-skinned, hardened to every
contradictory epithet that virtue could supply, and, on the
whole, armed to return such attentions; but all must have
admitted that they had invariably subordinated local to
national interests, and would continue to do so, whenever
forced to choose. C. F. Adams was sure to do what his

father had done, as his father had followed the steps of John Adams, and no doubt thereby earned his epithets.

The inevitable followed, as a child fresh from the nursery should have had the instinct to foresee, but the young man on the edge of life never dreamed. What motives or emotions drove his masters on their various paths he made no pretence of guessing; even at that age he preferred to admit his dislike for guessing motives; he knew only his own infantile ignorance, before which he stood amazed, and his innocent good-faith, always matter of simple-minded surprise. Critics who know ultimate truth will pronounce judgment on history; all that Henry Adams ever saw in man was a reflection of his own ignorance, and he never saw quite so much of it as in the winter of 1860–61. Every one knows the story; every one draws what conclusions suits his temper, and the conclusion matters now less than though it concerned the merits of Adam and Eve in the Garden of Eden; but in 1861 the conclusion made the sharpest lesson of life; it was condensed and concentrated education.

Rightly or wrongly the new President and his chief advisers in Washington decided that, before they could administer the Government, they must make sure of a government to administer, and that this chance depended on the action of Virginia. The whole ascendancy of the winter wavered between the effort of the cotton States to drag Virginia out, and the effort of the new President to keep Virginia in. Governor Seward representing the Administration in the Senate took the lead; Mr. Adams took the lead in the House; and as far as a private secretary knew, the party united on its tactics. In offering concessions to the border States, they had to run the risk, or incur the certainty, of dividing their own party, and they took this risk with open eyes. As Seward himself, in his gruff way, said at dinner, after Mr. Adams and he had made their speeches: "If there's no secession now, you and I are ruined."

They won their game; this was their affair and the affair of the historians who tell their story; their private secretaries had nothing to do with it except to follow their orders. On that side a secretary learned nothing and had nothing to learn. The sudden arrival of Mr. Lincoln in Washington on February 23, and the language of his inaugural address, were the final term of the winter's tactics, and closed the private secretary's interest in the matter forever. Perhaps he felt, even then, a good deal more interest in the appearance of another private secretary, of his own age, a young man named John Hay, who lighted on La Fayette Square at the same moment. Friends are born, not made, and Henry never mistook a friend except when in power. From the first slight meeting in February and March, 1861, he recognized Hay as a friend, and never lost sight of him at the future crossing of their paths; but, for the moment, his own task ended on March 4 when Hay's began. The winter's anxieties were shifted upon new shoulders, and Henry gladly turned back to Blackstone. He had tried to make himself useful, and had exerted energy that seemed to him portentous, acting in secret as newspaper correspondent, cultivating a large acquaintance and even haunting ballrooms where the simple, oldfashioned, Southern tone was pleasant even in the atmosphere of conspiracy and treason. The sum was next to nothing for education, because no one could teach; all were as ignorant as himself; none knew what should be done, or how to do it; all were trying to learn and were more bent on asking than on answering questions. The mass of ignorance in Washington was lighted up by no ray of knowledge. Society, from top to bottom, broke down.

From this law there was no exception, unless, perhaps,

that of old General Winfield Scott, who happened to be the only military figure that looked equal to the crisis. No one else either looked it, or was it, or could be it, by nature or training. Had young Adams been told that his life was to hang on the correctness of his estimate of the new President, he would have lost. He saw Mr. Lincoln but once; at the melancholy function called an Inaugural Ball. Of course he looked anxiously for a sign of character. He saw a long, awkward figure; a plain, ploughed face; a mind, absent in part, and in part evidently worried by white kid gloves; features that expressed neither self-satisfaction nor any other familiar Americanism, but rather the same painful sense of becoming educated and of needing education that tormented a private secretary, above all a lack of apparent force. Any private secretary in the least fit for his business would have thought, as Adams did, that no man living needed so much education as the new President but that all the education he could get would not be enough.

As far as a young man of anxious temperament could see, no one in Washington was fitted for his duties; or rather, no duties in March were fitted for the duties in April. The few people who thought they knew something were more in error than those who knew nothing. Education was matter of life and death, but all the education in the world would have helped nothing. Only one man in Adams's reach seemed to him supremely fitted by knowledge and experience to be an adviser and friend. This was Senator Sumner; and there, in fact, the young man's education began; there it ended.

Going over the experience again, long after all the great actors were dead, he struggled to see where he had blundered. In the effort to make acquaintances, he lost friends, but he would have liked much to know whether he could have helped it. He had necessarily followed

Seward and his father; he took for granted that his business was obedience, discipline, and silence; he supposed
the party to require it, and that the crisis overruled all personal doubts. He was thunderstruck to learn that Senator
Sumner privately denounced the course, regarded Mr.
Adams as betraying the principles of his life, and broke
off relations with his family.

Many a shock was Henry Adams to meet in the course
of a long life passed chiefly near politics and politicians,
but the profoundest lessons are not the lessons of reason;
they are sudden strains that permanently warp the mind.
He cared little or nothing about the point in discussion; he
was even willing to admit that Sumner might be right,
though in all great emergencies he commonly found that
every one was more or less wrong; he liked lofty moral
principle and cared little for political tactics; he felt a
profound respect for Sumner himself; but the shock
opened a chasm in life that never closed, and as long as life
lasted, he found himself invariably taking for granted, as
a political instinct, without waiting further experiment —
as he took for granted that arsenic poisoned — the rule that
a friend in power is a friend lost.

On his own score, he never admitted the rupture, and
never exchanged a word with Mr. Sumner on the subject,
then or afterwards, but his education — for good or bad —
made an enormous stride. One has to deal with all sorts of
unexpected morals in life, and, at this moment, he was
looking at hundreds of Southern gentlemen who believed
themselves singularly honest, but who seemed to him engaged in the plainest breach of faith and the blackest secret
conspiracy, yet they did not disturb his education. History
told of little else; and not one rebel defection — not even
Robert E. Lee's — cost young Adams a personal pang; but
Sumner's struck home.

This, then, was the result of the new attempt at education, down to March 4, 1861; this was all; and frankly, it seemed to him hardly what he wanted. The picture of Washington in March, 1861, offered education, but not the kind of education that led to good. The process that Matthew Arnold described as wandering between two worlds, one dead, the other powerless to be born, helps nothing. Washington was a dismal school. Even before the traitors had flown, the vultures descended on it in swarms that darkened the ground, and tore the carrion of political patronage into fragments and gobbets of fat and lean, on the very steps of the White House. Not a man there knew what his task was to be, or was fitted for it; every one without exception, Northern or Southern, was to learn his business at the cost of the public. Lincoln, Seward, Sumner, and the rest, could give no help to the young man seeking education; they knew less than he; within six weeks they were all to be taught their duties by the uprising of such as he, and their education was to cost a million lives and ten thousand million dollars, more or less, North and South, before the country could recover its balance and movement. Henry was a helpless victim, and, like all the rest, he could only wait for he knew not what, to send him he knew not where.

With the close of the session, his own functions ended. Ceasing to be private secretary he knew not what else to do but return with his father and mother to Boston in the middle of March, and, with childlike docility, sit down at a desk in the law-office of Horace Gray in Court Street, to begin again: "My Lords and Gentlemen"; dozing after a two o'clock dinner, or waking to discuss politics with the future Justice. There, in ordinary times, he would have remained for life, his attempt at education in treason having, like all the rest, disastrously failed.

8

Diplomacy

(1861)

Hardly a week passed when the newspapers announced
that President Lincoln had selected Charles Francis Adams
as his Minister to England. Once more, silently, Henry
put Blackstone back on its shelf. As Friar Bacon's head
sententiously announced many centuries before: Time had
passed! The Civil Law lasted a brief day; the Common
Law prolonged its shadowy existence for a week. The law,
altogether, as path of education, vanished in April, 1861,
leaving a million young men planted in the mud of a law-
less world, to begin a new life without education at all.
They asked few questions, but if they had asked millions
they would have got no answers. No one could help.
Looking back on this moment of crisis, nearly fifty years
afterwards, one could only shake one's white beard in
silent horror. Mr. Adams once more intimated that he
thought himself entitled to the services of one of his sons,
and he indicated Henry as the only one who could be
spared from more serious duties. Henry packed his trunk
again without a word. He could offer no protest. Ridiculous as he knew himself about to be in his new rôle, he was
less ridiculous than his betters. He was at least no public
official, like the thousands of improvised secretaries and

generals who crowded their jealousies and intrigues on the President. He was not a vulture of carrion — patronage. He knew that his father's appointment was the result of Governor Seward's personal friendship; he did not then know that Senator Sumner had opposed it; or the reasons which Sumner alleged for thinking it unfit; but he could have supplied proofs enough had Sumner asked for them, the strongest and most decisive being that, in his opinion, Mr. Adams had chosen a private secretary far more unfit than his chief. That Mr. Adams was unfit might well be, since it was hard to find a fit appointment in the list of possible candidates, except Mr. Sumner himself; and no one knew so well as this experienced Senator that the weakest of all Mr. Adams's proofs of fitness was his consent to quit a safe seat in Congress for an exceedingly unsafe seat in London with no better support than Senator Sumner, at the head of the Foreign Relations Committee, was likely to give him. In the family history, its members had taken many a dangerous risk, but never before had they taken one so desperate.

The private secretary troubled himself not at all about the unfitness of any one; he knew too little; and, in fact, no one, except perhaps Mr. Sumner, knew more. The President and Secretary of State knew least of all. As Secretary of Legation the Executive appointed the editor of a Chicago newspaper who had applied for the Chicago Post-Office; a good fellow, universally known as Charley Wilson, who had not a thought of staying in the post, or of helping the Minister. The Assistant Secretary was inherited from Buchanan's time, a hard worker, but socially useless. Mr. Adams made no effort to find efficient help; perhaps he knew no name to suggest; perhaps he knew too much of Washington; but he could hardly have hoped to find a staff of strength in his son.

The private secretary was more passive than his father,

for he knew not where to turn. Sumner alone could have smoothed his path by giving him letters of introduction, but if Sumner wrote letters, it was not with the effect of smoothing paths. No one, at that moment, was engaged in smoothing either paths or people. The private secretary was no worse off than his neighbors except in being called earlier into service. On April 13 the storm burst and rolled several hundred thousand young men like Henry Adams into the surf of a wild ocean, all helpless like himself, to be beaten about for four years by the waves of war. Adams still had time to watch the regiments form ranks before Boston State House in the April evenings and march southward, quietly enough, with the air of business they wore from their cradles, but with few signs or sounds of excitement. He had time also to go down the harbor to see his brother Charles quartered in Fort Independence before being thrown, with a hundred thousand more, into the furnace of the Army of the Potomac to get educated in a fury of fire. Few things were for the moment so trivial in importance as the solitary private secretary crawling down to the wretched old Cunard steamer Niagara at East Boston to start again for Liverpool. This time the pitcher of education had gone to the fountain once too often; it was fairly broken; and the young man had got to meet a hostile world without defence — or arms.

The situation did not seem even comic, so ignorant was the world of its humors; yet Minister Adams sailed for England, May 1, 1861, with much the same outfit as Admiral Dupont would have enjoyed if the Government had sent him to attack Port Royal with one cabin-boy in a rowboat. Luckily for the cabin-boy, he was alone. Had Secretary Seward and Senator Sumner given to Mr. Adams the rank of Ambassador and four times his salary, a palace in London, a staff of trained secretaries, and personal letters of introduction to the royal family and the whole peerage, the private secretary would have been cabin-boy still, with the extra burden of many masters; he was the most fortunate person in the party, having for master only his father who never fretted, never dictated, never disciplined, and whose idea of American diplomacy was that of the eighteenth century. Minister Adams remembered how his grandfather had sailed from Mount Wollaston in midwinter, 1778, on the little frigate Boston, taking his eleven-year-old son John Quincy with him, for secretary, on a diplomacy of adventure that had hardly a parallel for success. He remembered how John Quincy, in 1809, had sailed for Russia, with himself, a baby of two years old, to cope with Napoleon and the Czar Alexander single-handed, almost as much of an adventurer as John Adams before him, and almost as successful. He thought it natural that the Government should send him out as an adventurer also, with a twenty-three-year-old son, and he did not even notice that he left not a friend behind him. No doubt he could depend on Seward, but on whom could Seward depend? Certainly not on the Chairman of the Committee of Foreign Relations. Minister Adams had no friend in the Senate; he could hope for no favors, and he asked none. He thought it right to play the adventurer as his father and grandfather had done before him, without a murmur. This was a lofty view, and for him answered his objects, but it bore hard on cabin-boys, and when, in time, the young man realized what had happened, he felt it as a betrayal. He modestly thought himself unfit for the career of adventurer, and judged his father to be less fit than himself. For the first time America was posing as the champion of legitimacy and order. Her representatives should know how to play their rôle; they should wear the costume; but, in the mission attached to Mr. Adams in

1861, the only rag of legitimacy or order was the private secretary, whose stature was not sufficient to impose awe on the Court and Parliament of Great Britain.

One inevitable effect of this lesson was to make a victim of the scholar and to turn him into a harsh judge of his masters. If they overlooked him, he could hardly overlook them, since they stood with their whole weight on his body. By way of teaching him quickly, they sent out their new Minister to Russia in the same ship. Secretary Seward had occasion to learn the merits of Cassius M. Clay in the diplomatic service, but Mr. Seward's education profited less than the private secretary's, Cassius Clay as a teacher having no equal though possibly some rivals. No young man, not in Government pay, could be asked to draw, from such lessons, any confidence in himself, and it was notorious that, for the next two years, the persons were few indeed who felt, or had reason to feel, any sort of confidence in the Government; fewest of all among those who were in it. At home, for the most part, young men went to the war, grumbled and died; in England they might grumble or not; no one listened.

Above all, the private secretary could not grumble to his chief. He knew surprisingly little, but that much he did know. He never labored so hard to learn a language as he did to hold his tongue, and it affected him for life. The habit of reticence — of talking without meaning — is never effaced. He had to begin it at once. He was already an adept when the party landed at Liverpool, May 13, 1861, and went instantly up to London: a family of early Christian martyrs about to be flung into an arena of lions, under the glad eyes of Tiberius Palmerston. Though Lord Palmerston would have laughed his peculiar Palmerston laugh at figuring as Tiberius, he would have seen only evident resemblance in the Christian martyrs, for he had already arranged the ceremony.

Of what they had to expect, the Minister knew no more than his son. What he or Mr. Seward or Mr. Sumner may have thought is the affair of history and their errors concern historians. The errors of a private secretary concerned no one but himself, and were a large part of his education. He thought on May 12 that he was going to a friendly Government and people, true to the anti-slavery principles which had been their steadiest profession. For a hundred years the chief effort of his family had aimed at bringing the Government of England into intelligent co-operation with the objects and interests of America. His father was about to make a new effort, and this time the chance of success was promising. The slave States had been the chief apparent obstacle to good understanding. As for the private secretary himself, he was, like all Bostonians, instinctively English. He could not conceive the idea of a hostile England. He supposed himself, as one of the members of a famous anti-slavery family, to be welcome everywhere in the British Islands.

On May 13, he met the official announcement that England recognized the belligerency of the Confederacy. This beginning of a new education tore up by the roots nearly all that was left of Harvard College and Germany. He had to learn — the sooner the better — that his ideas were the reverse of truth; that in May, 1861, no one in England — literally no one — doubted that Jefferson Davis had made or would make a nation, and nearly all were glad of it, though not often saying so. They mostly imitated Palmerston, who, according to Mr. Gladstone, "desired the severance as a diminution of a dangerous power, but prudently held his tongue." The sentiment of anti-slavery had disappeared. Lord John Russell, as Foreign Secretary, had received the rebel emissaries, and had decided to recognize their belligerency before the arrival of Mr. Adams in order to fix the position of the British Government in advance.

The recognition of independence would then become an understood policy; a matter of time and occasion.

Whatever Minister Adams may have felt, the first effect of this shock upon his son produced only a dullness of comprehension — a sort of hazy inability to grasp the missile or realize the blow. Yet he realized that to his father it was likely to be fatal. The chances were great that the whole family would turn round and go home within a few weeks. The horizon widened out in endless waves of confusion. When he thought over the subject in the long leisure of later life, he grew cold at the idea of his situation had his father then shown himself what Sumner thought him to be — unfit for his post. That the private secretary was unfit for his — trifling though it were — was proved by his unreflecting confidence in his father. It never entered his mind that his father might lose his nerve or his temper, and yet in a subsequent knowledge of statesmen and diplomats extending over several generations, he could not certainly point out another who could have stood such a shock without showing it. He passed this long day, and tedious journey to London, without once thinking of the possibility that his father might make a mistake. Whatever the Minister thought, and certainly his thought was not less active than his son's, he showed no trace of excitement. His manner was the same as ever; his mind and temper were as perfectly balanced; not a word escaped; not a nerve twitched.

The test was final, for no other shock so violent and sudden could possibly recur. The worst was in full sight. For once the private secretary knew his own business, which was to imitate his father as closely as possible and hold his tongue. Dumped thus into Maurigy's Hotel at the foot of Regent Street, in the midst of a London season, without a friend or even an acquaintance, he preferred to laugh at his father's bewilderment before the waiter's

" 'amhandheggsir" for breakfast, rather than ask a question or express a doubt. His situation, if taken seriously, was too appalling to face. Had he known it better, he would only have thought it worse.

Politically or socially, the outlook was desperate, beyond retrieving or contesting. Socially, under the best of circumstances, a newcomer in London society needs years to establish a position, and Minister Adams had not a week or an hour to spare, while his son had not even a remote chance of beginning. Politically the prospect looked even worse, and for Secretary Seward and Senator Sumner it was so; but for the Minister, on the spot, as he came to realize exactly where he stood, the danger was not so imminent. Mr. Adams was always one of the luckiest of men, both in what he achieved and in what he escaped. The blow, which prostrated Seward and Sumner, passed over him. Lord John Russell had acted — had probably intended to act — kindly by him in forestalling his arrival. The blow must have fallen within three months, and would then have broken him down. The British Ministers were a little in doubt still — a little ashamed of themselves — and certain to wait the longer for their next step in proportion to the haste of their first.

This is not a story of the diplomatic adventures of Charles Francis Adams, but of his son Henry's adventures in search of an education, which, if not taken too seriously, tended to humor. The father's position in London was not altogether bad; the son's was absurd. Thanks to certain family associations, Charles Francis Adams naturally looked on all British Ministers as enemies; the only public occupation of all Adamses for a hundred and fifty years at least, in their brief intervals of quarrelling with State Street, had been to quarrel with Downing Street; and the British Government, well used to a liberal unpopularity abroad, even when officially rude liked to be personally civil. All diplomatic agents are liable to be put, so to speak, in a corner, and are none the worse for it. Minister Adams had nothing in especial to complain of; his position was good while it lasted, and he had only the chances of war to fear. The son had no such compensations. Brought over in order to help his father, he could conceive no way of rendering his father help, but he was clear that his father had got to help him. To him, the Legation was social ostracism, terrible beyond anything he had known. Entire solitude in the great society of London was doubly desperate because his duties as private secretary required him to know everybody and go with his father and mother everywhere they needed escort. He had no friend, or even enemy, to tell him to be patient. Had any one done it, he would surely have broken out with the reply that patience was the last resource of fools as well as of sages; if he was to help his father at all, he must do it at once, for his father would never so much need help again. In fact he never gave his father the smallest help, unless it were as a footman, clerk, or a companion for the younger children.

He found himself in a singular situation for one who was to be useful. As he came to see the situation closer, he began to doubt whether secretaries were meant to be useful. Wars were too common in diplomacy to disturb the habits of the diplomat. Most secretaries detested their chiefs, and wished to be anything but useful. At the St. James's Club, to which the Minister's son could go only as an invited guest, the most instructive conversation he ever heard among the young men of his own age who hung about the tables, more helpless than himself, was: "Quel chien de pays!" or, "Que tu es beau aujourd'hui, mon cher!" No one wanted to discuss affairs; still less to give or get information. That was the affair of their chiefs, who were also slow to assume work not specially ordered from their Courts. If the American Minister was in trouble to-day, the Russian Ambassador was in trouble yesterday and the Frenchman would be in trouble to-morrow. It would all come in the day's work. There was nothing professional in worry. Empires were always tumbling to pieces and diplomats were always picking them up.

This was his whole diplomatic education, except that he found rich veins of jealousy running between every chief and his staff. His social education was more barren still, and more trying to his vanity. His little mistakes in etiquette or address made him writhe with torture. He never forgot the first two or three social functions he attended: one an afternoon at Miss Burdett Coutts's in Stratton Place, where he hid himself in the embrasure of a window and hoped that no one noticed him; another was a garden-party given by the old anti-slavery Duchess Dowager of Sutherland at Chiswick, where the American Minister and Mrs. Adams were kept in conversation by the old Duchess till every one else went away except the young Duke and his cousins, who set to playing leap-frog on the lawn. At intervals during the next thirty years Henry Adams continued to happen upon the Duke, who, singularly enough, was always playing leap-frog. Still another nightmare he suffered at a dance given by the old Duchess Dowager of Somerset, a terrible vision in castanets, who seized him and forced him to perform a Highland fling before the assembled nobility and gentry, with the daughter of the Turkish Ambassador for partner. This might seem humorous to some, but to him the world turned to ashes.

When the end of the season came, the private secretary had not yet won a private acquaintance, and he hugged himself in his solitude when the story of the battle of Bull Run appeared in the *Times*. He felt only the wish to be more private than ever, for Bull Run was a worse diplomatic than military disaster. All this is history and can be read by public schools if they choose; but the curious and unexpected happened to the Legation, for the effect of Bull Run on them was almost strengthening. They no longer felt doubt. For the next year they went on only from week to week, ready to leave England at once, and never assuming more than three months for their limit. Europe was waiting to see them go. So certain was the end that no one cared to hurry it.

So far as a private secretary could see, this was all that saved his father. For many months he looked on himself as lost or finished in the character of private secretary; and as about to begin, without further experiment, a final education in the ranks of the Army of the Potomac where he would find most of his friends enjoying a much pleasanter life than his own. With this idea uppermost in his mind, he passed the summer and the autumn, and began the winter. Any winter in London is a severe trial; one's first winter is the most trying; but the month of December, 1861, in Mansfield Street, Portland Place, would have gorged a glutton of gloom.

One afternoon when he was struggling to resist complete nervous depression in the solitude of Mansfield Street, during the absence of the Minister and Mrs. Adams on a country visit, Reuter's telegram announcing the seizure of Mason and Slidell from a British mail-steamer was brought to the office. All three secretaries, public and private were there — nervous as wild beasts under the long strain on their endurance — and all three, though they knew it to be not merely their order of departure — not merely diplomatic rupture — but a declaration of war — broke into shouts of delight. They were glad to face the end. They saw it and cheered it! Since England was waiting only for its own moment to strike, they were eager to strike first.

They telegraphed the news to the Minister, who was

staying with Monckton Milnes at Fryston, in Yorkshire. How Mr. Adams took it, is told in the "Lives" of Lord Houghton and William E. Forster who was one of the Fryston party. The moment was for him the crisis of his diplomatic career; for the secretaries it was merely the beginning of another intolerable delay, as though they were a military outpost waiting orders to quit an abandoned position. At the moment of sharpest suspense, the Prince Consort sickened and died. Portland Place at Christmas in a black fog was never a rosy landscape, but in 1861 the most hardened Londoner lost his ruddiness. The private secretary had one source of comfort denied to them — he should not be private secretary long.

He was mistaken — of course! He had been mistaken at every point of his education, and, on this point, he kept up the same mistake for nearly seven years longer, always deluded by the notion that the end was near. To him the Trent Affair was nothing but one of many affairs which he had to copy in a delicate round hand into his books, yet it had one or two results personal to him which left no trace on the Legation records. One of these, and to him the most important, was to put an end forever to the idea of being "useful." Hitherto, as an independent and free citizen, not in the employ of the Government, he had kept up his relations with the American press. He had written pretty frequently to Henry J. Raymond, and Raymond had used his letters in the *New York Times*. He had also become fairly intimate with the two or three friendly newspapers in London, the *Daily News*, the *Star*, the weekly *Spectator;* and he had tried to give them news and views that should have a certain common character, and prevent clash. He had even gone down to Manchester to study the cotton famine, and wrote a long account of his visit which his brother Charles had published in the *Boston Courier*. Unfortunately it was printed

with his name, and instantly came back upon him in the
most crushing shape possible — that of a long, satirical
leader in the *London Times*. Luckily the *Times* did not
know its victim to be a part, though not an official, of
the Legation, and lost the chance to make its satire fatal;
but he instantly learned the narrowness of his escape from
old Joe Parkes, one of the traditional busy-bodies of
politics, who had haunted London since 1830, and who,
after rushing to the *Times* office, to tell them all they did
not know about Henry Adams, rushed to the Legation
to tell Adams all he did not want to know about the
Times. For a moment Adams thought his "usefulness"
at an end in other respects than in the press, but a day or
two more taught him the value of obscurity. He was
totally unknown; he had not even a club; London was
empty; no one thought twice about the *Times* article; no
one except Joe Parkes ever spoke of it; and the world had
other persons — such as President Lincoln, Secretary Seward, and Commodore Wilkes — for constant and favorite
objects of ridicule. Henry Adams escaped, but he never
tried to be useful again. The Trent Affair dwarfed individual effort. His education at least had reached the point
of seeing its own proportions. "Surtout point de zèle!"
Zeal was too hazardous a profession for a Minister's son
to pursue, as a volunteer manipulator, among Trent Affairs and rebel cruisers. He wrote no more letters and
meddled with no more newspapers, but he was still young,
and felt unkindly towards the editor of the *London
Times*.

Mr. Delane lost few opportunities of embittering him,
and he felt little or no hope of repaying these attentions;
but the Trent Affair passed like a snowstorm, leaving the
Legation, to its surprise, still in place. Although the private secretary saw in this delay — which he attributed to
Mr. Seward's good sense — no reason for changing his

opinion about the views of the British Government, he had no choice but to sit down again at his table, and go on copying papers, filing letters, and reading newspaper accounts of the incapacity of Mr. Lincoln and the brutality of Mr. Seward — or *vice versa*. The heavy months dragged on and winter slowly turned to spring without improving his position or spirits. Socially he had but one relief; and, to the end of life, he never forgot the keen gratitude he owed for it. During this tedious winter and for many months afterwards, the only gleams of sunshine were on the days he passed at Walton-on-Thames as the guest of Mr. and Mrs. Russell Sturgis at Mount Felix.

His education had unfortunately little to do with bankers, although old George Peabody and his partner, Junius Morgan, were strong allies. Joshua Bates was devoted, and no one could be kinder than Thomas Baring, whose little dinners in Upper Grosvenor Street were certainly the best in London; but none offered a refuge to compare with Mount Felix, and, for the first time, the refuge was a liberal education. Mrs. Russell Sturgis was one of the women to whom an intelligent boy attaches himself as closely as he can. Henry Adams was not a very intelligent boy, and he had no knowledge of the world, but he knew enough to understand that a cub needed shape. The kind of education he most required was that of a charming woman, and Mrs. Russell Sturgis, a dozen years older than himself, could have good-naturedly trained a school of such, without an effort, and with infinite advantage to them. Near her he half forgot the anxieties of Portland Place. During two years of miserable solitude, she was in this social polar winter, the single source of warmth and light.

Of course the Legation itself was home, and, under such pressure, life in it could be nothing but united. All the inmates made common cause, but this was no education. One lived, but was merely flayed alive. Yet, while this might be exactly true of the younger members of the household, it was not quite so with the Minister and Mrs. Adams. Very slowly, but quite steadily, they gained foothold. For some reason partly connected with American sources, British society had begun with violent social prejudice against Lincoln, Seward, and all the Republican leaders except Sumner. Familiar as the whole tribe of Adamses had been for three generations with the impenetrable stupidity of the British mind, and weary of the long struggle to teach it its own interests, the fourth generation could still not quite persuade itself that this new British prejudice was natural. The private secretary suspected that Americans in New York and Boston had something to do with it. The Copperhead was at home in Pall Mall. Naturally the Englishman was a coarse animal and liked coarseness. Had Lincoln and Seward been the ruffians supposed, the average Englishman would have liked them the better. The exceedingly quiet manner and the unassailable social position of Minister Adams in no way conciliated them. They chose to ignore him, since they could not ridicule him. Lord John Russell set the example. Personally the Minister was to be kindly treated; politically he was negligible; he was there to be put aside. London and Paris imitated Lord John. Every one waited to see Lincoln and his hirelings disappear in one vast *débâcle*. All conceived that the Washington Government would soon crumble, and that Minister Adams would vanish with the rest.

This situation made Minister Adams an exception among diplomats. European rulers for the most part fought and treated as members of one family, and rarely had in view the possibility of total extinction; but the Governments and society of Europe, for a year at least, regarded the Washington Government as dead, and its Ministers as nullities. Minister Adams was better received than most nullities because he made no noise. Little by little, in private, society took the habit of accepting him, not so much as a diplomat, but rather as a member of opposition, or an eminent counsel retained for a foreign Government. He was to be received and considered; to be cordially treated as, by birth and manners, one of themselves. This curiously English way of getting behind a stupidity gave the Minister every possible advantage over a European diplomat. Barriers of race, language, birth, habit, ceased to exist. Diplomacy held diplomats apart in order to save Governments, but Earl Russell could not hold Mr. Adams apart. He was undistinguishable from a Londoner. In society few Londoners were so widely at home. None had such double personality and corresponding double weight.

The singular luck that took him to Fryston to meet the shock of the Trent Affair under the sympathetic eyes of Monckton Milnes and William E. Forster never afterwards deserted him. Both Milnes and Forster needed support and were greatly relieved to be supported. They saw what the private secretary in May had overlooked, the hopeless position they were in if the American Minister made a mistake, and, since his strength was theirs, they lost no time in expressing to all the world their estimate of the Minister's character. Between them the Minister was almost safe.

One might discuss long whether, at that moment, Milnes or Forster were the more valuable ally, since they were influences of different kinds. Monckton Milnes was a social power in London, possibly greater than Londoners themselves quite understood, for in London society as elsewhere, the dull and the ignorant made a large majority, and dull men always laughed at Monckton Milnes.

Every bore was used to talk familiarly about "Dicky Milnes," the "cool of the evening"; and of course he himself affected social eccentricity, challenging ridicule with the indifference of one who knew himself to be the first wit in London, and a maker of men — of a great many men. A word from him went far. An invitation to his breakfast-table went farther. Behind his almost Falstaffian mask and laugh of Silenus, he carried a fine, broad, and high intelligence which no one questioned. As a young man he had written verses, which some readers thought poetry, and which were certainly not altogether prose. Later, in Parliament he made speeches, chiefly criticised as too good for the place and too high for the audience. Socially, he was one of two or three men who went everywhere, knew everybody, talked of everything, and had the ear of Ministers; but unlike most wits, he held a social position of his own that ended in a peerage, and he had a house in Upper Brook Street to which most clever people were exceedingly glad of admission. His breakfasts were famous, and no one liked to decline his invitations, for it was more dangerous to show timidity than to risk a fray. He was a voracious reader, a strong critic, an art connoisseur in certain directions, a collector of books, but above all he was a man of the world by profession, and loved the contacts — perhaps the collisions — of society. Not even Henry Brougham dared do the things he did, yet Brougham defied rebuff. Milnes was the good-nature of London; the Gargantuan type of its refinement and coarseness; the most universal figure of May Fair.

Compared with him, figures like Hayward, or Delane, or Venables, or Henry Reeve were quite secondary, but William E. Forster stood in a different class. Forster had nothing whatever to do with May Fair. Except in being a Yorkshireman he was quite the opposite of Milnes. He had at that time no social or political position; he never had a vestige of Milnes's wit or variety; he was a tall, rough, ungainly figure, affecting the singular form of self-defense which the Yorkshiremen and Lancashiremen seem to hold dear — the exterior roughness assumed to cover an internal, emotional, almost sentimental nature. Kindly he had to be, if only by his inheritance from a Quaker ancestry, but he was a Friend one degree removed. Sentimental and emotional he must have been, or he could never have persuaded a daughter of Dr. Arnold to marry him. Pure gold, without a trace of base metal; honest, unselfish, practical; he took up the Union cause and made himself its champion, as a true Yorkshireman was sure to do, partly because of his Quaker anti-slavery convictions, and partly because it gave him a practical opening in the House. As a new member, he needed a field.

Diffidence was not one of Forster's weaknesses. His practical sense and his personal energy soon established him in leadership, and made him a powerful champion, not so much for ornament as for work. With such a manager, the friends of the Union in England began to take heart. Minister Adams had only to look on as his true champions, the heavy-weights, came into action, and even the private secretary caught now and then a stray gleam of encouragement as he saw the ring begin to clear for these burly Yorkshiremen to stand up in a prize-fight likely to be as brutal as ever England had known. Milnes and Forster were not exactly light-weights, but Bright and Cobden were the hardest hitters in England, and with them for champions the Minister could tackle even Lord Palmerston without much fear of foul play.

In society John Bright and Richard Cobden were never seen, and even in Parliament they had no large following. They were classed as enemies of order, — anarchists, —

and anarchists they were if hatred of the so-called established orders made them so. About them was no sort of political timidity. They took bluntly the side of the Union against Palmerston whom they hated. Strangers to London society, they were at home in the American Legation, delightful dinner-company, talking always with reckless freedom. Cobden was the milder and more persuasive; Bright was the more dangerous to approach; but the private secretary delighted in both, and nourished an ardent wish to see them talk the same language to Lord John Russell from the gangway of the House.

With four such allies as these, Minister Adams stood no longer quite helpless. For the second time the British Ministry felt a little ashamed of itself after the Trent Affair, as well it might, and disposed to wait before moving again. Little by little, friends gathered about the Legation who were no fair-weather companions. The old anti-slavery, Exeter Hall, Shaftesbury clique turned out to be an annoying and troublesome enemy, but the Duke of Argyll was one of the most valuable friends the Minister found, both politically and socially, and the Duchess was as true as her mother. Even the private secretary shared faintly in the social profit of this relation, and never forgot dining one night at the Lodge, and finding himself after dinner engaged in instructing John Stuart Mill about the peculiar merits of an American protective system. In spite of all the probabilities, he convinced himself that it was not the Duke's claret which led him to this singular form of loquacity; he insisted that it was the fault of Mr. Mill himself who led him on by assenting to his point of view. Mr. Mill took no apparent pleasure in dispute, and in that respect the Duke would perhaps have done better; but the secretary had to admit that though at other periods of life he was sufficiently and even amply snubbed by Englishmen, he could never recall a single occasion during this trying year, when he had to complain of rudeness.

Friendliness he found here and there, but chiefly among his elders; not among fashionable or socially powerful people, either men or women; although not even this rule was quite exact, for Frederick Cavendish's kindness and intimate relations made Devonshire House almost familiar, and Lyulph Stanley's ardent Americanism created a certain cordiality with the Stanleys of Alderley whose house was one of the most frequented in London. Lorne, too, the future Argyll, was always a friend. Yet the regular course of society led to more literary intimacies. Sir Charles Trevelyan's house was one of the first to which young Adams was asked, and with which his friendly relations never ceased for near half a century, and then only when death stopped them. Sir Charles and Lady Lyell were intimates. Tom Hughes came into close alliance. By the time society began to reopen its doors after the death of the Prince Consort, even the private secretary occasionally saw a face he knew, although he made no more effort of any kind, but silently waited the end. Whatever might be the advantages of social relations to his father and mother, to him the whole business of diplomacy and society was futile. He meant to go home.

9

Foes
or Friends

(1862)

Of the year 1862 Henry Adams could never think without a shudder. The war alone did not greatly distress him; already in his short life he was used to seeing people wade in blood, and he could plainly discern in history, that man from the beginning had found his chief amusement in bloodshed; but the ferocious joy of destruction at its best requires that one should kill what one hates, and young Adams neither hated nor wanted to kill his friends the rebels, while he wanted nothing so much as to wipe England off the earth. Never could any good come from that besotted race! He was feebly trying to save his own life. Every day the British Government deliberately crowded him one step further into the grave. He could see it; the Legation knew it; no one doubted it; no one thought of questioning it. The Trent Affair showed where Palmerston and Russell stood. The escape of the rebel cruisers from Liverpool was not, in a young man's eyes, the sign of hesitation, but the proof of their fixed intention to intervene. Lord Russell's replies to Mr. Adams's notes were discourteous in their indifference, and, to an irritable young private secretary of twenty-four, were insolent in their disregard of truth. Whatever forms of phrase were usual in public to modify the harshness of invective, in private no political opponent in England, and few political friends, hesitated to say brutally of Lord John Russell that he lied. This was no great reproach, for, more or less, every statesman lied, but the intensity of the private secretary's rage sprang from his belief that Russell's form of defence covered intent to kill. Not for an instant did the Legation draw a free breath. The suspense was hideous and unendurable.

The Minister, no doubt, endured it, but he had support and consideration, while his son had nothing to think about but his friends who were mostly dying under McClellan in the swamps about Richmond, or his enemies who were exulting in Pall Mall. He bore it as well as he could till midsummer, but, when the story of the second Bull Run appeared, he could bear it no longer, and after a sleepless night, walking up and down his room without reflecting that his father was beneath him, he announced at breakfast his intention to go home into the army. His mother seemed to be less impressed by the announcement than by the walking over her head, which was so unlike her as to surprise her son. His father, too, received the announcement quietly. No doubt they expected it, and had taken their measures in advance. In those days, parents got used to all sorts of announcements from their children. Mr. Adams took his son's defection as quietly as he took Bull Run; but his son never got the chance to go. He found obstacles constantly rising in his path. The remonstrances of his brother Charles, who was himself in the Army of the Potomac, and whose opinion had always the greatest weight with Henry, had much to do with delaying action; but he felt, of his own accord, that if he deserted his post in London, and found the Capuan comforts he expected in Virginia where he would have only bullets to wound him, he would never forgive himself for leaving his father and mother alone to be devoured by the wild beasts of the British amphitheatre. This reflection might not have stopped him, but his father's suggestion was decisive. The Minister pointed out that it was too late for him to take part in the actual campaign, and that long before next spring they would all go home together.

The young man had copied too many affidavits about rebel cruisers to miss the point of this argument, so he sat down again to copy some more. Consul Dudley at Liverpool provided a continuous supply. Properly, the affidavits were no business of the private secretary, but practically the private secretary did a second secretary's work, and was glad to do it, if it would save Mr. Seward the trouble of sending more secretaries of his own selection to help the Minister. The work was nothing, and no one ever complained of it; not even Moran, the Secretary of Legation after the departure of Charley Wilson, though he might sit up all night to copy. Not the work, but the play exhausted. The effort of facing a hostile society was bad enough, but that of facing friends was worse. After terrific disasters like the seven days before Richmond and the second Bull Run, friends needed support; a tone of bluff would have been fatal, for the average mind sees quickest through a bluff; nothing answers but candor; yet private secretaries never feel candid, however much they feel the reverse, and therefore they must affect candor; not always a simple act when one is exasperated, furious, bitter, and choking with tears over the blunders and incapacity of one's Government. If one shed tears, they must be shed on one's pillow. Least of all, must one throw extra strain on the Minister, who had all he could carry without being fretted in his family. One must read one's *Times* every morning over one's muffin without reading aloud — "Another disastrous Federal Defeat"; and one might not even indulge in harmless profanity. Self-restraint among friends required much more effort than keeping a quiet face before enemies. Great men were the worst blunderers. One day the private secretary smiled, when standing with the crowd in the throne-room while the endless procession made bows to the royal family, at hearing, behind his shoulder, one Cabinet Minister remark gaily to another: "So the Federals have got another licking!" The point of the remark was its truth. Even a private secretary had learned to control his tones and guard his features and betray no joy over the "lickings" of an enemy — in the enemy's presence.

London was altogether beside itself on one point, in especial; it created a nightmare of its own, and gave it the shape of Abraham Lincoln. Behind this it placed another demon, if possible more devilish, and called it Mr. Seward. In regard to these two men, English society seemed demented. Defence was useless; explanation was vain; one could only let the passion exhaust itself. One's best friends were as unreasonable as enemies, for the belief in poor Mr. Lincoln's brutality and Seward's ferocity became a dogma of popular faith. The last time Henry Adams saw Thackeray, before his sudden death at Christmas in 1863, was in entering the house of Sir Henry Holland for an evening reception. Thackeray was pulling on his coat downstairs, laughing because, in his usual blind way, he had stumbled into the wrong house and not found it out till he shook hands with old Sir Henry, whom he knew very well, but who was not the host he expected. Then his tone changed as he spoke of his — and Adams's — friend, Mrs. Frank Hampton, of South Carolina, whom

he had loved as Sally Baxter and painted as Ethel Newcome. Though he had never quite forgiven her marriage,
his warmth of feeling revived when he heard that she had
died of consumption at Columbia while her parents and
sister were refused permission to pass through the lines
to see her. In speaking of it, Thackeray's voice trembled
and his eyes filled with tears. The coarse cruelty of Lincoln and his hirelings was notorious. He never doubted
that the Federals made a business of harrowing the ten-
derest feelings of women — particularly of women — in
order to punish their opponents. On quite insufficient
evidence he burst into violent reproach. Had Adams carried in his pocket the proofs that the reproach was unjust,
he would have gained nothing by showing them. At that
moment Thackeray, and all London society with him,
needed the nervous relief of expressing emotion; for if
Mr. Lincoln was not what they said he was — what were
they?

For like reason, the members of the Legation kept silence, even in private, under the boorish Scotch jibes of
Carlyle. If Carlyle was wrong, his diatribes would give
his true measure, and this measure would be a low one,
for Carlyle was not likely to be more sincere or more
sound in one thought than in another. The proof that a
philosopher does not know what he is talking about is apt
to sadden his followers before it reacts on himself. Demo-
lition of one's idols is painful, and Carlyle had been an
idol. Doubts cast on his stature spread far into general
darkness like shadows of a setting sun. Not merely the
idols fell, but also the habit of faith. If Carlyle, too, was
a fraud, what were his scholars and school?

Society as a rule was civil, and one had no more reason to complain than every other diplomatist has had, in
like conditions, but one's few friends in society were
mere ornament. The Legation could not dream of con-

testing social control. The best they could do was to escape mortification, and by this time their relations were good enough to save the Minister's family from that annoyance. Now and then, the fact could not be wholly disguised that some one had refused to meet — or to receive — the Minister; but never an open insult, or any expression of which the Minister had to take notice. Diplomacy served as a buffer in times of irritation, and no diplomat who knew his business fretted at what every diplomat — and none more commonly than the English — had to expect; therefore Henry Adams, though not a diplomat and wholly unprotected, went his way peacefully enough, seeing clearly that society cared little to make his acquaintance, but seeing also no reason why society should discover charms in him of which he was himself unconscious. He went where he was asked; he was always courteously received; he was, on the whole, better treated than at Washington; and he held his tongue.

For a thousand reasons, the best diplomatic house in London was Lord Palmerston's, while Lord John Russell's was one of the worst. Of neither host could a private secretary expect to know anything. He might as well have expected to know the Grand Lama. Personally Lord Palmerston was the last man in London that a cautious private secretary wanted to know. Other Prime Ministers may perhaps have lived who inspired among diplomatists as much distrust as Palmerston, and yet between Palmerston's word and Russell's word, one hesitated to decide, and gave years of education to deciding, whether either could be trusted, or how far. The Queen herself in her famous memorandum of August 12, 1850, gave her opinion of Palmerston in words that differed little from words used by Lord John Russell, and both the Queen and Russell said in substance only what Cobden and Bright said in private. Every diplomatist agreed with them, yet the diplomatic standard of trust seemed to be other than the parliamentarian. No professional diplomatists worried about falsehoods. Words were with them forms of expression which varied with individuals, but falsehood was more or less necessary to all. The worst liars were the candid. What diplomatists wanted to know was the motive that lay beyond the expression. In the case of Palmerston they were unanimous in warning new colleagues that they might expect to be sacrificed by him to any momentary personal object. Every new Minister or Ambassador at the Court of St. James received this preliminary lesson that he must, if possible, keep out of Palmerston's reach. The rule was not secret or merely diplomatic. The Queen herself had emphatically expressed the same opinion officially. If Palmerston had an object to gain, he would go down to the House of Commons and betray or misrepresent a foreign Minister, without concern for his victim. No one got back on him with a blow equally mischievous — not even the Queen — for, as old Baron Brunnow described him: "C'est une peau de rhinocère!" Having gained his point, he laughed, and his public laughed with him, for the usual British — or American — public likes to be amused, and thought it very amusing to see these beribboned and bestarred foreigners caught and tossed and gored on the horns of this jovial, slashing, devil-may-care British bull.

Diplomatists have no right to complain of mere lies; it is their own fault, if, educated as they are, the lies deceive them; but they complain bitterly of traps. Palmerston was believed to lay traps. He was the *enfant terrible* of the British Government. On the other hand, Lady Palmerston was believed to be good and loyal. All the diplomats and their wives seemed to think so, and took their troubles to her, believing that she would try to help them. For this reason among others, her evenings at home — Saturday Reviews, they were called — had great vogue. An ignorant young American could not be expected to explain it. Cambridge House was no better for entertaining than a score of others. Lady Palmerston was no longer young or handsome, and could hardly at any age have been vivacious. The people one met there were never smart and seldom young; they were largely diplomatic, and diplomats are commonly dull; they were largely political, and politicians rarely decorate or beautify an evening party; they were sprinkled with literary people, who are notoriously unfashionable; the women were of course ill-dressed and middle-aged; the men looked mostly bored or out of place; yet, beyond a doubt, Cambridge House was the best, and perhaps the only political house in London, and its success was due to Lady Palmerston, who never seemed to make an effort beyond a friendly recognition. As a lesson in social education, Cambridge House gave much subject for thought. First or last, one was to know dozens of statesmen more powerful and more agreeable than Lord Palmerston; dozens of ladies more beautiful and more painstaking than Lady Palmerston; but no political house so successful as Cambridge House. The world never explains such riddles. The foreigners said only that Lady Palmerston was "sympathique."

The small fry of the Legations were admitted there, or tolerated, without a further effort to recognize their existence, but they were pleased because rarely tolerated anywhere else, and there they could at least stand in a corner and look at a bishop or even a duke. This was the social diversion of young Adams. No one knew him — not even the lackeys. The last Saturday evening he ever attended, he gave his name as usual at the foot of the staircase, and was rather disturbed to hear it shouted up as "Mr. Handrew Hadams!" He tried to correct it, and the footman shouted more loudly: "Mr. Hanthony Hadams!"

With some temper he repeated the correction, and was finally announced as "Mr. Halexander Hadams," and under this name made his bow for the last time to Lord Palmerston who certainly knew no better.

Far down the staircase one heard Lord Palmerston's laugh as he stood at the door receiving his guests, talking probably to one of his henchmen, Delane, Borthwick, or Hayward, who were sure to be near. The laugh was singular, mechanical, wooden, and did not seem to disturb his features. "Ha! . . . Ha! . . . Ha!" Each was a slow, deliberate ejaculation, and all were in the same tone, as though he meant to say: "Yes! . . . Yes! . . . Yes!" by way of assurance. It was a laugh of 1810 and the Congress of Vienna. Adams would have much liked to stop a moment and ask whether William Pitt and the Duke of Wellington had laughed so; but young men attached to foreign Ministers asked no questions at all of Palmerston and their chiefs asked as few as possible. One made the usual bow and received the usual glance of civility; then passed on to Lady Palmerston, who was always kind in manner, but who wasted no remarks; and so to Lady Jocelyn with her daughter, who commonly had something friendly to say; then went through the diplomatic corps, Brunnow, Musurus, Azeglio, Apponyi, Van de Weyer, Bille, Tricoupi, and the rest, finally dropping into the hands of some literary accident as strange there as one's self. The routine varied little. There was no attempt at entertainment. Except for the desperate isolation of these two first seasons, even secretaries would have found the effort almost as mechanical as a levee at St. James's Palace.

Lord Palmerston was not Foreign Secretary; he was Prime Minister, but he loved foreign affairs and could no more resist scoring a point in diplomacy than in whist. Ministers of foreign powers, knowing his habits, tried to hold him at arms'-length, and, to do this, were obliged to court the actual Foreign Secretary, Lord John Russell, who, on July 30, 1861, was called up to the House of Lords as an earl. By some process of personal affiliation, Minister Adams succeeded in persuading himself that he could trust Lord Russell more safely than Lord Palmerston. His son, being young and ill-balanced in temper, thought there was nothing to choose. Englishmen saw little difference between them, and Americans were bound to follow English experience in English character. Minister Adams had much to learn, although with him as well as with his son, the months of education began to count as æons.

Just as Brunnow predicted, Lord Palmerston made his rush at last, as unexpected as always, and more furiously than though still a private secretary of twenty-four. Only a man who had been young with the battle of Trafalgar could be fresh and jaunty to that point, but Minister Adams was not in a position to sympathize with octogenarian youth and found himself in a danger as critical as that of his numerous predecessors. It was late one afternoon in June, 1862, as the private secretary returned, with the Minister, from some social function, that he saw his father pick up a note from his desk and read it in silence. Then he said curtly: "Palmerston wants a quarrel!" This was the point of the incident as he felt it. Palmerston wanted a quarrel; he must not be gratified; he must be stopped. The matter of quarrel was General Butler's famous woman-order at New Orleans, but the motive was the belief in President Lincoln's brutality that had taken such deep root in the British mind. Knowing Palmerston's habits, the Minister took for granted that he meant to score a diplomatic point by producing this note in the House of Commons. If he did this at once, the Minister was lost; the quarrel was made; and one new victim to Palmerston's passion for popularity was sacrificed.

The moment was nervous — as far as the private secretary knew, quite the most critical moment in the records
of American diplomacy — but the story belongs to history, not to education, and can be read there by any one
who cares to read it. As a part of Henry Adams's education it had a value distinct from history. That his father
succeeded in muzzling Palmerston without a public scandal, was well enough for the Minister, but was not enough
for a private secretary who liked going to Cambridge
House, and was puzzled to reconcile contradictions. That
Palmerston had wanted a quarrel was obvious; why, then,
did he submit so tamely to being made the victim of the
quarrel? The correspondence that followed his note was
conducted feebly on his side, and he allowed the United
States Minister to close it by a refusal to receive further
communications from him except through Lord Russell.
The step was excessively strong, for it broke off private
relations as well as public, and cost even the private secretary his invitations to Cambridge House. Lady Palmerston tried her best, but the two ladies found no resource
except tears. They had to do with an American Minister
perplexed in the extreme. Not that Mr. Adams lost his
temper, for he never felt such a weight of responsibility,
and was never more cool; but he could conceive no other
way of protecting his Government, not to speak of himself, than to force Lord Russell to interpose. He believed
that Palmerston's submission and silence were due to Russell. Perhaps he was right; at the time, his son had no doubt
of it, though afterwards he felt less sure. Palmerston
wanted a quarrel; the motive seemed evident; yet when
the quarrel was made, he backed out of it; for some reason
it seemed that he did not want it — at least, not then. He
never showed resentment against Mr. Adams at the time
or afterwards. He never began another quarrel. Incredible
as it seemed, he behaved like a well-bred gentleman who

felt himself in the wrong. Possibly this change may have been due to Lord Russell's remonstrances, but the private secretary would have felt his education in politics more complete had he ever finally made up his mind whether Palmerston was more angry with General Butler, or more annoyed at himself, for committing what was in both cases an unpardonable *bêtise*.

At the time, the question was hardly raised, for no one doubted Palmerston's attitude or his plans. The season was near its end, and Cambridge House was soon closed. The Legation had troubles enough without caring to publish more. The tide of English feeling ran so violently against it that one could only wait to see whether General McClellan would bring it relief. The year 1862 was a dark spot in Henry Adams's life, and the education it gave was mostly one that he gladly forgot. As far as he was aware, he made no friends; he could hardly make enemies; yet towards the close of the year he was flattered by an invitation from Monckton Milnes to Fryston, and it was one of many acts of charity towards the young that gave Milnes immortality. Milnes made it his business to be kind. Other people criticised him for his manner of doing it, but never imitated him. Naturally, a dispirited, disheartened private secretary was exceedingly grateful, and never forgot the kindness, but it was chiefly as education that this first country visit had value. Commonly, country visits are much alike, but Monckton Milnes was never like anybody, and his country parties served his purpose of mixing strange elements. Fryston was one of a class of houses that no one sought for its natural beauties, and the winter mists of Yorkshire were rather more evident for the absence of the hostess on account of them, so that the singular guests whom Milnes collected to enliven his December had nothing to do but astonish each other, if anything could astonish such men. Of the five,

Adams alone was tame; he alone added nothing to the wit or humor, except as a listener; but they needed a listener and he was useful. Of the remaining four, Milnes was the oldest, and perhaps the sanest in spite of his superficial eccentricities, for Yorkshire sanity was true to a standard of its own, if not to other conventions; yet even Milnes startled a young American whose Boston and Washington mind was still fresh. He would not have been startled by the hard-drinking, horse-racing Yorkshireman of whom he had read in books; but Milnes required a knowledge of society and literature that only himself possessed, if one were to try to keep pace with him. He had sought contact with everybody and everything that Europe could offer. He knew it all from several points of view, and chiefly as humorous.

The second of the party was also of a certain age; a quiet, well-mannered, singularly agreeable gentleman of the literary class. When Milnes showed Adams to his room to dress for dinner, he stayed a moment to say a word about this guest, whom he called Stirling of Keir. His sketch closed with the hint that Stirling was violent only on one point — hatred of Napoleon III. On that point, Adams was himself sensitive, which led him to wonder how bad the Scotch gentleman might be. The third was a man of thirty or thereabouts, whom Adams had already met at Lady Palmerston's carrying his arm in a sling. His figure and bearing were sympathetic — almost pathetic — with a certain grave and gentle charm, a pleasant smile, and an interesting story. He was Laurence Oliphant, just from Japan, where he had been wounded in the fanatics' attack on the British Legation. He seemed exceptionally sane and peculiarly suited for country houses, where every man would enjoy his company, and every woman would adore him. He had not then published "Piccadilly"; perhaps he was writing it; while, like all the young men about the Foreign Office, he contributed to *The Owl*.

The fourth was a boy, or had the look of one, though in fact a year older than Adams himself. He resembled in action — and in this trait, was remotely followed, a generation later, by another famous young man, Robert Louis Stevenson — a tropical bird, high-crested, long-beaked, quick-moving, with rapid utterance and screams of humor, quite unlike any English lark or nightingale. One could hardly call him a crimson macaw among owls, and yet no ordinary contrast availed. Milnes introduced him as Mr. Algernon Swinburne. The name suggested nothing. Milnes was always unearthing new coins and trying to give them currency. He had unearthed Henry Adams who knew himself to be worthless and not current. When Milnes lingered a moment in Adams's room to add that Swinburne had written some poetry, not yet published, of really extraordinary merit, Adams only wondered what more Milnes would discover, and whether by chance he could discover merit in a private secretary. He was capable of it.

In due course this party of five men sat down to dinner with the usual club manners of ladyless dinner-tables, easy and formal at the same time. Conversation ran first to Oliphant who told his dramatic story simply, and from him the talk drifted off into other channels, until Milnes thought it time to bring Swinburne out. Then, at last, if never before, Adams acquired education. What he had sought so long, he found; but he was none the wiser; only the more astonished. For once, too, he felt at ease, for the others were no less astonished than himself, and their astonishment grew apace. For the rest of the evening Swinburne figured alone; the end of dinner made the monologue only freer, for in 1862, even when ladies were not in the house, smoking was forbidden, and guests usually smoked in the stables or the kitchen; but Monck-ton Milnes was a licensed libertine who let his guests smoke in Adams's bedroom, since Adams was an Ameri-can-German barbarian ignorant of manners; and there after dinner all sat — or lay — till far into the night, listen-ing to the rush of Swinburne's talk. In a long experience, before or after, no one ever approached it; yet one had heard accounts of the best talking of the time, and read accounts of talkers in all time, among the rest, of Voltaire, who seemed to approach nearest the pattern.

That Swinburne was altogether new to the three types of men-of-the-world before him; that he seemed to them quite original, wildly eccentric, astonishingly gifted, and convulsingly droll, Adams could see; but what more he was, even Milnes hardly dared say. They could not be-lieve his incredible memory and knowledge of literature, classic, mediæval, and modern; his faculty of reciting a play of Sophocles or a play of Shakespeare, forward or backward, from end to beginning; or Dante, or Villon, or Victor Hugo. They knew not what to make of his rhetorical recitation of his own unpublished ballads — "Faustine"; the "Four Boards of the Coffin Lid"; the "Ballad of Burdens" — which he declaimed as though they were books of the Iliad. It was singular that his most ap-preciative listener should have been the author only of pretty verses like "We wandered by the brookside," and "She seemed to those that saw them meet"; and who never cared to write in any other tone; but Milnes took every-thing into his sympathies, including Americans like young Adams whose standards were stiffest of all, while Swin-burne, though millions of ages far from them, united them by his humor even more than by his poetry. The story of his first day as a member of Professor Stubbs's household was professionally clever farce, if not high comedy, in a young man who could write a Greek ode or a Provençal chanson as easily as an English quatrain.

Late at night when the symposium broke up, Stirling of Keir wanted to take with him to his chamber a copy of "Queen Rosamund," the only volume Swinburne had then published, which was on the library table, and Adams offered to light him down with his solitary bedroom candle. All the way, Stirling was ejaculating explosions of wonder, until at length, at the foot of the stairs and at the climax of his imagination, he paused, and burst out: "He's a cross between the devil and the Duke of Argyll!"

To appreciate the full merit of this description, a judicious critic should have known both, and Henry Adams knew only one — at least in person — but he understood that to a Scotchman the likeness meant something quite portentous, beyond English experience, supernatural, and what the French call *moyenâgeux*, or mediæval with a grotesque turn. That Stirling as well as Milnes should regard Swinburne as a prodigy greatly comforted Adams, who lost his balance of mind at first in trying to imagine that Swinburne was a natural product of Oxford, as muffins and pork-pies of London, at once the cause and effect of dyspepsia. The idea that one has actually met a real genius dawns slowly on a Boston mind, but it made entry at last.

Then came the sad reaction, not from Swinburne whose genius never was in doubt, but from the Boston mind which, in its uttermost flights, was never *moyenâgeux*. One felt the horror of Longfellow and Emerson, the doubts of Lowell and the humor of Holmes, at the wild Walpurgis-night of Swinburne's talk. What could a shy young private secretary do about it? Perhaps, in his good nature, Milnes thought that Swinburne might find a friend in Stirling or Oliphant, but he could hardly have fancied Henry Adams rousing in him even an interest. Adams could no more interest Algernon Swinburne than he could interest Encke's comet. To Swinburne he could be no more than a worm. The quality of genius was an education almost ultimate, for one touched there the limits of the human mind on that side; but one could only receive; one had nothing to give — nothing even to offer.

Swinburne tested him then and there by one of his favorite tests — Victor Hugo; for to him the test of Victor Hugo was the surest and quickest of standards. French poetry is at best a severe exercise for foreigners; it requires extraordinary knowledge of the language and rare refinement of ear to appreciate even the recitation of French verse; but unless a poet has both, he lacks something of poetry. Adams had neither. To the end of his life he never listened to a French recitation with pleasure, or felt a sense of majesty in French verse; but he did not care to proclaim his weakness, and he tried to evade Swinburne's vehement insistence by parading an affection for Alfred de Musset. Swinburne would have none of it; de Musset was unequal; he did not sustain himself on the wing.

Adams would have given a world or two, if he owned one, to sustain himself on the wing like de Musset, or even like Hugo; but his education as well as his ear was at fault, and he succumbed. Swinburne tried him again on Walter Savage Landor. In truth the test was the same, for Swinburne admired in Landor's English the qualities that he felt in Hugo's French; and Adams's failure was equally gross, for, when forced to despair, he had to admit that both Hugo and Landor bored him. Nothing more was needed. One who could feel neither Hugo nor Landor was lost.

The sentence was just and Adams never appealed from it. He knew his inferiority in taste as he might know it in smell. Keenly mortified by the dullness of his senses and instincts, he knew he was no companion for Swinburne; probably he could be only an annoyance; no number of centuries could ever educate him to Swinburne's level, even in technical appreciation; yet he often wondered whether there was nothing he had to offer that was worth the poet's acceptance. Certainly such mild homage as the American insect would have been only too happy to bring, had he known how, was hardly worth the acceptance of any one. Only in France is the attitude of prayer possible; in England it became absurd. Even Monckton Milnes, who felt the splendors of Hugo and Landor, was almost as helpless as an American private secretary in personal contact with them. Ten years afterwards Adams met him at the Geneva Conference, fresh from Paris, bubbling with delight at a call he had made on Hugo: "I was shown into a large room," he said, "with women and men seated in chairs against the walls, and Hugo at one end throned. No one spoke. At last Hugo raised his voice solemnly, and uttered the words: 'Quant à moi, je crois en Dieu!' Silence followed. Then a woman responded as if in deep meditation: 'Chose sublime! un Dieu qui croit en Dieu!' "

With the best of will, one could not do this in London; the actors had not the instinct of the drama; and yet even a private secretary was not wholly wanting in instinct. As soon as he reached town he hurried to Pickering's for a copy of "Queen Rosamund," and at that time, if Swinburne was not joking, Pickering had sold seven copies. When the "Poems and Ballads" came out, and met their great success and scandal, he sought one of the first copies from Moxon. If he had sinned and doubted at all, he wholly repented and did penance before "Atalanta in Calydon," and would have offered Swinburne a solemn worship as Milnes's female offered Hugo, if it would have pleased the poet. Unfortunately it was worthless.

The three young men returned to London, and each went his own way. Adams's interest in making friends was something desperate, but "the London season," Milnes used to say, "is a season for making acquaintances and losing friends"; there was no intimate life. Of Swinburne he saw no more till Monckton Milnes summoned his whole array of Frystonians to support him in presiding at the dinner of the Authors' Fund, when Adams found himself seated next to Swinburne, famous then, but no nearer. They never met again. Oliphant he met oftener; all the world knew and loved him; but he too disappeared in the way that all the world knows. Stirling of Keir, after one or two efforts, passed also from Adams's vision into Sir William Stirling-Maxwell. The only record of his wonderful visit to Fryston may perhaps exist still in the registers of the St. James's Club, for immediately afterwards Milnes proposed Henry Adams for membership, and unless his memory erred, the nomination was seconded by Tricoupi and endorsed by Laurence Oliphant and Evelyn Ashley. The list was a little singular for variety, but on the whole it suggested that the private secretary was getting on.

10

Political Morality

(1862)

On Moran's promotion to be Secretary, Mr. Seward inquired whether Minister Adams would like the place of Assistant Secretary for his son. It was the first — and last — office ever offered him, if indeed he could claim what was offered in fact to his father. To them both, the change seemed useless. Any young man could make some sort of Assistant Secretary; only one, just at that moment, could make an Assistant Son. More than half his duties were domestic; they sometimes required long absences; they always required independence of the Government service. His position was abnormal. The British Government by courtesy allowed the son to go to Court as Attaché, though he was never attached, and after five or six years' toleration, the decision was declared irregular. In the Legation, as private secretary, he was liable to do Secretary's work. In society, when official, he was attached to the Minister; when unofficial, he was a young man without any position at all. As the years went on, he began to find advantages in having no position at all except that of young man. Gradually he aspired to become a gentle-man; just a member of society like the rest. The position was irregular; at that time many positions were irregular; yet it lent itself to a sort of irregular education that seemed to be the only sort of education the young man was ever to get.

Such as it was, few young men had more. The spring and summer of 1863 saw a great change in Secretary Seward's management of foreign affairs. Under the stimulus of danger, he too got education. He felt, at last, that his official representatives abroad needed support. Officially he could give them nothing but despatches, which were of no great value to any one; and at best the mere weight of an office had little to do with the public. Governments were made to deal with Governments, not with private individuals or with the opinions of foreign society. In order to affect European opinion, the weight of American opinion had to be brought to bear personally, and had to be backed by the weight of American interests. Mr. Seward set vigorously to work and sent over every important American on whom he could lay his hands. All came to the Legation more or less intimately, and Henry Adams had a chance to see them all, bankers or bishops, who did their work quietly and well, though, to the outsider, the work seemed wasted and the "influential classes" more indurated with prejudice than ever. The waste was only apparent; the work all told in the end, and meanwhile it helped education.

Two or three of these gentlemen were sent over to aid the Minister and to coöperate with him. The most interesting of these was Thurlow Weed, who came to do what the private secretary himself had attempted two years before, with boyish ignorance of his own powers. Mr. Weed took charge of the press, and began, to the amused astonishment of the secretaries, by making what the Legation had learned to accept as the invariable mistake of every amateur diplomat; he wrote letters to the *London Times*. Mistake or not, Mr. Weed soon got into his hands the threads of management, and did quietly and smoothly all that was to be done. With his work the private secretary had no connection; it was he that interested. Thurlow Weed was a complete American education in himself. His mind was naturally strong and beautifully balanced; his temper never seemed ruffled; his manners were carefully perfect in the style of benevolent simplicity, the tradition of Benjamin Franklin. He was the model of political management and patient address; but the trait that excited enthusiasm in a private secretary was his faculty of irresistibly conquering confidence. Of all flowers in the garden of education, confidence was becoming the rarest; but before Mr. Weed went away, young Adams followed him about not only obediently — for obedience had long since become a blind instinct — but rather with sympathy and affection, much like a little dog.

The sympathy was not due only to Mr. Weed's skill of management, although Adams never met another such master, or any one who approached him; nor was the confidence due to any display of professions, either moral or social, by Mr. Weed. The trait that astounded and confounded cynicism was his apparent unselfishness. Never, in any man who wielded such power, did Adams meet anything like it. The effect of power and publicity on all men is the aggravation of self, a sort of tumor that ends by killing the victim's sympathies; a diseased appetite, like a passion for drink or perverted tastes; one can scarcely use expressions too strong to describe the violence of egotism it stimulates; and Thurlow Weed was one of the exceptions; a rare immune. He thought apparently not of himself, but of the person he was talking with. He held himself naturally in the background. He was not jealous. He grasped power, but not office. He distributed offices by handfuls without caring to take them. He had the instinct of empire: he gave, but he did not receive. This rare superiority to the politicians he controlled, a trait that private secretaries never met in the politicians themselves, excited Adams's wonder and curiosity, but when he tried to get behind it, and to educate himself from the stores of Mr. Weed's experience, he found the study still more fascinating. Management was an instinct with Mr. Weed; an object to be pursued for its own sake, as one plays cards; but he appeared to play with men as though they were only cards; he seemed incapable of feeling himself one of them. He took them and played them for their face-value; but once, when he had told, with his usual humor, some stories of his political experience which were strong even for the Albany lobby, the private secretary made bold to ask him outright: "Then, Mr. Weed, do you think that no politician can be trusted?" Mr. Weed hesitated for a moment; then said in his mild manner: "I never advise a young man to begin by thinking so."

This lesson, at the time, translated itself to Adams in a moral sense, as though Mr. Weed had said: "Youth needs illusions!" As he grew older he rather thought that Mr. Weed looked on it as a question of how the game should be played. Young men most needed experience. They could not play well if they trusted to a general rule. Every card had a relative value. Principles had better be left aside; values were enough. Adams knew that he could never learn to play politics in so masterly a fashion as this: his education and his nervous system equally forbade it, although he admired all the more the impersonal faculty of the political master who could thus efface himself and his temper in the game. He noticed that most of the greatest politicians in history had seemed to regard men as counters. The lesson was the more interesting because another famous New Yorker came over at the same time who liked to discuss the same problem. Secretary Seward sent William M. Evarts to London as law counsel, and Henry began an acquaintance with Mr. Evarts that soon became intimate. Evarts was as individual as Weed was impersonal; like most men, he cared little for the game, or how it was played, and much for the stakes, but he played it in a large and liberal way, like Daniel Webster, "a great advocate employed in politics." Evarts was also an economist of morals, but with him the question was rather how much morality one could afford. "The world can absorb only doses of truth," he said; "too much would kill it." One sought education in order to adjust the dose.

The teachings of Weed and Evarts were practical, and the private secretary's life turned on their value. England's power of absorbing truth was small. Englishmen, such as Palmerston, Russell, Bethell, and the society represented by the *Times* and *Morning Post*, as well as the Tories represented by Disraeli, Lord Robert Cecil, and the *Standard*, offered a study in education that sickened a young student with anxiety. He had begun — contrary to Mr. Weed's advice — by taking their bad faith for granted. Was he wrong? To settle this point became the main object of the diplomatic education so laboriously pursued, at a cost already stupendous, and promising to become ruinous. Life changed front, according as one thought one's self dealing with honest men or with rogues.

Thus far, the private secretary felt officially sure of dishonesty. The reasons that satisfied him had not altogether satisfied his father, and of course his father's doubts gravely shook his own convictions, but, in practice, if only for safety, the Legation put little or no confidence in Ministers, and there the private secretary's diplomatic education began. The recognition of belligerency, the management of the Declaration of Paris, the Trent Affair, all strengthened the belief that Lord Russell had started in May, 1861, with the assumption that the Confederacy was established; every step he had taken proved his persistence in the same idea; he never would consent to put obstacles in the way of recognition; and he was waiting only for the proper moment to interpose. All these points seemed so fixed — so self-evident — that no one in the Legation would have doubted or even discussed them except that Lord Russell obstinately denied the whole charge, and persisted in assuring Minister Adams of his honest and impartial neutrality.

With the insolence of youth and zeal, Henry Adams jumped at once to the conclusion that Earl Russell — like other statesmen — lied; and, although the Minister thought differently, he had to act as though Russell were false. Month by month the demonstration followed its mathematical stages; one of the most perfect educational courses in politics and diplomacy that a young man ever had a chance to pursue. The most costly tutors in the world were provided for him at public expense — Lord Palmerston, Lord Russell, Lord Westbury, Lord Selborne, Mr. Gladstone, Lord Granville, and their associates, paid by the British Government; William H. Seward, Charles Francis Adams, William Maxwell Evarts, Thurlow Weed, and other considerable professors employed by the American Government; but there was only one student to profit by this immense staff of teachers. The private secretary alone sought education.

To the end of his life he labored over the lessons then taught. Never was demonstration more tangled. Hegel's metaphysical doctrine of the identity of opposites was simpler and easier to understand. Yet the stages of demonstration were clear. They began in June, 1862, after the escape of one rebel cruiser, by the remonstrances of the Minister against the escape of "No. 290," which was imminent. Lord Russell declined to act on the evidence. New evidence was sent in every few days, and with it, on July 24, was included Collier's legal opinion: "It appears difficult to make out a stronger case of infringement of the Foreign Enlistment Act, which, if not enforced on this occasion, is little better than a dead letter." Such language implied almost a charge of collusion with the rebel agents — an intent to aid the Confederacy. In spite of the warning, Earl Russell let the ship, four days afterwards, escape.

Young Adams had nothing to do with law; that was business of his betters. His opinion of law hung on his opinion of lawyers. In spite of Thurlow Weed's advice, could one afford to trust human nature in politics? History said not. Sir Robert Collier seemed to hold that Law agreed with History. For education the point was vital. If one could not trust a dozen of the most respected private characters in the world, composing the Queen's Ministry, one could trust no mortal man.

Lord Russell felt the force of this inference, and undertook to disprove it. His effort lasted till his death. At first he excused himself by throwing the blame on the law officers. This was a politician's practice, and the lawyers overruled it. Then he pleaded guilty to criminal negligence, and said in his "Recollections": — "I assent entirely to the opinion of the Lord Chief Justice of England that the Alabama ought to have been detained during the four days I was waiting for the opinion of the law officers. But I think that the fault was not that of the commissioners of customs, it was my fault as Secretary of State for Foreign Affairs." This concession brought all parties on common ground. Of course it was his fault! The true issue lay not in the question of his fault, but of his intent. To a young man, getting an education in politics, there could be no sense in history unless a constant course of faults implied a constant motive.

For his father the question was not so abstruse; it was a practical matter of business to be handled as Weed or Evarts handled their bargains and jobs. Minister Adams held the convenient belief that, in the main, Russell was true, and the theory answered his purposes so well that he died still holding it. His son was seeking education, and wanted to know whether he could, in politics, risk trusting any one. Unfortunately no one could then decide; no one knew the facts. Minister Adams died without knowing them. Henry Adams was an older man than his father in 1862, before he learned a part of them. The most curious fact, even then, was that Russell believed in his own good faith and that Argyll believed in it also.

Argyll betrayed a taste for throwing the blame on Bethell, Lord Westbury, then Lord Chancellor, but this escape helped Adams not at all. On the contrary, it complicated the case of Russell. In England, one half of society enjoyed throwing stones at Lord Palmerston, while the other half delighted in flinging mud at Earl Russell, but every one of every party united in pelting Westbury with every missile at hand. The private secretary had no doubts about him, for he never professed to be moral. He was the head and heart of the whole rebel contention, and his opinions on neutrality were as clear as they were on morality. The private secretary had nothing to do with him, and regretted it, for Lord Westbury's wit and wisdom were great; but as far as his authority went, he affirmed the law that in politics no man should be trusted.

Russell alone insisted on his honesty of intention and persuaded both the Duke and the Minister to believe him. Every one in the Legation accepted his assurances as the only assertions they could venture to trust. They knew he expected the rebels to win in the end, but they believed he would not actively interpose to decide it. On that — on nothing else — they rested their frail hopes of remaining a day longer in England. Minister Adams remained six years longer in England; then returned to America to lead a busy life till he died in 1886 still holding the same faith in Earl Russell, who had died in 1878. In 1889, Spencer Walpole published the official life of Earl Russell, and told a part of the story which had never been known to the Minister and which astounded his son, who burned with curiosity to know what his father would have said of it.

The story was this: The Alabama escaped, by Russell's confessed negligence, on July 28, 1862. In America the Union armies had suffered great disasters before Richmond and at the second Bull Run, August 29–30, followed by Lee's invasion of Maryland, September 7, the news of which, arriving in England on September 14, roused the natural idea that the crisis was at hand. The next news was expected by the Confederates to announce the fall of Washington or Baltimore. Palmerston instantly, September 14, wrote to Russell: "If this should happen, would it not be time for us to consider whether in such a state of things England and France might not address the contending parties and recommend an arrangement on the basis of separation?"

This letter, quite in the line of Palmerston's supposed opinions, would have surprised no one, if it had been communicated to the Legation; and indeed, if Lee had captured Washington, no one could have blamed Palmerston for offering intervention. Not Palmerston's letter but

Russell's reply, merited the painful attention of a young man seeking a moral standard for judging politicians: —

GOTHA, September, 17, 1862.

My dear Palmerston: —

Whether the Federal army is destroyed or not, it is clear that it is driven back to Washington and has made no progress in subduing the insurgent States. Such being the case, I agree with you that the time is come for offering mediation to the United States Government with a view to the recognition of the independence of the Confederates. I agree further that in case of failure, we ought ourselves to recognize the Southern States as an independent State. For the purpose of taking so important a step, I think we must have a meeting of the Cabinet. The 23d or 30th would suit me for the meeting.

We ought then, if we agree on such a step, to propose it first to France, and then on the part of England and France, to Russia and other powers, as a measure decided upon by us.

We ought to make ourselves safe in Canada, not by sending more troops there, but by concentrating those we have in a few defensible posts before the winter sets in. . . .

Here, then, appeared in its fullest force, the practical difficulty in education which a mere student could never overcome; a difficulty not in theory, or knowledge, or even want of experience, but in the sheer chaos of human nature. Lord Russell's course had been consistent from the first, and had all the look of rigid determination to recognize the Southern Confederacy "with a view" to breaking up the Union. His letter of September 17 hung directly on his encouragement of the Alabama and his protection of the rebel navy; while the whole of his plan had its root in the Proclamation of Belligerency, May 13, 1861. The policy had every look of persistent forethought, but it took for granted the deliberate dishonesty of three famous men: Palmerston, Russell, and Gladstone. This dishonesty, as concerned Russell, was denied by Russell himself, and disbelieved by Argyll, Forster, and most of America's friends in England, as well as by Minister Adams. What the Minister would have thought had he seen this letter of September 17, his son would have greatly liked to know, but he would have liked still more to know what the Minister would have thought of Palmerston's answer, dated September 23: —

> ... It is evident that a great conflict is taking place to the northwest of Washington, and its issue must have a great effect on the state of affairs. If the Federals sustain a great defeat, they may be at once ready for mediation, and the iron should be struck while it is hot. If, on the other hand, they should have the best of it, we may wait a while and see what may follow. . . .

The rôles were reversed. Russell wrote what was expected from Palmerston, or even more violently; while Palmerston wrote what was expected from Russell, or even more temperately. The private secretary's view had been altogether wrong, which would not have much surprised even him, but he would have been greatly astonished to learn that the most confidential associates of these men knew little more about their intentions than was known in the Legation. The most trusted member of the Cabinet was Lord Granville, and to him Russell next wrote. Granville replied at once decidedly opposing recognition of the Confederacy, and Russell sent the reply to Palmerston, who returned it October 2, with the mere suggestion of waiting for further news from America. At the same time Granville wrote to another member of the Cabinet, Lord Stanley of Alderley, a letter published forty years afterwards in Granville's "Life" (I, 442) — to the private secretary altogether the most curious and instructive relic of the whole lesson in politics: —

> . . . I have written to Johnny my reasons for thinking it decidedly premature. I, however, suspect you will settle to do so. Pam., Johnny, and Gladstone would be in favor of it, and probably Newcastle. I do not know about the others. It appears to me a great mistake. . . .

Out of a Cabinet of a dozen members, Granville, the best informed of them all, could pick only three who would favor recognition. Even a private secretary thought he knew as much as this, or more. Ignorance was not confined to the young and insignificant, nor were they the only victims of blindness. Granville's letter made only one point clear. He knew of no fixed policy or conspiracy. If any existed, it was confined to Palmerston, Russell, Gladstone, and perhaps Newcastle. In truth, the Legation knew, then, all that was to be known, and the true fault of education was to suspect too much.

By that time, October 3, news of Antietam and of Lee's retreat into Virginia had reached London. The Emancipation Proclamation arrived. Had the private secretary known all that Granville or Palmerston knew, he would surely have thought the danger past, at least for a time, and any man of common sense would have told him to stop worrying over phantoms. This healthy lesson would have been worth much for practical education, but it was quite upset by the sudden rush of a new actor upon the stage with a rhapsody that made Russell seem sane, and all education superfluous.

This new actor, as every one knows, was William Ewart Gladstone, then Chancellor of the Exchequer. If, in the domain of the world's politics, one point was fixed, one value ascertained, one element serious, it was the British Exchequer; and if one man lived who could be certainly counted as sane by overwhelming interest, it was the man who had in charge the finances of England. If education had the smallest value, it should have shown its force in Gladstone, who was educated beyond all record of English training. From him, if from no one else, the poor student could safely learn.

Here is what he learned! Palmerston notified Gladstone, September 24, of the proposed intervention: "If I am not mistaken, you would be inclined to approve such a course." Gladstone replied the next day: "He was glad to learn what the Prime Minister had told him; and for two reasons especially he desired that the proceedings should be prompt: the first was the rapid progress of the Southern arms and the extension of the area of Southern feeling; the second was the risk of violent impatience in the cotton-towns of Lancashire such as would prejudice the dignity and disinterestedness of the proffered mediation."

Had the puzzled student seen this letter, he must have concluded from it that the best educated statesman England ever produced did not know what he was talking about, an assumption which all the world would think quite inadmissible from a private secretary — but this was a trifle. Gladstone having thus arranged, with Palmerston and Russell, for intervention in the American war, reflected on the subject for a fortnight from September 25 to October 7, when he was to speak on the occasion of a great dinner at Newcastle. He decided to announce the Government's policy with all the force his personal and official authority could give it. This decision was no sudden impulse; it was the result of deep reflection pursued to the last moment. On the morning of October 7, he entered in his diary: "Reflected further on what I should say about Lancashire and America, for both these subjects are critical." That evening at dinner, as the mature fruit of his long study, he deliberately pronounced the famous phrase: —

... We know quite well that the people of the Northern States have not yet drunk of the cup — they are still trying to hold it far from their lips — which all the rest of the world see they nevertheless must drink of. We may have our own opinions about slavery; we may be for or against the South; but there is no doubt that Jefferson Davis and other leaders of the South have made an army; they are making, it appears, a navy; and they have made, what is more than either, they have made a nation. . . .

Looking back, forty years afterwards, on this episode, one asked one's self painfully what sort of a lesson a young man should have drawn, for the purposes of his education, from this world-famous teaching of a very great master. In the heat of passion at the moment, one drew some harsh moral conclusions: Were they incorrect? Posed bluntly as rules of conduct, they led to the worst possible practices. As morals, one could detect no shade of difference between Gladstone and Napoleon except to the advantage of Napoleon. The private secretary saw none; he accepted the teacher in that sense; he took his lesson of political morality as learned, his notice to quit as duly served, and supposed his education to be finished.

Every one thought so, and the whole City was in a turmoil. Any intelligent education ought to end when it is complete. One would then feel fewer hesitations and would handle a surer world. The old-fashioned logical drama required unity and sense; the actual drama is a pointless puzzle, without even an intrigue. When the curtain fell on Gladstone's speech, any student had the right to suppose the drama ended; none could have affirmed that it was about to begin; that one's painful lesson was thrown away.

Even after forty years, most people would refuse to believe it; they would still insist that Gladstone, Russell, and Palmerston were true villains of melodrama. The evidence against Gladstone in special seemed overwhelming. The word "must" can never be used by a responsible Minister of one Government towards another, as Gladstone used it. No one knew so well as he that he and his own officials and friends at Liverpool were alone "making" a rebel navy, and that Jefferson Davis had next to nothing to do with it. As Chancellor of the Exchequer he was the Minister most interested in knowing that Palmerston, Russell, and himself were banded together by mutual pledge to make the Confederacy a nation the next week, and that the Southern leaders had as yet no hope of "making a nation" but in them. Such thoughts occurred to every one at the moment and time only added to their force. Never in the history of political turpitude had any brigand of modern civilization offered a worse example. The proof of it was that it outraged even Palmerston, who immediately put up Sir George Cornewall Lewis to repudiate the Chancellor of the Exchequer, against whom he turned his press at the same time. Palmerston had no notion of letting his hand be forced by Gladstone.

Russell did nothing of the kind; if he agreed with Palmerston, he followed Gladstone. Although he had just created a new evangel of non-intervention for Italy, and preached it like an apostle, he preached the gospel of intervention in America as though he were a mouthpiece of the Congress of Vienna. On October 13, he issued his call for the Cabinet to meet, on October 23, for discussion of the "duty of Europe to ask both parties, in the most friendly

and conciliatory terms, to agree to a suspension of arms."
Meanwhile Minister Adams, deeply perturbed and profoundly anxious, would betray no sign of alarm, and pur-
posely delayed to ask explanation. The howl of anger
against Gladstone became louder every day, for every one
knew that the Cabinet was called for October 23, and then
could not fail to decide its policy about the United States.
Lord Lyons put off his departure for America till October 25 expressly to share in the conclusions to be discussed
on October 23. When Minister Adams at last requested an
interview, Russell named October 23 as the day. To the
last moment every act of Russell showed that, in his mind,
the intervention was still in doubt.

When Minister Adams, at the interview, suggested that
an explanation was due him, he watched Russell with natural interest, and reported thus: —

> ... His lordship took my allusion at once, though not
> without a slight indication of embarrassment. He said
> that Mr. Gladstone had been evidently much misunder-
> stood. I must have seen in the newspapers the letters
> which contained his later explanations. That he had cer-
> tain opinions in regard to the nature of the struggle in
> America, as on all public questions, just as other Eng-
> lishmen had, was natural enough. And it was the fashion
> here for public men to express such as they held in their
> public addresses. Of course it was not for him to dis-
> avow anything on the part of Mr. Gladstone; but he
> had no idea that in saying what he had, there was a seri-
> ous intention to justify any of the inferences that had
> been drawn from it of a disposition in the Government
> now to adopt a new policy....

A student trying to learn the processes of politics in a
free government could not but ponder long on the moral
to be drawn from this "explanation" of Mr. Gladstone by

Earl Russell. The point set for study as the first condition of political life, was whether any politician could be believed or trusted. The question which a private secretary asked himself, in copying this despatch of October 24, 1862, was whether his father believed, or should believe, one word of Lord Russell's "embarrassment." The "truth" was not known for thirty years, but when published, seemed to be the reverse of Earl Russell's statement. Mr. Gladstone's speech had been drawn out by Russell's own policy of intervention and had no sense except to declare the "disposition in the Government now to adopt" that new policy. Earl Russell never disavowed Gladstone, although Lord Palmerston and Sir George Cornewall Lewis instantly did so. As far as the curious student could penetrate the mystery, Gladstone exactly expressed Earl Russell's intent.

As political education, this lesson was to be crucial; it would decide the law of life. All these gentlemen were superlatively honorable; if one could not believe them, Truth in politics might be ignored as a delusion. Therefore the student felt compelled to reach some sort of idea that should serve to bring the case within a general law. Minister Adams felt the same compulsion. He bluntly told Russell that while he was "willing to acquit" Gladstone of "any deliberate intention to bring on the worst effects," he was bound to say that Gladstone was doing it quite as certainly as if he had one; and to this charge, which struck more sharply at Russell's secret policy than at Gladstone's public defence of it, Russell replied as well as he could: —

    . . . His lordship intimated as guardedly as possible that Lord Palmerston and other members of the Government regretted the speech, and Mr. Gladstone himself was not disinclined to correct, as far as he could, the misinterpretation which had been made of it. It was still their intention to adhere to the rule of perfect neutrality in the struggle, and to let it come to its natural end without the smallest interference, direct or otherwise. But he could not say what circumstances might happen from month to month in the future. I observed that the policy he mentioned was satisfactory to us, and asked if I was to understand him as saying that no change of it was now proposed. To which he gave his assent. . . .

Minister Adams never knew more. He retained his belief that Russell could be trusted, but that Palmerston could not. This was the diplomatic tradition, especially held by the Russian diplomats. Possibly it was sound, but it helped in no way the education of a private secretary. The cat's-paw theory offered no safer clue, than the frank, old-fashioned, honest theory of villainy. Neither the one nor the other was reasonable.

No one ever told the Minister that Earl Russell, only a few hours before, had asked the Cabinet to intervene, and that the Cabinet had refused. The Minister was led to believe that the Cabinet meeting was not held, and that its decision was informal. Russell's biographer said that, "with this memorandum [of Russell's, dated October 13] the cabinet assembled from all parts of the country on October 23; but . . . members of the Cabinet doubted the policy of moving, or moving at that time." The Duke of Newcastle and Sir George Grey joined Granville in opposition. As far as known, Russell and Gladstone stood alone. "Considerations such as these prevented the matter being pursued any further."

Still no one has distinctly said that this decision was formal; perhaps the unanimity of opposition made the formal Cabinet unnecessary; but it is certain that, within an hour or two before or after this decision, "his lordship

said [to the United States Minister] that the policy of the
Government was to adhere to a strict neutrality and to
leave this struggle to settle itself." When Mr. Adams, not
satisfied even with this positive assurance, pressed for a
categorical answer: "I asked him if I was to understand
that policy as not now to be changed; he said: Yes!"

John Morley's comment on this matter, in the "Life of
Gladstone," forty years afterwards, would have interested
the Minister, as well as his private secretary: "If this relation be accurate," said Morley of a relation officially published at the time, and never questioned, "then the Foreign
Secretary did not construe strict neutrality as excluding
what diplomatists call good offices." For a vital lesson in
politics, Earl Russell's construction of neutrality mattered
little to the student, who asked only Russell's intent, and
cared only to know whether his construction had any
other object than to deceive the Minister.

In the grave one can afford to be lavish of charity, and
possibly Earl Russell may have been honestly glad to reassure his personal friend Mr. Adams; but to one who is still
in the world even if not of it, doubts are as plenty as days.
Earl Russell totally deceived the private secretary, whatever he may have done to the Minister. The policy of
abstention was not settled on October 23. Only the next
day, October 24, Gladstone circulated a rejoinder to G. C.
Lewis, insisting on the duty of England, France, and Russia to intervene by representing, "with moral authority
and force, the opinion of the civilized world upon the conditions of the case." Nothing had been decided. By some
means, scarcely accidental, the French Emperor was led
to think that his influence might turn the scale, and only
ten days after Russell's categorical "Yes!" Napoleon officially invited him to say "No!" He was more than ready to
do so. Another Cabinet meeting was called for November
11, and this time Gladstone himself reports the debate: —

Nov. 11. We have had our Cabinet to-day and meet
again tomorrow. I am afraid we shall do little or nothing
in the business of America. But I will send you definite
intelligence. Both Lords Palmerston and Russell are
right.

Nov. 12. The United States affair has ended and not
well. Lord Russell rather turned tail. He gave way without resolutely fighting out his battle. However, though
we decline for the moment, the answer is put upon
grounds and in terms which leave the matter very open
for the future.

Nov. 13. I think the French will make our answer
about America public; at least it is very possible. But I
hope they may not take it as a positive refusal, or at any
rate that they may themselves act in the matter. It will
be clear that we concur with them, that the war should
cease. Palmerston gave to Russell's proposal a feeble and
half-hearted support.

Forty years afterwards, when every one except himself,
who looked on at this scene, was dead, the private secretary of 1862 read these lines with stupor, and hurried to
discuss them with John Hay, who was more astounded
than himself. All the world had been at cross-purposes,
had misunderstood themselves and the situation, had followed wrong paths, drawn wrong conclusions, had
known none of the facts. One would have done better to
draw no conclusions at all. One's diplomatic education
was a long mistake.

These were the terms of this singular problem as they
presented themselves to the student of diplomacy in 1862:
Palmerston, on September 14, under the impression that
the President was about to be driven from Washington
and the Army of the Potomac dispersed, suggested to Russell that in such a case, intervention might be feasible.
Russell instantly answered that, in any case, he wanted to

intervene and should call a Cabinet for the purpose. Palmerston hesitated; Russell insisted; Granville protested. Meanwhile the rebel army was defeated at Antietam, September 17, and driven out of Maryland. Then Gladstone, October 7, tried to force Palmerston's hand by treating the intervention as a *fait accompli*. Russell assented, but Palmerston put up Sir George Cornewall Lewis to contradict Gladstone and treated him sharply in the press, at the very moment when Russell was calling a Cabinet to make Gladstone's words good. On October 23, Russell assured Adams that no change in policy was now proposed. On the same day he had proposed it, and was voted down. Instantly Napoleon III appeared as the ally of Russell and Gladstone with a proposition which had no sense except as a bribe to Palmerston to replace America, from pole to pole, in her old dependence on Europe, and to replace England in her old sovereignty of the seas, if Palmerston would support France in Mexico. The young student of diplomacy, knowing Palmerston, must have taken for granted that Palmerston inspired this motion and would support it; knowing Russell and his Whig antecedents, he would conceive that Russell must oppose it; knowing Gladstone and his lofty principles, he would not doubt that Gladstone violently denounced the scheme. If education was worth a straw, this was the only arrangement of persons that a trained student would imagine possible, and it was the arrangement actually assumed by nine men out of ten, as history. In truth, each valuation was false. Palmerston never showed favor to the scheme and gave it only "a feeble and half-hearted support." Russell gave way without resolutely fighting out "*his* battle." The only resolute, vehement, conscientious champion of Russell, Napoleon, and Jefferson Davis was Gladstone.

Other people could afford to laugh at a young man's blunders, but to him the best part of life was thrown away if he learned such a lesson wrong. Henry James had not yet taught the world to read a volume for the pleasure of seeing the lights of his burning-glass turned on alternate sides of the same figure. Psychological study was still simple, and at worst — or at best — English character was never subtle. Surely no one would believe that complexity was the trait that confused the student of Palmerston, Russell, and Gladstone. Under a very strong light human nature will always appear complex and full of contradictions, but the British statesman would appear, on the whole, among the least complex of men.

Complex these gentlemen were not. Disraeli alone might, by contrast, be called complex, but Palmerston, Russell, and Gladstone deceived only by their simplicity. Russell was the most interesting to a young man because his conduct seemed most statesmanlike. Every act of Russell, from April, 1861, to November, 1862, showed the clearest determination to break up the Union. The only point in Russell's character about which the student thought no doubt to be possible was its want of good faith. It was thoroughly dishonest, but strong. Habitually Russell said one thing and did another. He seemed unconscious of his own contradictions even when his opponents pointed them out, as they were much in the habit of doing, in the strongest language. As the student watched him deal with the Civil War in America, Russell alone showed persistence, even obstinacy, in a definite determination, which he supported, as was necessary, by the usual definite falsehoods. The young man did not complain of the falsehoods; on the contrary, he was vain of his own insight in detecting them; but he was wholly upset by the idea that Russell should think himself true.

Young Adams thought Earl Russell a statesman of the old school, clear about his objects and unscrupulous in his methods — dishonest but strong. Russell ardently asserted that he had no objects, and that though he might be weak he was above all else honest. Minister Adams leaned to Russell personally and thought him true, but officially, in practice, treated him as false. *Punch*, before 1862, commonly drew Russell as a schoolboy telling lies, and afterwards as prematurely senile, at seventy. Education stopped there. No one, either in or out of England, ever offered a rational explanation of Earl Russell.

Palmerston was simple — so simple as to mislead the student altogether — but scarcely more consistent. The world thought him positive, decided, reckless; the record proved him to be cautious, careful, vacillating. Minister Adams took him for pugnacious and quarrelsome; the "Lives" of Russell, Gladstone, and Granville show him to have been good-tempered, conciliatory, avoiding quarrels. He surprised the Minister by refusing to pursue his attack on General Butler. He tried to check Russell. He scolded Gladstone. He discouraged Napoleon. Except Disraeli none of the English statesmen were so cautious as he in talking of America. Palmerston told no falsehoods; made no professions; concealed no opinions; was detected in no double-dealing. The most mortifying failure in Henry Adams's long education was that, after forty years of confirmed dislike, distrust, and detraction of Lord Palmerston, he was obliged at last to admit himself in error, and to consent in spirit — for by that time he was nearly as dead as any of them — to beg his pardon.

Gladstone was quite another story, but with him a student's difficulties were less because they were shared by all the world including Gladstone himself. He was the sum of contradictions. The highest education could reach, in this analysis, only a reduction to the absurd, but no absurdity that a young man could reach in 1862 would have approached the level that Mr. Gladstone admitted, avowed, proclaimed, in his confessions of 1896, which brought all reason and all hope of education to a still-stand: —

> I have yet to record an undoubted error, the most singular and palpable, I may add the least excusable of them all, especially since it was committed so late as in the year 1862 when I had outlived half a century. . . . I declared in the heat of the American struggle that Jefferson Davis had made a nation. . . . Strange to say, this declaration, most unwarrantable to be made by a Minister of the Crown with no authority other than his own, was not due to any feeling of partisanship for the South or hostility to the North. . . . I really, though most strangely, believed that it was an act of friendliness to all America to recognize that the struggle was virtually at an end. . . . That my opinion was founded upon a false estimate of the facts was the very least part of my fault. I did not perceive the gross impropriety of such an utterance from a Cabinet Minister of a power allied in blood and language, and bound to loyal neutrality; the case being further exaggerated by the fact that we were already, so to speak, under indictment before the world for not (as was alleged) having strictly enforced the laws of neutrality in the matter of the cruisers. My offense was indeed only a mistake, but one of incredible grossness, and with such consequences of offence and alarm attached to it, that my failing to perceive them justly exposed me to very severe blame. It illustrates vividly that incapacity which my mind so long retained, and perhaps still exhibits, an incapacity of viewing subjects all round. . . .

Long and patiently — more than patiently — sympathetically, did the private secretary, forty years afterwards in the twilight of a life of study, read and re-read and reflect upon this confession. Then, it seemed, he had seen nothing correctly at the time. His whole theory of conspiracy — of policy — of logic and connection in the affairs of man, resolved itself into "incredible grossness." He felt no rancor, for he had won the game; he forgave, since he must admit, the "incapacity of viewing subjects all round" which had so nearly cost him life and fortune; he was willing even to believe. He noted, without irritation, that Mr. Gladstone, in his confession, had not alluded to the understanding between Russell, Palmerston, and himself; had even wholly left out his most "incredible" act, his ardent support of Napoleon's policy, a policy which even Palmerston and Russell had supported feebly, with only half a heart. All this was indifferent. Granting, in spite of evidence, that Gladstone had no set plan of breaking up the Union; that he was party to no conspiracy; that he saw none of the results of his acts which were clear to every one else; granting in short what the English themselves seemed at last to conclude — that Gladstone was not quite sane; that Russell was verging on senility; and that Palmerston had lost his nerve — what sort of education should have been the result of it? How should it have affected one's future opinions and acts?

Politics cannot stop to study psychology. Its methods are rough; its judgments rougher still. All this knowledge would not have affected either the Minister or his son in 1862. The sum of the individuals would still have seemed, to the young man, one individual — a single will or intention — bent on breaking up the Union "as a diminution of a dangerous power." The Minister would still have found his interest in thinking Russell friendly and Palmerston hostile. The individual would still have been identical with the mass. The problem would have been the same; the answer equally obscure. Every student would, like the private secretary, answer for himself alone.

11

The
Battle
of the
Rams

(1863)

Minister Adams troubled himself little about what he did not see of an enemy. His son, a nervous animal, made life a terror by seeing too much. Minister Adams played his hand as it came, and seldom credited his opponents with greater intelligence than his own. Earl Russell suited him; perhaps a certain personal sympathy united them; and indeed Henry Adams never saw Russell without being amused by his droll likeness to John Quincy Adams. Apart from this shadowy personal relation, no doubt the Minister was diplomatically right; he had nothing to lose and everything to gain by making a friend of the Foreign Secretary, and whether Russell were true or false mattered less, because, in either case, the American Legation could act only as though he were false. Had the Minister known Russell's determined effort to betray and ruin him in October, 1862, he could have scarcely used stronger expressions

than he did in 1863. Russell must have been greatly annoyed by Sir Robert Collier's hint of collusion with the
rebel agents in the Alabama Case, but he hardened himself
to hear the same innuendo repeated in nearly every note
from the Legation. As time went on, Russell was compelled, though slowly, to treat the American Minister as
serious. He admitted nothing so unwillingly, for the
nullity or fatuity of the Washington Government was his
idée fixe; but after the failure of his last effort for joint
intervention on November 12, 1862, only one week
elapsed before he received a note from Minister Adams repeating his charges about the Alabama, and asking in very
plain language for redress. Perhaps Russell's mind was naturally slow to understand the force of sudden attack, or
perhaps age had affected it; this was one of the points that
greatly interested a student, but young men have a passion
for regarding their elders as senile, which was only in part
warranted in this instance by observing that Russell's generation were mostly senile from youth. They had never
got beyond 1815. Both Palmerston and Russell were in this
case. Their senility was congenital, like Gladstone's Oxford training and High Church illusions, which caused
wild eccentricities in his judgment. Russell could not conceive that he had misunderstood and mismanaged Minister
Adams from the start, and when, after November 12, he
found himself on the defensive, with Mr. Adams taking
daily a stronger tone, he showed mere confusion and helplessness.

Thus, whatever the theory, the action of diplomacy had
to be the same. Minister Adams was obliged to imply collusion between Russell and the rebels. He could not even
stop at criminal negligence. If, by an access of courtesy,
the Minister were civil enough to admit that the escape
of the Alabama had been due to criminal negligence, he
could make no such concession in regard to the ironclad

rams which the Lairds were building; for no one could be so simple as to believe that two armored ships-of-war could be built publicly, under the eyes of the Government, and go to sea like the Alabama, without active and incessant collusion. The longer Earl Russell kept on his mask of assumed ignorance, the more violently in the end, the Minister would have to tear it off. Whatever Mr. Adams might personally think of Earl Russell, he must take the greatest possible diplomatic liberties with him if this crisis were allowed to arrive.

As the spring of 1863 drew on, the vast field cleared itself for action. A campaign more beautiful— better suited for training the mind of a youth eager for training — has not often unrolled itself for study, from the beginning, before a young man perched in so commanding a position. Very slowly, indeed, after two years of solitude, one began to feel the first faint flush of new and imperial life. One was twenty-five years old, and quite ready to assert it; some of one's friends were wearing stars on their collars; some had won stars of a more enduring kind. At moments one's breath came quick. One began to dream the sensation of wielding unmeasured power. The sense came, like vertigo, for an instant, and passed, leaving the brain a little dazed, doubtful, shy. With an intensity more painful than that of any Shakespearean drama, men's eyes were fastened on the armies in the field. Little by little, at first only as a shadowy chance of what might be, if things could be rightly done, one began to feel that, somewhere behind the chaos in Washington power was taking shape; that it was massed and guided as it had not been before. Men seemed to have learned their business — at a cost that ruined — and perhaps too late. A private secretary knew better than most people how much of the new power was to be swung in London, and almost exactly when; but the diplomatic campaign had to wait for the military campaign to lead. The student could only study.

Life never could know more than a single such climax. In that form, education reached its limits. As the first great blows began to fall, one curled up in bed in the silence of night, to listen with incredulous hope. As the huge masses struck, one after another, with the precision of machinery, the opposing mass, the world shivered. Such development of power was unknown. The magnificent resistance and the return shocks heightened the suspense. During the July days Londoners were stupid with unbelief. They were learning from the Yankees how to fight.

An American saw in a flash what all this meant to England, for one's mind was working with the acceleration of the machine at home; but Englishmen were not quick to see their blunders. One had ample time to watch the process, and had even a little time to gloat over the repayment of old scores. News of Vicksburg and Gettysburg reached London one Sunday afternoon, and it happened that Henry Adams was asked for that evening to some small reception at the house of Monckton Milnes. He went early in order to exchange a word or two of congratulation before the rooms should fill, and on arriving he found only the ladies in the drawing-room; the gentlemen were still sitting over their wine. Presently they came in, and, as luck would have it, Delane of the *Times* came first. When Milnes caught sight of his young American friend, with a whoop of triumph he rushed to throw both arms about his neck and kiss him on both cheeks. Men of later birth who knew too little to realize the passions of 1863 — backed by those of 1813 — and reënforced by those of 1763 — might conceive that such publicity embarrassed a private secretary who came from Boston and called himself shy; but that evening, for the first time in his life, he happened not to be thinking of himself. He was thinking of

Delane, whose eye caught his, at the moment of Milnes's embrace. Delane probably regarded it as a piece of Milnes's foolery; he had never heard of young Adams, and never dreamed of his resentment at being ridiculed in the *Times;* he had no suspicion of the thought floating in the mind of the American Minister's son, for the British mind is the slowest of all minds, as the files of the *Times* proved, and the capture of Vicksburg had not yet penetrated Delane's thick cortex of fixed ideas. Even if he had read Adams's thought he would have felt for it only the usual amused British contempt for all that he had not been taught at school. It needed a whole generation for the *Times* to reach Milnes's standpoint.

Had the Minister's son carried out the thought, he would surely have sought an introduction to Delane on the spot, and assured him that he regarded his own personal score as cleared off — sufficiently settled, then and there — because his father had assumed the debt, and was going to deal with Mr. Delane himself. "You come next!" would have been the friendly warning. For nearly a year the private secretary had watched the board arranging itself for the collision between the Legation and Delane who stood behind the Palmerston Ministry. Mr. Adams had been steadily strengthened and reënforced from Washington in view of the final struggle. The situation had changed since the Trent Affair. The work was efficiently done; the organization was fairly complete. No doubt, the Legation itself was still as weakly manned and had as poor an outfit as the Legations of Guatemala or Portugal. Congress was always jealous of its diplomatic service, and the Chairman of the Committee of Foreign Relations was not likely to press assistance on the Minister to England. For the Legation not an additional clerk was offered or asked. The Secretary, the Assistant Secretary, and the private secretary did all the work that the Minister did not do. A clerk at five dollars a week would have done the work as well or better, but the Minister could trust no clerk; without express authority he could admit no one into the Legation; he strained a point already by admitting his son. Congress and its committees were the proper judges of what was best for the public service, and if the arrangement seemed good to them, it was satisfactory to a private secretary who profited by it more than they did. A great staff would have suppressed him. The whole Legation was a sort of improvised, volunteer service, and he was a volunteer with the rest. He was rather better off than the rest, because he was invisible and unknown. Better or worse, he did his work with the others, and if the secretaries made any remarks about Congress, they made no complaints, and knew that none would have received a moment's attention.

If they were not satisfied with Congress, they were satisfied with Secretary Seward. Without appropriations for the regular service, he had done great things for its support. If the Minister had no secretaries, he had a staff of active consuls; he had a well-organized press; efficient legal support; and a swarm of social allies permeating all classes. All he needed was a victory in the field, and Secretary Stanton undertook that part of diplomacy. Vicksburg and Gettysburg cleared the board, and, at the end of July, 1863, Minister Adams was ready to deal with Earl Russell or Lord Palmerston or Mr. Gladstone or Mr. Delane, or any one else who stood in his way; and by the necessity of the case, was obliged to deal with all of them shortly.

Even before the military climax at Vicksburg and Gettysburg the Minister had been compelled to begin his attack; but this was history, and had nothing to do with education. The private secretary copied the notes into his private books, and that was all the share he had in the matter, except to talk in private.

No more volunteer services were needed; the volunteers were in a manner sent to the rear; the movement was too serious for skirmishing. All that a secretary could hope to gain from the affair was experience and knowledge of politics. He had a chance to measure the motive forces of men; their qualities of character; their foresight; their tenacity of purpose.

In the Legation no great confidence was felt in stopping the rams. Whatever the reason, Russell seemed immovable. Had his efforts for intervention in September, 1862, been known to the Legation in September, 1863, the Minister must surely have admitted that Russell had, from the first, meant to force his plan of intervention on his colleagues. Every separate step since April, 1861, led to this final coercion. Although Russell's hostile activity of 1862 was still secret — and remained secret for some five-and-twenty years — his *animus* seemed to be made clear by his steady refusal to stop the rebel armaments. Little by little, Minister Adams lost hope. With loss of hope came the raising of tone, until at last, after stripping Russell of every rag of defence and excuse, he closed by leaving him loaded with connivance in the rebel armaments, and ended by the famous sentence: "It would be superfluous in me to point out to your lordship that this is war!"

What the Minister meant by this remark was his own affair; what the private secretary understood by it, was a part of his education. Had his father ordered him to draft an explanatory paragraph to expand the idea as he grasped it, he would have continued thus: —

"It would be superfluous: 1st. Because Earl Russell not only knows it already, but has meant it from the start. 2d. Because it is the only logical and necessary consequence of his unvarying action. 3d. Because Mr. Adams is not pointing out to *him* that 'this is war,' but is pointing it out to the world, to complete the record."

This would have been the matter-of-fact sense in which the private secretary copied into his books the matter-of-fact statement with which, without passion or excitement, the Minister announced that a state of war existed. To his copying eye, as clerk, the words, though on the extreme verge of diplomatic propriety, merely stated a fact, without novelty, fancy, or rhetoric. The fact had to be stated in order to make clear the issue. The war was Russell's war — Adams only accepted it.

Russell's reply to this note of September 5 reached the Legation on September 8, announcing at last to the anxious secretaries that "instructions have been issued which will prevent the departure of the two ironclad vessels from Liverpool." The members of the modest Legation in Portland Place accepted it as Grant had accepted the capitulation of Vicksburg. The private secretary conceived that, as Secretary Stanton had struck and crushed by superior weight the rebel left on the Mississippi, so Secretary Seward had struck and crushed the rebel right in England, and he never felt a doubt as to the nature of the battle. Though Minister Adams should stay in office till he were ninety, he would never fight another campaign of life and death like this; and though the private secretary should covet and attain every office in the gift of President or people, he would never again find education to compare with the life-and-death alternative of this two-year-and-a-half struggle in London, as it had racked and thumb-screwed him in its shifting phases; but its practical value as education turned on his correctness of judgment in measuring the men and their forces. He felt respect for Russell as for Palmerston because they represented traditional England and an English policy, respectable enough in itself, but which, for four generations, every Adams had fought and exploited as the chief source of his political fortunes. As he understood it, Russell had followed this policy steadily, ably, even vigorously, and had brought it to the moment of execution. Then he had met wills stronger than his own, and, after persevering to the last possible instant, had been beaten. Lord North and George Canning had a like experience.

This was only the idea of a boy, but, as far as he ever knew, it was also the idea of his Government. For once, the volunteer secretary was satisfied with his Government. Commonly the self-respect of a secretary, private or public, depends on, and is proportional to, the severity of his criticism, but in this case the English campaign seemed to him as creditable to the State Department as the Vicksburg campaign to the War Department, and more decisive. It was well planned, well prepared, and well executed. He could never discover a mistake in it. Possibly he was biassed by personal interest, but his chief reason for trusting his own judgment was that he thought himself to be one of only half a dozen persons who knew something about it. When others criticised Mr. Seward, he was rather indifferent to their opinions because he thought they hardly knew what they were talking about, and could not be taught without living over again the London life of 1862. To him Secretary Seward seemed immensely strong and steady in leadership; but this was no discredit to Russell or Palmerston or Gladstone. They, too, had shown power, patience and steadiness of purpose. They had persisted for two years and a half in their plan for breaking up the Union, and had yielded at last only in the jaws of war. After a long and desperate struggle, the American Minister had trumped their best card and won the game.

Again and again, in after life, he went back over the ground to see whether he could detect error on either side. He found none. At every stage the steps were both probable and proved. All the more he was disconcerted that

Russell should indignantly and with growing energy, to his dying day, deny and resent the axiom of Adams's whole contention, that from the first he meant to break up the Union. Russell affirmed that he meant nothing of the sort; that he had meant nothing at all; that he meant to do right; that he did not know what he meant. Driven from one defence after another, he pleaded at last, like Gladstone, that he had no defence. Concealing all he could conceal — burying in profound secrecy his attempt to break up the Union in the autumn of 1862 — he affirmed the louder his scrupulous good faith. What was worse for the private secretary, to the total derision and despair of the lifelong effort for education, as the final result of combined practice, experience, and theory — he proved it.

Henry Adams had, as he thought, suffered too much from Russell to admit any plea in his favor; but he came to doubt whether this admission really favored him. Not until long after Earl Russell's death was the question reopened. Russell had quitted office in 1866; he died in 1878; the biography was published in 1889. During the Alabama controversy and the Geneva Conference in 1872, his course as Foreign Secretary had been sharply criticised, and he had been compelled to see England pay more than £3,000,000 penalty for his errors. On the other hand, he brought forward — or his biographer for him — evidence tending to prove that he was not consciously dishonest, and that he had, in spite of appearances, acted without collusion, agreement, plan, or policy, as far as concerned the rebels. He had stood alone, as was his nature. Like Gladstone, he had thought himself right.

In the end, Russell entangled himself in a hopeless ball of admissions, denials, contradictions, and resentments which led even his old colleagues to drop his defence, as they dropped Gladstone's; but this was not enough for the student of diplomacy who had made a certain theory his law of life, and wanted to hold Russell up against himself; to show that he had foresight and persistence of which he was unaware. The effort became hopeless when the biography in 1889 published papers which upset all that Henry Adams had taken for diplomatic education; yet he sat down once more, when past sixty years old, to see whether he could unravel the skein.

Of the obstinate effort to bring about an armed intervention, on the lines marked out by Russell's letter to Palmerston from Gotha, 17 September, 1862, nothing could be said beyond Gladstone's plea in excuse for his speech in pursuance of the same effort, that it was "the most singular and palpable error," "the least excusable," "a mistake of incredible grossness," which passed defence; but while Gladstone threw himself on the mercy of the public for his speech, he attempted no excuse for Lord Russell who led him into the "incredible grossness" of announcing the Foreign Secretary's intent. Gladstone's offence, "singular and palpable," was not the speech alone, but its cause — the policy that inspired the speech, "I weakly supposed . . . I really, though most strangely, believed that it was an act of friendliness." Whatever absurdity Gladstone supposed, Russell supposed nothing of the sort. Neither he nor Palmerston "most strangely believed" in any proposition so obviously and palpably absurd, nor did Napoleon delude himself with philanthropy. Gladstone, even in his confession, mixed up policy, speech, motives, and persons, as though he were trying to confuse chiefly himself.

There Gladstone's activity seems to have stopped. He did not reappear in the matter of the rams. The rebel influence shrank in 1863, as far as is known, to Lord Russell alone, who wrote on September 1 that he could not interfere in any way with those vessels, and thereby brought on himself Mr. Adams's declaration of war on September 5. A student held that, in this refusal, he was merely following his policy of September, 1862, and of every step he had taken since 1861.

The student was wrong. Russell proved that he had been feeble, timid, mistaken, senile, but not dishonest. The evidence is convincing. The Lairds had built these ships in reliance on the known opinion of the law-officers that the statute did not apply, and a jury would not convict. Minister Adams replied that, in this case, the statute should be amended, or the ships stopped by exercise of the political power. Bethell rejoined that this would be a violation of neutrality; one must preserve the *status quo*. Tacitly Russell connived with Laird, and, had he meant to interfere, he was bound to warn Laird that the defect of the statute would no longer protect him, but he allowed the builders to go on till the ships were ready for sea. Then, on September 3, two days before Mr. Adams's "superfluous" letter, he wrote to Lord Palmerston begging for help; "The conduct of the gentlemen who have contracted for the two ironclads at Birkenhead is so very suspicious," — he began, and this he actually wrote in good faith and deep confidence to Lord Palmerston, his chief, calling "the conduct" of the rebel agents "suspicious" when no one else in Europe or America felt any suspicion about it, because the whole question turned not on the rams, but on the technical scope of the Foreign Enlistment Act, — "that I have thought it necessary to direct that they should be detained," not, of course, under the statute, but on the ground urged by the American Minister, of international obligation above the statute. "The Solicitor General has been consulted and concurs in the measure as one of policy though not of strict law. We shall thus test the law, and, if we have to pay damages, we have satisfied the opinion

which prevails here as well as in America that that kind
of neutral hostility should not be allowed to go on without some attempt to stop it."

For naïveté that would be unusual in an unpaid attaché
of Legation, this sudden leap from his own to his opponent's ground, after two years and a half of dogged resistance, might have roused Palmerston to inhuman scorn,
but instead of derision, well earned by Russell's old attacks
on himself, Palmerston met the appeal with wonderful
loyalty. "On consulting the law officers he found that
there was no lawful ground for meddling with the ironclads," or, in unprofessional language, that he could trust
neither his law officers nor a Liverpool jury; and therefore
he suggested buying the ships for the British Navy. As
proof of "criminal negligence" in the past, this suggestion
seemed decisive, but Russell, by this time, was floundering
in other troubles of negligence, for he had neglected to
notify the American Minister. He should have done so at
once, on September 3. Instead he waited till September 4,
and then merely said that the matter was under "serious
and anxious consideration." This note did not reach the
Legation till three o'clock on the afternoon of September 5 — after the "superfluous" declaration of war had
been sent. Thus, Lord Russell had sacrificed the Lairds:
had cost his Ministry the price of two ironclads, besides
the Alabama Claims — say, in round numbers, twenty million dollars — and had put himself in the position of appearing to yield only to a threat of war. Finally he wrote
to the Admiralty a letter which, from the American point
of view, would have sounded youthful from an Eton
schoolboy: —

September 14, 1863.

My Dear Duke: —

It is of the utmost importance and urgency that the
ironclads building at Birkenhead should not go to

America to break the blockade. They belong to
Monsieur Bravay of Paris. If you will offer to buy them
on the part of the Admiralty you will get money's
worth if he accepts your offer; and if he does not, it
will be presumptive proof that they are already bought
by the Confederates. I should state that we have suggested to the Turkish Government to buy them; but
you can easily settle that matter with the Turks. . . .

The hilarity of the secretaries in Portland Place would
have been loud had they seen this letter and realized the
muddle of difficulties into which Earl Russell had at last
thrown himself under the impulse of the American Minister; but, nevertheless, these letters upset from top to bottom the results of the private secretary's diplomatic
education forty years after he had supposed it complete.
They made a picture different from anything he had conceived and rendered worthless his whole painful diplomatic experience.

To reconstruct, when past sixty, an education useful
for any practical purpose, is no practical problem, and
Adams saw no use in attacking it as only theoretical. He
no longer cared whether he understood human nature or
not; he understood quite as much of it as he wanted; but
he found in the "Life of Gladstone" (II, 464) a remark
several times repeated that gave him matter for curious
thought. "I *always* hold," said Mr. Gladstone, "that politicians are the men whom, as a rule, it is most difficult to
comprehend"; and he added, by way of strengthening it:
"For my own part, I never have thus understood, or
thought I understood, *above one or two.*"

Earl Russell was certainly not one of the two.

Henry Adams thought he also had understood one or
two; but the American type was more familiar. Perhaps
this was the sufficient result of his diplomatic education;
it seemed to be the whole.

12

Eccentricity

(1863)

Knowledge of human nature is the beginning and end of political education, but several years of arduous study in the neighborhood of Westminster led Henry Adams to think that knowledge of English human nature had little or no value outside of England. In Paris, such a habit stood in one's way; in America, it roused all the instincts of native jealousy. The English mind was one-sided, eccentric, systematically unsystematic, and logically illogical. The less one knew of it, the better.

This heresy, which scarcely would have been allowed to penetrate a Boston mind — it would, indeed, have been shut out by instinct as a rather foolish exaggeration — rested on an experience which Henry Adams gravely thought he had a right to think conclusive — for him. That it should be conclusive for any one else never occurred to him, since he had no thought of educating anybody else. For him — alone — the less English education he got, the better!

For several years, under the keenest incitement to watchfulness, he observed the English mind in contact with itself and other minds. Especially with the American the contact was interesting because the limits and defects of the American mind were one of the favorite topics of the European. From the old-world point of view, the American had no mind; he had an economic thinking-machine which could work only on a fixed line. The American mind exasperated the European as a buzz-saw might exasperate a pine forest. The English mind disliked the French mind because it was antagonistic, unreasonable, perhaps hostile, but recognized it as at least a thought. The American mind was not a thought at all; it was a convention, superficial, narrow, and ignorant; a mere cutting instrument, practical, economical, sharp, and direct.

The English themselves hardly conceived that their mind was either economical, sharp, or direct; but the defect that most struck an American was its enormous waste in eccentricity. Americans needed and used their whole energy, and applied it with close economy; but English society was eccentric by law and for sake of the eccentricity itself.

The commonest phrase overheard at an English club or dinner-table was that So-and-So "is quite mad." It was no offence to So-and-So; it hardly distinguished him from his fellows; and when applied to a public man, like Gladstone, it was qualified by epithets much more forcible. Eccentricity was so general as to become hereditary distinction. It made the chief charm of English society as well as its chief terror.

The American delighted in Thackeray as a satirist, but Thackeray quite justly maintained that he was not a satirist at all, and that his pictures of English society were exact and good-natured. The American, who could not believe it, fell back on Dickens, who, at all events, had the vice of exaggeration to extravagance, but Dickens's English audience thought the exaggeration rather in manner or style, than in types. Mr. Gladstone himself went to see Sothern act Dundreary, and laughed till his face was distorted —

not because Dundreary was exaggerated, but because he was ridiculously like the types that Gladstone had seen — or might have seen — in any club in Pall Mall. Society swarmed with exaggerated characters; it contained little else.

Often this eccentricity bore all the marks of strength; perhaps it was actual exuberance of force, a birthmark of genius. Boston thought so. The Bostonian called it national character — native vigor — robustness — honesty — courage. He respected and feared it. British self-assertion, bluff, brutal, blunt as it was, seemed to him a better and nobler thing than the acuteness of the Yankee or the polish of the Parisian. Perhaps he was right. These questions of taste, of feeling, of inheritance, need no settlement. Every one carries his own inch-rule of taste, and amuses himself by applying it, triumphantly, wherever he travels. Whatever others thought, the cleverest Englishmen held that the national eccentricity needed correction, and were beginning to correct it. The savage satires of Dickens and the gentler ridicule of Matthew Arnold against the British middle class were but a part of the rebellion, for the middle class were no worse than their neighbors in the eyes of an American in 1863; they were even a very little better in the sense that one could appeal to their interests, while a university man, like Gladstone, stood outside of argument. From none of them could a young American afford to borrow ideas.

The private secretary, like every other Bostonian, began by regarding British eccentricity as a force. Contact with it, in the shape of Palmerston, Russell, and Gladstone, made him hesitate; he saw his own national type — his father, Weed, Evarts, for instance — deal with the British, and show itself certainly not the weaker; certainly sometimes the stronger. Biassed though he were, he could hardly be biassed to such a degree as to mistake the effects of force on others, and while — labor as he might — Earl Russell and his state papers seemed weak to a secretary, he could not see that they seemed strong to Russell's own followers. Russell might be dishonest or he might be merely obtuse —the English type might be brutal or might be only stupid — but strong, in either case, it was not, nor did it seem strong to Englishmen.

Eccentricity was not always a force; Americans were deeply interested in deciding whether it was always a weakness. Evidently, on the hustings or in Parliament, among eccentricities, eccentricity was at home; but in private society the question was not easy to answer. That English society was infinitely more amusing because of its eccentricities, no one denied. Barring the atrocious insolence and brutality which Englishmen and especially Englishwomen showed to each other — very rarely, indeed, to foreigners — English society was much more easy and tolerant than American. One must expect to be treated with exquisite courtesy this week and be totally forgotten the next, but this was the way of the world, and education consisted in learning to turn one's back on others with the same unconscious indifference that others showed among themselves. The smart of wounded vanity lasted no long time with a young man about town who had little vanity to smart, and who, in his own country, would have found himself in no better position. He had nothing to complain of. No one was ever brutal to him. On the contrary, he was much better treated than ever he was likely to be in Boston — let alone New York or Washington — and if his reception varied inconceivably between extreme courtesy and extreme neglect, it merely proved that he had become, or was becoming, at home. Not from a sense of personal griefs or disappointments did he labor over this part of the social problem, but only because his education was becoming English, and the further it went, the less it promised.

By natural affinity the social eccentrics commonly sympathized with political eccentricity. The English mind took naturally to rebellion — when foreign — and it felt particular confidence in the Southern Confederacy because of its combined attributes — foreign rebellion of English blood — which came nearer ideal eccentricity than could be reached by Poles, Hungarians, Italians or Frenchmen. All the English eccentrics rushed into the ranks of rebel sympathizers, leaving few but well-balanced minds to attach themselves to the cause of the Union. None of the English leaders on the Northern side were marked eccentrics. William E. Forster was a practical, hard-headed Yorkshireman, whose chief ideals in politics took shape as working arrangements on an economical base. Cobden, considering the one-sided conditions of his life, was remarkably well balanced. John Bright was stronger in his expressions than either of them, but with all his self-assertion he stuck to his point, and his point was practical. He did not, like Gladstone, box the compass of thought; "furiously earnest," as Monckton Milnes said, "on both sides of every question"; he was rather, on the whole, a consistent conservative of the old Commonwealth type, and seldom had to defend inconsistencies. Monckton Milnes himself was regarded as an eccentric, chiefly by those who did not know him, but his fancies and hobbies were only ideas a little in advance of the time; his manner was eccentric, but not his mind, as any one could see who read a page of his poetry. None of them, except Milnes, was a university man. As a rule, the Legation was troubled very little, if at all, by indiscretions, extravagances, or contradictions among its English friends. Their work was largely judicious, practical, well considered, and almost too cautious. The "cranks" were all rebels, and the list was portentous. Perhaps it might be headed by old Lord Brougham, who had the audacity to appear at a July 4th reception at the Legation, led by Joe Parkes, and claim his old credit as "Attorney General to Mr. Madison." The Church was rebel, but the dissenters were mostly with the Union. The universities were rebel, but the university men who enjoyed most public confidence — like Lord Granville, Sir George Cornewall Lewis, Lord Stanley, Sir George Grey — took infinite pains to be neutral for fear of being thought eccentric. To most observers, as well as to the *Times*, the *Morning Post*, and the *Standard*, a vast majority of the English people seemed to follow the professional eccentrics; even the emotional philanthropists took that direction; Lord Shaftesbury and Carlyle, Fowell Buxton, and Gladstone, threw their sympathies on the side which they should naturally have opposed, and did so for no reason except their eccentricity; but the "canny" Scots and Yorkshiremen were cautious.

This eccentricity did not mean strength. The proof of it was the mismanagement of the rebel interests. No doubt the first cause of this trouble lay in the Richmond Government itself. No one understood why Jefferson Davis chose Mr. Mason as his agent for London at the same time that he made so good a choice as Mr. Slidell for Paris. The Confederacy had plenty of excellent men to send to London, but few who were less fitted than Mason. Possibly Mason had a certain amount of common sense, but he seemed to have nothing else, and in London society he counted merely as one eccentric more. He enjoyed a great opportunity; he might even have figured as a new Benjamin Franklin with all society at his feet; he might have roared as lion of the season and made the social path of the American Minister almost impassable; but Mr. Adams had his usual luck in enemies, who were always his most valuable allies if his friends only let them alone. Mason was his greatest diplomatic triumph. He had his collision with Palmerston; he drove Russell off the field; he swept the board before Cockburn; he overbore Slidell; but he never lifted a finger against Mason, who became his bulwark of defence.

Possibly Jefferson Davis and Mr. Mason shared two defects in common which might have led them into this serious mistake. Neither could have had much knowledge of the world, and both must have been unconscious of humor. Yet at the same time with Mason, President Davis sent out Slidell to France and Mr. Lamar to Russia. Some twenty years later, in the shifting search for the education he never found, Adams became closely intimate at Washington with Lamar, then Senator from Mississippi, who had grown to be one of the calmest, most reasonable and most amiable Union men in the United States, and quite unusual in social charm. In 1860 he passed for the worst of Southern fire-eaters, but he was an eccentric by environment, not by nature; above all his Southern eccentricities, he had tact and humor; and perhaps this was a reason why Mr. Davis sent him abroad with the others, on a futile mission to St. Petersburg. He would have done better in London, in place of Mason. London society would have delighted in him; his stories would have won success; his manners would have made him loved; his oratory would have swept every audience; even Monckton Milnes could never have resisted the temptation of having him to breakfast between Lord Shaftesbury and the Bishop of Oxford.

Lamar liked to talk of his brief career in diplomacy, but he never spoke of Mason. He never alluded to Confederate management or criticised Jefferson Davis's administration. The subject that amused him was his English allies. At that moment — the early summer of 1863 — the rebel party in England were full of confidence, and felt strong enough to challenge the American Legation to a show of power. They knew better than the Legation what they could depend upon: that the law officers and commissioners of customs at Liverpool dared not prosecute the ironclad ships; that Palmerston, Russell, and Gladstone were ready to recognize the Confederacy; that the Emperor Napoleon would offer them every inducement to do it. In a manner they owned Liverpool and especially the firm of Laird who were building their ships. The political member of the Laird firm was Lindsay, about whom the whole web of rebel interests clung — rams, cruisers, munitions, and Confederate loan; social introductions and parliamentary tactics. The firm of Laird, with a certain dignity, claimed to be champion of England's navy; and public opinion, in the summer of 1863, still inclined towards them.

Never was there a moment when eccentricity, if it were a force, should have had more value to the rebel interest; and the managers must have thought so, for they adopted or accepted as their champion an eccentric of eccentrics; a type of 1820; a sort of Brougham of Sheffield, notorious for poor judgment and worse temper. Mr. Roebuck had been a tribune of the people, and, like tribunes of most other peoples, in growing old, had grown fatuous. He was regarded by the friends of the Union as rather a comical personage — a favorite subject for *Punch* to laugh at — with a bitter tongue and a mind enfeebled even more than common by the political epidemic of egotism. In all England they could have found no opponent better fitted to give away his own case. No American man of business would have paid him attention; yet the Lairds, who certainly knew their own affairs best, let Roebuck represent them and take charge of their interests.

With Roebuck's doings, the private secretary had no concern except that the Minister sent him down to the House of Commons on June 30, 1863, to report the result of Roebuck's motion to recognize the Southern Confederacy. The Legation felt no anxiety, having Vicksburg already in its pocket, and Bright and Forster to say so; but the private secretary went down and was admitted under the gallery on the left, to listen, with great content, while John Bright, with astonishing force, caught and shook and tossed Roebuck, as a big mastiff shakes a wiry, ill-conditioned, toothless, bad-tempered Yorkshire terrier. The private secretary felt an artistic sympathy with Roebuck, for, from time to time, by way of practice, Bright in a friendly way was apt to shake him too, and he knew how it was done. The manner counted for more than the words. The scene was interesting, but the result was not in doubt.

All the more sharply he was excited, near the year 1879, in Washington, by hearing Lamar begin a story after dinner, which, little by little, became dramatic, recalling the scene in the House of Commons. The story, as well as one remembered, began with Lamar's failure to reach St. Petersburg at all, and his consequent detention in Paris waiting instructions. The motion to recognize the Confederacy was about to be made, and, in prospect of the debate, Mr. Lindsay collected a party at his villa on the Thames to bring the rebel agents into relations with Roebuck. Lamar was sent for, and came. After much conversation of a general sort, such as is the usual object or resource of the English Sunday, finding himself alone with Roebuck, Lamar, by way of showing interest, bethought himself of John Bright and asked Roebuck whether he expected Bright to take part in the debate: "No, sir!" said Roebuck sententiously; "Bright and I have met before. It was the old story — the story of the swordfish and the whale! No, sir! Mr. Bright will not cross swords with me again!"

Thus assured, Lamar went with the more confidence

to the House on the appointed evening, and was placed under the gallery, on the right, where he listened to Roebuck and followed the debate with such enjoyment as an experienced debater feels in these contests, until, as he said, he became aware that a man, with a singularly rich voice and imposing manner, had taken the floor, and was giving Roebuck the most deliberate and tremendous pounding he ever witnessed, "until at last," concluded Lamar, "it dawned on my mind that the sword-fish was getting the worst of it."

Lamar told the story in the spirit of a joke against himself rather than against Roebuck; but such jokes must have been unpleasantly common in the experience of the rebel agents. They were surrounded by cranks of the worst English species, who distorted their natural eccentricities and perverted their judgment. Roebuck may have been an extreme case, since he was actually in his dotage, yet this did not prevent the Lairds from accepting his lead, or the House from taking him seriously. Extreme eccentricity was no bar, in England, to extreme confidence; sometimes it seemed a recommendation; and unless it caused financial loss, it rather helped popularity.

The question whether British eccentricity was ever strength weighed heavily in the balance of education. That Roebuck should mislead the rebel agents on so strange a point as that of Bright's courage was doubly characteristic because the Southern people themselves had this same barbaric weakness of attributing want of courage to opponents, and owed their ruin chiefly to such ignorance of the world. Bright's courage was almost as irrational as that of the rebels themselves. Every one knew that he had the courage of a prize-fighter. He struck, in succession, pretty nearly every man in England that could be reached by a blow, and when he could not reach the individual he struck the class, or when the class was too small for him, the whole people of England. At times he had the whole country on his back. He could not act on the defensive; his mind required attack. Even among friends at the dinner-table he talked as though he were denouncing them, or some one else, on a platform; he measured his phrases, built his sentences, cumulated his effects, and pounded his opponents, real or imagined. His humor was glow, like iron at dull heat; his blow was elementary, like the thrash of a whale.

On day in early spring, March 26, 1863, the Minister requested his private secretary to attend a Trades-Union Meeting at St. James's Hall, which was the result of Professor Beesly's patient efforts to unite Bright and the Trades-Unions on an American platform. The secretary went to the meeting and made a report which reposes somewhere on file in the State Department to this day, as harmless as such reports should be; but it contained no mention of what interested young Adams most — Bright's psychology. With singular skill and oratorical power, Bright managed at the outset, in his opening paragraph, to insult or outrage every class of Englishman commonly considered respectable, and, for fear of any escaping, he insulted them repeatedly under consecutive heads. The rhetorical effect was tremendous: —

"Privilege thinks it has a great interest in the American contest," he began in his massive, deliberate tones; "and every morning with blatant voice, it comes into our streets and curses the American Republic. Privilege has beheld an afflicting spectacle for many years past. It has beheld thirty million of men happy and prosperous, without emperors — without king (*cheers*) — without the surroundings of a court (*renewed cheers*) — without nobles, except such as are made by eminence in intellect and virtue — without State bishops and State priests, those vendors of the love that works salvation (*cheers*) — without great armies and great navies — without a great debt and great taxes — and Privilege has shuddered at what might happen to old Europe if this great experiment should succeed."

An ingenious man, with an inventive mind, might have managed, in the same number of lines, to offend more Englishmen than Bright struck in this sentence; but he must have betrayed artifice and hurt his oratory. The audience cheered furiously, and the private secretary felt peace in his much troubled mind, for he knew how careful the Ministry would be, once they saw Bright talk republican principles before Trades-Unions; but, while he did not, like Roebuck, see reason to doubt the courage of a man who, after quarrelling with the Trades-Unions, quarrelled with all the world outside the Trades-Unions, he did feel a doubt whether to class Bright as eccentric or conventional. Every one called Bright "un-English," from Lord Palmerston to William E. Forster; but to an American he seemed more English than any of his critics. He was a liberal hater, and what he hated he reviled after the manner of Milton, but he was afraid of no one. He was almost the only man in England, or, for that matter, in Europe, who hated Palmerston and was not afraid of him, or of the press or the pulpit, the clubs or the bench, that stood behind him. He loathed the whole fabric of sham religion, sham loyalty, sham aristocracy, and sham socialism. He had the British weakness of believing only in himself and his own conventions. In all this, an American saw, if one may make the distinction, much racial eccentricity, but little that was personal. Bright was singularly well poised; but he used singularly strong language.

Long afterwards, in 1880, Adams happened to be living again in London for a season, when James Russell

Lowell was transferred there as Minister; and as Adams's relations with Lowell had become closer and more intimate with years, he wanted the new Minister to know some of his old friends. Bright was then in the Cabinet, and no longer the most radical member even there, but he was still a rare figure in society. He came to dinner, along with Sir Francis Doyle and Sir Robert Cunliffe, and as usual did most of the talking. As usual also, he talked of the things most on his mind. Apparently it must have been some reform of the criminal law which the Judges opposed, that excited him, for at the end of dinner, over the wine, he took possession of the table in his old way, and ended with a superb denunciation of the Bench, spoken in his massive manner, as though every word were a hammer, smashing what it struck: —

"For two hundred years, the Judges of England sat on the Bench, condemning to the penalty of death every man, woman, and child who stole property to the value of five shillings; and, during all that time, not one Judge ever remonstrated against the law. We English are a nation of brutes, and ought to be exterminated to the last man."

As the party rose from table and passed into the drawing-room, Adams said to Lowell that Bright was very fine. "Yes!" replied Lowell; "but too violent!"

Precisely this was the point that Adams doubted. Bright knew his Englishmen better than Lowell did — better than England did. He knew what amount of violence in language was necessary to drive an idea into a Lancashire or Yorkshire head. He knew that no violence was enough to affect a Somersetshire or Wiltshire peasant. Bright kept his own head cool and clear. He was not excited; he never betrayed excitement. As for his denunciation of the English Bench, it was a very old story, not original with him. That the English were a nation of brutes was a commonplace generally admitted by Englishmen and universally accepted by foreigners; while the matter of their extermination could be treated only as unpractical, on their deserts, because they were probably not very much worse than their neighbors. Had Bright said that the French, Spaniards, Germans, or Russians were a nation of brutes and ought to be exterminated, no one would have found fault; the whole human race, according to the highest authority, has been exterminated once already for the same reason, and only the rainbow protects them from a repetition of it. What shocked Lowell was that he denounced his own people.

Adams felt no moral obligation to defend Judges, who, as far as he knew, were the only class of society specially adapted to defend themselves; but he was curious — even anxious — as a point of education, to decide for himself whether Bright's language was violent for its purpose. He thought not. Perhaps Cobden did better by persuasion, but that was another matter. Of course, even Englishmen sometimes complained of being so constantly told that they were brutes and hypocrites, although they were told little else by their censors, and bore it, on the whole, meekly; but the fact that it was true in the main troubled the ten-pound voter much less than it troubled Newman, Gladstone, Ruskin, Carlyle, and Matthew Arnold. Bright was personally disliked by his victims, but not distrusted. They never doubted what he would do next, as they did with John Russell, Gladstone, and Disraeli. He betrayed no one, and he never advanced an opinion in practical matters which did not prove to be practical.

The class of Englishmen who set out to be the intellectual opposites of Bright, seemed to an American bystander the weakest and most eccentric of all. These were the trimmers, the political economists, the anti-slavery and doctrinaire class, the followers of de Tocqueville, and of John Stuart Mill. As a class, they were timid — with good reason — and timidity, which is high wisdom in philosophy, sicklies the whole cast of thought in action. Numbers of these men haunted London society, all tending to free-thinking, but never venturing much freedom of thought. Like the anti-slavery doctrinaires of the forties and fifties, they became mute and useless when slavery struck them in the face. For type of these eccentrics, literature seems to have chosen Henry Reeve, at least to the extent of biography. He was a bulky figure in society, always friendly, good-natured, obliging, and useful; almost as universal as Milnes and more busy. As editor of the *Edinburgh Review* he had authority and even power, although the *Review* and the whole Whig doctrinaire school had begun — as the French say — to date; and of course the literary and artistic sharpshooters of 1867 — like Frank Palgrave — frothed and foamed at the mere mention of Reeve's name. Three-fourths of their fury was due only to his ponderous manner. London society abused its rights of personal criticism by fixing on every too conspicuous figure some word or phrase that stuck to it. Every one had heard of Mrs. Grote as "the origin of the word grotesque." Every one had laughed at the story of Reeve approaching Mrs. Grote, with his usual somewhat florid manner, asking in his literary dialect how her husband the historian was: "And how is the learned Grotius?" "Pretty well, thank you, Puffendorf!" One winced at the word, as though it were a drawing of Forain.

No one would have been more shocked than Reeve had he been charged with want of moral courage. He proved his courage afterwards by publishing the "Greville Memoirs," braving the displeasure of the Queen. Yet the *Edinburgh Review* and its editor avoided taking sides except where sides were already fixed. Americanism would have been bad form in the liberal *Edinburgh Review;* it would have seemed eccentric even for a Scotchman, and Reeve was a Saxon of Saxons. To an American this attitude of oscillating reserve seemed more eccentric than the reckless hostility of Brougham or Carlyle, and more mischievous, for he never could be sure what preposterous commonplace it might encourage.

The sum of these experiences in 1863 left the conviction that eccentricity was weakness. The young American who should adopt English thought was lost. From the facts, the conclusion was correct, yet, as usual, the conclusion was wrong. The years of Palmerston's last Cabinet, 1859 to 1865, were avowedly years of truce — of arrested development. The British system like the French, was in its last stage of decomposition. Never had the British mind shown itself so *décousu* — so unravelled, at sea, floundering in every sort of historical shipwreck. Eccentricities had a free field. Contradictions swarmed in State and Church. England devoted thirty years of arduous labor to clearing away only a part of the *débris*. A young American in 1863 could see little or nothing of the future. He might dream, but he could not foretell, the suddenness with which the old Europe, with England in its wake, was to vanish in 1870. He was in deadwater, and the parti-colored, fantastic cranks swam about his boat, as though he were the ancient mariner, and they saurians of the prime.

13

The
Perfection
of Human
Society

(1864)

Minister Adams's success in stopping the rebel rams fixed his position once for all in English society. From that moment he could afford to drop the character of diplomatist, and assume what, for an American Minister in London, was an exclusive diplomatic advantage, the character of a kind of American Peer of the Realm. The British never did things by halves. Once they recognized a man's right to social privileges, they accepted him as one of themselves. Much as Lord Derby and Mr. Disraeli were accepted as leaders of Her Majesty's domestic Opposition, Minister Adams had a rank of his own as a kind of leader of Her Majesty's American Opposition. Even the *Times* conceded it. The years of struggle were over, and Minister Adams rapidly gained a position which would have caused his father or grandfather to stare with incredulous envy.

This Anglo-American form of diplomacy was chiefly

undiplomatic, and had the peculiar effect of teaching a habit of diplomacy useless or mischievous everywhere but in London. Nowhere else in the world could one expect to figure in a rôle so unprofessional. The young man knew no longer what character he bore. Private secretary in the morning, son in the afternoon, young man about town in the evening, the only character he never bore was that of diplomatist, except when he wanted a card to some great function. His diplomatic education was at an end; he seldom met a diplomat, and never had business with one; he could be of no use to them, or they to him; but he drifted inevitably into society, and, do what he might, his next education must be one of English social life. Tossed between the horns of successive dilemmas, he reached his twenty-sixth birthday without the power of earning five dollars in any occupation. His friends in the army were almost as badly off, but even army life ruined a young man less fatally than London society. Had he been rich, this form of ruin would have mattered nothing; but the young men of 1865 were none of them rich; all had to earn a living; yet they had reached high positions of responsibility and power in camps and Courts, without a dollar of their own and with no tenure of office.

Henry Adams had failed to acquire any useful education; he should at least have acquired social experience. Curiously enough, he failed here also. From the European or English point of view, he had no social experience, and never got it. Minister Adams happened on a political interregnum owing to Lord Palmerston's personal influence from 1860 to 1865; but this political interregnum was less marked than the social still-stand during the same years. The Prince Consort was dead; the Queen had retired; the Prince of Wales was still a boy. In its best days, Victorian society had never been "smart." During the forties, under the influence of Louis Philippe, Courts affected to be simple, serious and middle class; and they succeeded. The taste of Louis Philippe was *bourgeois* beyond any taste except that of Queen Victoria. Style lingered in the background with the powdered footman behind the yellow chariot, but speaking socially the Queen had no style save what she inherited. Balmoral was a startling revelation of royal taste. Nothing could be worse than the toilettes at Court unless it were the way they were worn. One's eyes might be dazzled by jewels, but they were heirlooms, and if any lady appeared well dressed, she was either a foreigner or "fast." Fashion was not fashionable in London until the Americans and the Jews were let loose. The style of London toilette universal in 1864 was grotesque, like Monckton Milnes on horseback in Rotten Row.

Society of this sort might fit a young man in some degree for editing Shakespeare or Swift, but had little relation with the society of 1870, and none with that of 1900. Owing to other causes, young Adams never got the full training of such style as still existed. The embarrassments of his first few seasons socially ruined him. His own want of experience prevented his asking introductions to the ladies who ruled society; his want of friends prevented his knowing who these ladies were; and he had every reason to expect snubbing if he put himself in evidence. This sensitiveness was thrown away on English society, where men and women treated each others' advances much more brutally than those of strangers, but young Adams was son and private secretary too; he could not be as thick-skinned as an Englishman. He was not alone. Every young diplomat, and most of the old ones, felt awkward in an English house from a certainty that they were not precisely wanted there, and a possibility that they might be told so.

If there was in those days a country house in England

which had a right to call itself broad in views and large in tastes, it was Bretton in Yorkshire; and if there was a hostess who had a right to consider herself fashionable as well as charming, it was Lady Margaret Beaumont; yet one morning at breakfast there, sitting by her side — not for his own merits — Henry Adams heard her say to herself in her languid and liberal way, with her rich voice and musing manner, looking into her tea-cup: "I don't think I care for foreigners!" Horror-stricken, not so much on his own account as on hers, the young man could only execute himself as gaily as he might: "But Lady Margaret, please make one small exception for me!" Of course she replied what was evident, that she did not call him a foreigner, and her genial Irish charm made the slip of tongue a happy courtesy; but none the less she knew that, except for his momentary personal introduction, he was in fact a foreigner, and there was no imaginable reason why she should like him, or any other foreigner, unless it were because she was bored by natives. She seemed to feel that her indifference needed a reason to excuse itself in her own eyes, and she showed the subconscious sympathy of the Irish nature which never feels itself perfectly at home even in England. She, too, was some shadowy shade un-English.

Always conscious of this barrier, while the war lasted the private secretary hid himself among the herd of foreigners till he found his relations fixed and unchangeable. He never felt himself in society, and he never knew definitely what was meant as society by those who were in it. He saw far enough to note a score of societies which seemed quite independent of each other. The smartest was the smallest, and to him almost wholly strange. The largest was the sporting world, also unknown to him except through the talk of his acquaintances. Between or beyond these lay groups of nebulous societies. His lawyer friends, like Evarts, frequented legal circles where one still sat over the wine and told anecdotes of the bench and bar; but he himself never set eyes on a judge except when his father took him to call on old Lord Lyndhurst, where they found old Lord Campbell, both abusing old Lord Brougham. The Church and the Bishops formed several societies which no secretary ever saw except as an interloper. The Army; the Navy; the Indian Service; the medical and surgical professions; City people; artists; county families; the Scotch, and indefinite other subdivisions of society existed, which were as strange to each other as they were to Adams. At the end of eight or ten seasons in London society he professed to know less about it, or how to enter it, than he did when he made his first appearance at Miss Burdett Coutts's in May, 1861.

Sooner or later every young man dropped into a set or circle, and frequented the few houses that were willing to harbor him. An American who neither hunted nor raced, neither shot nor fished nor gambled, and was not marriageable, had no need to think of society at large. Ninety-nine houses in every hundred were useless to him, a greater bore to him than he to them. Thus the question of getting into — or getting out of — society which troubled young foreigners greatly, settled itself after three or four years of painful speculation. Society had no unity; one wandered about in it like a maggot in cheese; it was not a hansom cab, to be got into, or out of, at dinner-time.

Therefore he always professed himself ignorant of society; he never knew whether he had been in it or not, but from the accounts of his future friends, like General Dick Taylor or George Smalley, and of various ladies who reigned in the seventies, he inclined to think that he knew very little about it. Certain great houses and certain great functions of course he attended, like every one else who could get cards, but even of these the number was small that kept an interest or helped education. In seven years he could remember only two that seemed to have any meaning for him, and he never knew what that meaning was. Neither of the two was official; neither was English in interest; and both were scandals to the philosopher while they scarcely enlightened men of the world.

One was at Devonshire House, an ordinary, unpremeditated evening reception. Naturally every one went to Devonshire House if asked, and the rooms that night were fairly full of the usual people. The private secretary was standing among the rest, when Mme. de Castiglione entered, the famous beauty of the Second Empire. How beautiful she may have been, or indeed what sort of beauty she was, Adams never knew, because the company, consisting of the most refined and aristocratic society in the world, instantly formed a lane, and stood in ranks to stare at her, while those behind mounted on chairs to look over their neighbors' heads; so that the lady walked through this polite mob, stared completely out of countenance, and fled the house at once. This was all!

The other strange spectacle was at Stafford House, April 13, 1864, when, in a palace gallery that recalled Paolo Veronese's pictures of Christ in his scenes of miracle, Garibaldi, in his gray capote over his red shirt, received all London, and three duchesses literally worshipped at his feet. Here, at all events, a private secretary had surely caught the last and highest touch of social experience; but what it meant — what social, moral, or mental development it pointed out to the searcher of truth — was not a matter to be treated fully by a leader in the *Morning Post* or even by a sermon in Westminster Abbey. Mme. de Castiglione and Garibaldi covered, between them, too much space for simple measurement; their curves were too complex for mere arithmetic. The task of bringing the two into any common relation with an ordered social system tending to orderly development — in London or elsewhere — was well fitted for Algernon Swinburne or Victor Hugo, but was beyond any process yet reached by the education of Henry Adams, who would probably, even then, have rejected, as superficial or supernatural, all the views taken by any of the company who looked on with him at these two interesting and perplexing sights.

From the Court, or Court society, a mere private secretary got nothing at all, or next to nothing, that could help him on his road through life. Royalty was in abeyance. One was tempted to think in these years, 1860–65, that the nicest distinction between the very best society and the second-best, was their attitude towards royalty. The one regarded royalty as a bore, and avoided it, or quietly said that the Queen had never been in society. The same thing might have been said of fully half the peerage. Adams never knew even the names of half the rest; he never exchanged ten words with any member of the royal family; he never knew any one in those years who showed interest in any member of the royal family, or who would have given five shillings for the opinion of any royal person on any subject; or cared to enter any royal or noble presence, unless the house was made attractive by as much social effort as would have been necessary in other countries where no rank existed. No doubt, as one of a swarm, young Adams slightly knew various gilded youth who frequented balls and led such dancing as was most in vogue, but they seemed to set no value on rank; their anxiety was only to know where to find the best partners before midnight, and the best supper after midnight. To the American, as to Arthur Pendennis or Barnes Newcome, the value of social position and knowledge was evident enough; he valued it at rather more than it was worth to him; but it was a shadowy thing which seemed to vary with every street corner; a thing which had shifting standards, and which no one could catch outright. The half-dozen leaders and beauties of his time, with great names and of the utmost fashion, made some of the poorest marriages, and the least showy careers.

Tired at looking on at society from the outside, Adams grew to loathe the sight of his Court dress; to groan at every announcement of a Court ball; and to dread every invitation to a formal dinner. The greatest social event gave not half the pleasure that one could buy for ten shillings at the opera when Patti sang Cherubino or Gretchen, and not a fourth of the education. Yet this was not the opinion of the best judges. Lothrop Motley, who stood among the very best, said to him early in his apprenticeship that the London dinner and the English country house were the perfection of human society. The young man meditated over it, uncertain of its meaning. Motley could not have thought the dinner itself perfect, since there was not then — outside of a few bankers or foreigners — a good cook or a good table in London, and nine out of ten of the dinners that Motley ate came from Gunter's, and all were alike. Every one, especially in young society, complained bitterly that Englishmen did not know a good dinner when they ate it, and could not order one if they were given *carte blanche*. Henry Adams was not a judge, and knew no more than they, but he heard the complaints, and he could not think that Motley meant to praise the English *cuisine*.

Equally little could Motley have meant that dinners were good to look at. Nothing could be worse than the toilettes; nothing less artistic than the appearance of the company. One's eyes might be dazzled by family diamonds, but, if an American woman were present, she was sure to make comments about the way the jewels were worn. If there was a well-dressed lady at table, she was either an American or "fast." She attracted as much notice as though she were on the stage. No one could possibly admire an English dinner-table.

Least of all did Motley mean that the taste or the manners were perfect. The manners of English society were notorious, and the taste was worse. Without exception every American woman rose in rebellion against English manners. In fact, the charm of London which made most impression on Americans was the violence of its contrasts; the extreme badness of the worst, making background for the distinction, refinement, or wit of a few, just as the extreme beauty of a few superb women was more effective against the plainness of the crowd. The result was mediæval, and amusing; sometimes coarse to a degree that might have startled a roustabout, and sometimes courteous and considerate to a degree that suggested King Arthur's Round Table; but this artistic contrast was surely not the perfection that Motley had in his mind. He meant something scholarly, worldly, and modern; he was thinking of his own tastes.

Probably he meant that, in his favorite houses, the tone was easy, the talk was good, and the standard of scholarship was high. Even there he would have been forced to qualify his adjectives. No German would have admitted that English scholarship was high, or that it was scholarship at all, or that any wish for scholarship existed in England. Nothing that seemed to smell of the shop or of the lecture-room was wanted. One might as well have talked of Renan's Christ at the table of the Bishop of London, as talk of German philology at the table of an Oxford don. Society, if a small literary class could be called society, wanted to be amused in its old way. Sydney Smith, who had amused, was dead; so was Macaulay, who instructed if he did not amuse; Thackeray died at Christmas, 1863;

Dickens never felt at home, and seldom appeared, in society; Bulwer Lytton was not sprightly; Tennyson detested strangers; Carlyle was mostly detested by them; Darwin never came to town; the men of whom Motley must have been thinking were such as he might meet at Lord Houghton's breakfasts: Grote, Jowett, Milman, or Froude; Browning, Matthew Arnold, or Swinburne; Bishop Wilberforce, Venables, or Hayward; or perhaps Gladstone, Robert Lowe, or Lord Granville. A relatively small class, commonly isolated, suppressed, and lost at the usual London dinner, such society as this was fairly familiar even to a private secretary, but to the literary American it might well seem perfection since he could find nothing of the sort in America. Within the narrow limits of this class, the American Legation was fairly at home; possibly a score of houses, all liberal, and all literary, but perfect only in the eyes of a Harvard College historian. They could teach little worth learning, for their tastes were antiquated and their knowledge was ignorance to the next generation. What was altogether fatal for future purposes, they were only English.

A social education in such a medium was bound to be useless in any other, yet Adams had to learn it to the bottom. The one thing needful for a private secretary, was that he should not only seem, but should actually be, at home. He studied carefully, and practised painfully, what seemed to be the favorite accomplishments of society. Perhaps his nervousness deceived him; perhaps he took for an ideal of others what was only his reflected image; but he conceived that the perfection of human society required that a man should enter a drawing-room where he was a total stranger, and place himself on the hearth-rug, his back to the fire, with an air of expectant benevolence, without curiosity, much as though he had dropped in at a charity concert, kindly disposed to applaud the performers and to overlook mistakes. This ideal rarely succeeded in youth, and towards thirty it took a form of modified insolence and offensive patronage; but about sixty it mellowed into courtesy, kindliness, and even deference to the young which had extraordinary charm both in women and in men. Unfortunately Adams could not wait till sixty for education; he had his living to earn; and the English air of patronage would earn no income for him anywhere else.

After five or six years of constant practice, any one can acquire the habit of going from one strange company to another without thinking much of one's self or of them, as though silently reflecting that "in a world where we are all insects, no insect is alien; perhaps they are human in parts"; but the dreamy habit of mind which comes from solitude in crowds is not fitness for social success except in London. Everywhere else it is injury. England was a social kingdom whose social coinage had no currency elsewhere.

Englishwomen, from the educational point of view, could give nothing until they approached forty years old. Then they become very interesting — very charming — to the man of fifty. The young American was not worth the young Englishwoman's notice, and never received it. Neither understood the other. Only in the domestic relation, in the country — never in society at large — a young American might accidentally make friends with an Englishwoman of his own age, but it never happened to Henry Adams. His susceptible nature was left to the mercy of American girls, which was professional duty rather than education as long as diplomacy held its own.

Thus he found himself launched on waters where he had never meant to sail, and floating along a stream which carried him far from his port. His third season in London society saw the end of his diplomatic education, and began for him the social life of a young man who felt at home in England — more at home there than anywhere else. With this feeling, the mere habit of going to garden-parties, dinners, receptions, and balls had nothing to do. One might go to scores without a sensation of home. One might stay in no end of country houses without forgetting that one was a total stranger and could never be anything else. One might bow to half the dukes and duchesses in England, and feel only the more strange. Hundreds of persons might pass with a nod and never come nearer. Close relation in a place like London is a personal mystery as profound as chemical affinity. Thousands pass, and one separates himself from the mass to attach himself to another, and so make, little by little, a group.

One morning, April 27, 1863, he was asked to breakfast with Sir Henry Holland, the old Court physician who had been acquainted with every American Minister since Edward Everett, and was a valuable social ally, who had the courage to try to be of use to everybody, and who, while asking the private secretary to breakfast one day, was too discreet to betray what he might have learned about rebel doings at his breakfast-table the day before. He had been friendly with the Legation, in the teeth of society, and was still bearing up against the weight of opinion, so that young Adams could not decline his invitations, although they obliged him to breakfast in Brook Street at nine o'clock in the morning, alternately with Mr. James M. Mason. Old Dr. Holland was himself as hale as a hawk, driving all day bare-headed about London, and eating Welsh rarebit every night before bed; he thought that any young man should be pleased to take his early muffin in Brook Street, and supply a few crumbs of war news for the daily peckings of eminent patients. Meekly, when summoned, the private secretary went, and on reaching the front door, this particular morning, he found there another young man in the act of rapping the knocker. They entered the breakfast-room together, where they were introduced to each other, and Adams learned that the other guest was a Cambridge undergraduate, Charles Milnes Gaskell, son of James Milnes Gaskell, the Member for Wenlock; another of the Yorkshire Milneses, from Thornes near Wakefield. Fate had fixed Adams to Yorkshire. By another chance it happened that young Milnes Gaskell was intimate at Cambridge with William Everett who was also about to take his degree. A third chance inspired Mr. Evarts with a fancy for visiting Cambridge, and led William Everett to offer his services as host. Adams acted as courier to Mr. Evarts, and at the end of May they went down for a few days, when William Everett did the honors as host with a kindness and attention that made his cousin sorely conscious of his own social shortcomings. Cambridge was pretty, and the dons were kind. Mr. Evarts enjoyed his visit, but this was merely a part of the private secretary's day's work. What affected his whole life was the intimacy then begun with Milnes Gaskell and his circle of undergraduate friends, just about to enter the world.

Intimates are predestined. Adams met in England a thousand people, great and small; jostled against every one, from royal princes to gin-shop loafers; attended endless official functions and private parties; visited every part of the United Kingdom and was not quite a stranger at the Legations in Paris and Rome; he knew the societies of certain country houses, and acquired habits of Sunday-afternoon calls; but all this gave him nothing to do, and was life wasted. For him nothing whatever could be gained by escorting American ladies to drawing-rooms or American gentlemen to levees at St. James's Palace, or bowing solemnly to people with great titles, at Court balls, or even by awkwardly jostling royalty at garden-parties;

all this was done for the Government, and neither President Lincoln nor Secretary Seward would ever know enough of their business to thank him for doing what they did not know how to get properly done by their own servants; but for Henry Adams — not private secretary — all the time taken up by such duties was wasted. On the other hand, his few personal intimacies concerned him alone, and the chance that made him almost a Yorkshireman was one that must have started under the Heptarchy.

More than any other county in England, Yorkshire retained a sort of social independence of London. Scotland itself was hardly more distinct. The Yorkshire type had always been the strongest of the British strains; the Norwegian and the Dane were a different race from the Saxon. Even Lancashire had not the mass and the cultivation of the West Riding. London could never quite absorb Yorkshire, which, in its turn had no great love for London and freely showed it. To a certain degree, evident enough to Yorkshiremen, Yorkshire was not English — or was all England, as they might choose to express it. This must have been the reason why young Adams was drawn there rather than elsewhere. Monckton Milnes alone took the trouble to draw him, and possibly Milnes was the only man in England with whom Henry Adams, at that moment, had a chance of calling out such an un-English effort. Neither Oxford nor Cambridge nor any region south of the Humber contained a considerable house where a young American would have been sought as a friend. Eccentricity alone did not account for it. Monckton Milnes was a singular type, but his distant cousin, James Milnes Gaskell, was another, quite as marked, in an opposite sense. Milnes never seemed willing to rest; Milnes Gaskell never seemed willing to move. In his youth one of a very famous group — Arthur Hallam, Tennyson, Manning, Gladstone, Francis Doyle — and regarded as one of the most promising; an adorer of George Canning; in Parliament since coming of age; married into the powerful connection of the Wynns of Wynstay; rich according to Yorkshire standards; intimate with his political leaders; he was one of the numerous Englishmen who refuse office rather than make the effort of carrying it, and want power only to make it a source of indolence. He was a voracious reader and an admirable critic; he had forty years of parliamentary tradition on his memory; he liked to talk and to listen; he liked his dinner and, in spite of George Canning, his dry champagne; he liked wit and anecdote; but he belonged to the generation of 1830, a generation which could not survive the telegraph and railway, and which even Yorkshire could hardly produce again. To an American he was a character even more unusual and more fascinating than his distant cousin Lord Houghton.

Mr. Milnes Gaskell was kind to the young American whom his son brought to the house, and Mrs. Milnes Gaskell was kinder, for she thought the American perhaps a less dangerous friend than some Englishman might be, for her son, and she was probably right. The American had the sense to see that she was herself one of the most intelligent and sympathetic women in England; her sister, Miss Charlotte Wynn, was another; and both were of an age and a position in society that made their friendship a compliment as well as a pleasure. Their consent and approval settled the matter. In England, the family is a serious fact; once admitted to it, one is there for life. London might utterly vanish from one's horizon, but as long as life lasted, Yorkshire lived for its friends.

In the year 1857, Mr. James Milnes Gaskell, who had sat for thirty years in Parliament as one of the Members for the borough of Wenlock in Shropshire, bought Wenlock Abbey and the estate that included the old monastic buildings. This new, or old, plaything amused Mrs. Milnes

Gaskell. The Prior's house, a charming specimen of fifteenth-century architecture, had been long left to decay as a farmhouse. She put it in order, and went there to spend a part of the autumn of 1864. Young Adams was one of her first guests, and drove about Wenlock Edge and the Wrekin with her, learning the loveliness of this exquisite country, and its stores of curious antiquity. It was a new and charming existence; an experience greatly to be envied — ideal repose and rural Shakespearian peace — but a few years of it were likely to complete his education, and fit him to act a fairly useful part in life as an Englishman, an ecclesiastic, and a contemporary of Chaucer.

14

Dilettantism

(1865–1866)

The campaign of 1864 and the reëlection of Mr. Lincoln
in November set the American Minister on so firm a footing that he could safely regard his own anxieties as over,
and the anxieties of Earl Russell and the Emperor Napoleon as begun. With a few months more his own term of
four years would come to an end, and even though the
questions still under discussion with England should somewhat prolong his stay, he might look forward with some
confidence to his return home in 1865. His son no longer
fretted. The time for going into the army had passed. If
he were to be useful at all, it must be as a son, and as a son
he was treated with the widest indulgence and trust. He
knew that he was doing himself no good by staying in
London, but thus far in life he had done himself no good
anywhere, and reached his twenty-seventh birthday without having advanced a step, that he could see, beyond his
twenty-first. For the most part, his friends were worse off
than he. The war was about to end and they were to be
set adrift in a world they would find altogether strange.

At this point, as though to cut the last thread of relation,
six months were suddenly dropped out of his life in England. The London climate had told on some of the family;

the physicians prescribed a winter in Italy. Of course the private secretary was detached as their escort, since this was one of his professional functions; and he passed six months, gaining an education as Italian courier, while the Civil War came to its end. As far as other education went, he got none, but he was amused. Travelling in all possible luxury, at some one else's expense, with diplomatic privileges and position, was a form of travel hitherto untried. The Cornice in *vettura* was delightful; Sorrento in winter offered hills to climb and grottoes to explore, and Naples near by to visit; Rome at Easter was an experience necessary for the education of every properly trained private secretary; the journey north by *vettura* through Perugia and Sienna was a dream; the Splügen Pass, if not equal to the Stelvio, was worth seeing; Paris had always something to show. The chances of accidental education were not so great as they had been, since one's field of experience had grown large; but perhaps a season at Baden Baden in these later days of its brilliancy offered some chances of instruction, if it were only the sight of fashionable Europe and America on the race-course watching the Duke of Hamilton, in the middle, improving his social advantages by the conversation of Cora Pearl.

The assassination of President Lincoln fell on the party while they were at Rome, where it seemed singularly fitting to that nursery of murderers and murdered, as though America were also getting educated. Again one went to meditate on the steps of the Santa Maria in Ara Cœli, but the lesson seemed as shallow as before. Nothing happened. The travellers changed no plan or movement. The Minister did not recall them to London. The season was over before they returned; and when the private secretary sat down again at his desk in Portland Place before a mass of copy in arrears, he saw before him a world so changed as to be beyond connection with the past. His

identity, if one could call a bundle of disconnected memories an identity, seemed to remain; but his life was once
more broken into separate pieces; he was a spider and had
to spin a new web in some new place with a new attachment.

All his American friends and contemporaries who were
still alive looked singularly commonplace without uni-
forms, and hastened to get married and retire into back
streets and suburbs until they could find employment.
Minister Adams, too, was going home "next fall," and
when the fall came, he was going home "next spring," and
when the spring came, President Andrew Johnson was at
loggerheads with the Senate, and found it best to keep
things unchanged. After the usual manner of public servants who had acquired the habit of office and lost the
faculty of will, the members of the Legation in London
continued the daily routine of English society, which,
after becoming a habit, threatened to become a vice. Had
Henry Adams shared a single taste with the young Englishmen of his time, he would have been lost; but the
custom of pounding up and down Rotten Row every day,
on a hack, was not a taste, and yet was all the sport he
shared. Evidently he must set to work; he must get a new
education; he must begin a career of his own.

Nothing was easier to say, but even his father admitted
two careers to be closed. For the law, diplomacy had unfitted him; for diplomacy he already knew too much. Any
one who had held, during the four most difficult years
of American diplomacy, a position at the centre of action,
with his hands actually touching the lever of power, could
not beg a post of Secretary at Vienna or Madrid in order
to bore himself doing nothing until the next President
should do him the honor to turn him out. For once all his
advisers agreed that diplomacy was not possible.

In any ordinary system he would have been called back

to serve in the State Department, but, between the President and the Senate, service of any sort became a delusion. The choice of career was more difficult than the education which had proved impracticable. Adams saw no road; in fact there was none. All his friends were trying one path or another, but none went a way that he could have taken. John Hay passed through London in order to bury himself in second-rate Legations for years, before he drifted home again to join Whitelaw Reid and George Smalley on the *Tribune*. Frank Barlow and Frank Bartlett carried Major-Generals' commissions into small law business. Miles stayed in the army. Henry Higginson, after a desperate struggle, was forced into State Street; Charles Adams wandered about, with brevet-brigadier rank, trying to find employment. Scores of others tried experiments more or less unsuccessful. Henry Adams could see easy ways of making a hundred blunders; he could see no likely way of making a legitimate success. Such as it was, his so-called education was wanted nowhere.

One profession alone seemed possible — the press. In 1860 he would have said that he was born to be an editor, like at least a thousand other young graduates from American colleges who entered the world every year enjoying the same conviction; but in 1866 the situation was altered; the possession of money had become doubly needful for success, and double energy was essential to get money. America had more than doubled her scale. Yet the press was still the last resource of the educated poor who could not be artists and would not be tutors. Any man who was fit for nothing else could write an editorial or a criticism. The enormous mass of misinformation accumulated in ten years of nomad life could always be worked off on a helpless public, in diluted doses, if one could but secure a table in the corner of a newspaper office. The press was an inferior pulpit; an anonymous schoolmaster; a cheap boarding-school; but it was still the nearest approach to a career for the literary survivor of a wrecked education. For the press, then, Henry Adams decided to fit himself, and since he could not go home to get practical training, he set to work to do what he could in London.

He knew, as well as any reporter on the *New York Herald*, that this was not an American way of beginning, and he knew a certain number of other drawbacks which the reporter could not see so clearly. Do what he might, he drew breath only in the atmosphere of English methods and thoughts; he could breathe none other. His mother — who should have been a competent judge, since her success and popularity in England exceeded that of her husband — averred that every woman who lived a certain time in England came to look and dress like an English-woman, no matter how she struggled. Henry Adams felt himself catching an English tone of mind and processes of thought, though at heart more hostile to them than ever. As though to make him more helpless and wholly distort his life, England grew more and more agreeable and amusing. Minister Adams became, in 1866, almost a historical monument in London; he held a position alto-gether his own. His old opponents disappeared. Lord Pal-merston died in October, 1865; Lord Russell tottered on six months longer, but then vanished from power; and in July, 1866, the conservatives came into office. Tradi-tionally the Tories were easier to deal with than the Whigs, and Minister Adams had no reason to regret the change. His personal relations were excellent and his per-sonal weight increased year by year. On that score the private secretary had no cares, and not much copy. His own position was modest, but it was enough; the life he led was agreeable; his friends were all he wanted, and, except that he was at the mercy of politics, he felt much at ease. Of his daily life he had only to reckon so many breakfasts; so many dinners; so many receptions, balls, theatres, and country-parties; so many cards to be left; so many Americans to be escorted – the usual routine of every young American in a Legation; all counting for nothing in sum, because, even if it had been his official duty – which it was not – it was mere routine, a single, continuous, unbroken act, which led to nothing and no-where except Portland Place and the grave.

The path that led somewhere was the English habit of mind which deepened its ruts every day. The English mind was like the London drawing-room, a comfortable and easy spot, filled with bits and fragments of incoherent furnitures, which were never meant to go together, and could be arranged in any relation without making a whole, except by the square room. Philosophy might dispute about innate ideas till the stars died out in the sky, but about innate tastes no one, except perhaps a collie dog, has the right to doubt; least of all, the Englishman, for his tastes are his being; he drifts after them as unconsciously as a honey-bee drifts after his flowers, and, in England, every one must drift with him. Most young Englishmen drifted to the race-course or the moors or the hunting-field; a few towards books; one or two followed some form of science; and a number took to what, for want of a better name, they called Art. Young Adams inherited a certain taste for the same pursuit from his father who in-sisted that he had it not, because he could not see what his son thought he saw in Turner. The Minister, on the other hand, carried a sort of æsthetic rag-bag of his own, which he regarded as amusement, and never called art. So he would wander off on a Sunday to attend service suc-cessively in all the city churches built by Sir Christopher Wren; or he would disappear from the Legation day after day to attend coin sales at Sotheby's, where his son attended alternate sales of drawings, engravings, or watercolors. Neither knew enough to talk much about the other's tastes, but the only difference between them was a slight difference of direction. The Minister's mind like his writings showed a correctness of form and line that his son would have been well pleased had he inherited.

Of all supposed English tastes, that of art was the most alluring and treacherous. Once drawn into it, one had small chance of escape, for it had no centre or circumference, no beginning, middle, or end, no origin, no object, and no conceivable result as education. In London one met no corrective. The only American who came by, capable of teaching, was William Hunt, who stopped to paint the portrait of the Minister which now completes the family series at Harvard College. Hunt talked constantly, and was, or afterwards became, a famous teacher, but Henry Adams did not know enough to learn. Perhaps, too, he had inherited or acquired a stock of tastes, as young men must, which he was slow to outgrow. Hunt had no time to sweep out the rubbish of Adams's mind. The portrait finished, he went.

As often as he could, Adams ran over to Paris, for sunshine, and there always sought out Richardson in his attic in the Rue du Bac, or wherever he lived, and they went off to dine at the Palais Royal, and talk of whatever interested the students of the Beaux Arts. Richardson, too, had much to say, but had not yet seized his style. Adams caught very little of what lay in his mind, and the less, because, to Adams, everything French was bad except the restaurants, while the continuous life in England made French art seem worst of all. This did not prove that English art, in 1866, was good; far from it; but it helped to make bric-à-brac of all art, after the manner of England.

Not in the Legation, or in London, but in Yorkshire

at Thornes, Adams met the man that pushed him furthest
in this English garden of innate disorder called taste. The
older daughter of the Milnes Gaskells had married Francis
Turner Palgrave. Few Americans will ever ask whether
any one has described the Palgraves, but the family was
one of the most describable in all England at that day.
Old Sir Francis, the father, had been much the greatest
of all the historians of early England, the only one who
was un-English; and the reason of his superiority lay in
his name, which was Cohen, and his mind which was
Cohen also, or at least not English. He changed his name
to Palgrave in order to please his wife. They had a band
of remarkable sons: Francis Turner, Gifford, Reginald,
Inglis; all of whom made their mark. Gifford was perhaps the most eccentric, but his "Travels" in Arabia were
famous, even among the famous travels of that generation.
Francis Turner — or, as he was commonly called, Frank
Palgrave — unable to work off his restlessness in travel like
Gifford, and stifled in the atmosphere of the Board of
Education, became a critic. His art-criticisms helped to
make the *Saturday Review* a terror to the British artist.
His literary taste, condensed into the "Golden Treasury,"
helped Adams to more literary education than he ever
got from any taste of his own. Palgrave himself held rank
as one of the minor poets; his hymns had vogue. As an
art-critic he was too ferocious to be liked; even Holman
Hunt found his temper humorous; among many rivals, he
may perhaps have had a right to claim the much-disputed
rank of being the most unpopular man in London; but he
liked to teach, and asked only for a docile pupil. Adams
was docile enough, for he knew nothing and liked to
listen. Indeed, he had to listen, whether he liked or not,
for Palgrave's voice was strident, and nothing could stop
him. Literature, painting, sculpture, architecture were
open fields for his attacks, which were always intelligent

if not always kind, and when these failed, he readily descended to meaner levels. John Richard Green, who was Palgrave's precise opposite, and whose Irish charm of touch and humor defended him from most assaults, used to tell with delight of Palgrave's call on him just after he had moved into his new Queen Anne house in Kensington Square: "Palgrave called yesterday, and the first thing he said was, 'I've counted three anachronisms on your front doorstep.' "

Another savage critic, also a poet, was Thomas Woolner, a type almost more emphatic than Palgrave in a society which resounded with emphasis. Woolner's sculpture showed none of the rough assertion that Woolner himself showed, when he was not making supernatural effort to be courteous, but his busts were remarkable, and his work altogether was, in Palgrave's clamorous opinion, the best of his day. He took the matter of British art — or want of art — seriously, almost ferociously, as a personal grievance and torture; at times he was rather terrifying in the anarchistic wrath of his denunciation. As Henry Adams felt no responsibility for English art, and had no American art to offer for sacrifice, he listened with enjoyment to language much like Carlyle's, and accepted it without a qualm. On the other hand, as a third member of this critical group, he fell in with Stopford Brooke whose tastes lay in the same direction, and whose expression was modified by clerical propriety. Among these men, one wandered off into paths of education much too devious and slippery for an American foot to follow. He would have done better to go on the race-track, as far as concerned a career.

Fortunately for him he knew too little ever to be an art-critic, still less an artist. For some things ignorance is good, and art is one of them. He knew he knew nothing, and had not the trained eye or the keen instinct that trusted itself; but he was curious, as he went on, to find out how much others knew. He took Palgrave's word as final about a drawing of Rembrandt or Michael Angelo, and he trusted Woolner implicitly about a Turner; but when he quoted their authority to any dealer, the dealer pooh-poohed it, and declared that it had no weight in the trade. If he went to a sale of drawings or paintings, at Sotheby's or Christie's, an hour afterwards, he saw these same dealers watching Palgrave or Woolner for a point, and bidding over them. He rarely found two dealers agree in judgment. He once bought a water-color from the artist himself, out of his studio, and had it doubted an hour afterwards by the dealer to whose place he took it for framing. He was reduced to admit that he could not prove its authenticity; internal evidence was against it.

One morning in early July, 1867, Palgrave stopped at the Legation in Portland Place on his way downtown, and offered to take Adams to Sotheby's, where a small collection of old drawings was on show. The collection was rather a curious one, said to be that of Sir Anthony Westcomb, from Liverpool, with an undisturbed record of a century, but with nothing to attract notice. Probably none but collectors or experts examined the portfolios. Some dozens of these were always on hand, following every sale, and especially on the lookout for old drawings, which became rarer every year. Turning rapidly over the numbers, Palgrave stopped at one containing several small drawings, one marked as Rembrandt, one as Rafael; and putting his finger on the Rafael, after careful examination; "I should buy this," he said; "it looks to me like one of those things that sell for five shillings one day, and fifty pounds the next." Adams marked it for a bid, and the next morning came down to the auction. The numbers sold slowly, and at noon he thought he might safely go to lunch. When he came back, half an hour afterwards, the drawing was gone. Much annoyed at his own stupidity, since Palgrave had expressly said he wanted the drawing for himself if he had not in a manner given it to Adams, the culprit waited for the sale to close, and then asked the clerk for the name of the buyer. It was Holloway, the art-dealer, near Covent Garden, whom he slightly knew. Going at once to the shop he waited till young Holloway came in, with his purchases under his arm, and without attempt at preface, he said: "You bought to-day, Mr. Holloway, a number that I wanted. Do you mind letting me have it?" Holloway took out the parcel, looked over the drawings, and said that he had bought the number for the sake of the Rembrandt, which he thought possibly genuine; taking that out, Adams might have the rest for the price he paid for the lot — twelve shillings.

Thus, down to that moment, every expert in London had probably seen these drawings. Two of them — only two — had thought them worth buying at any price, and of these two, Palgrave chose the Rafael, Holloway the one marked as Rembrandt. Adams, the purchaser of the Rafael, knew nothing whatever on the subject, but thought he might credit himself with education to the value of twelve shillings, and call the drawing nothing. Such items of education commonly came higher.

He took the drawing to Palgrave. It was closely pasted to an old, rather thin, cardboard mount, and, on holding it up to the window, one could see lines on the reverse. "Take it down to Reed at the British Museum," said Palgrave; "he is Curator of the drawings, and, if you ask him, he will have it taken off the mount." Adams amused himself for a day or two by searching Rafael's works for the figure, which he found at last in the Parnasso, the figure of Horace, of which, as it happened — though Adams did not know it — the British Museum owned a much finer drawing. At last he took the dirty, little, unfinished red-chalk sketch to Reed whom he found in the Curator's room, with some of the finest Rafael drawings in existence, hanging on the walls. "Yes!" said Mr. Reed; "I noticed this at the sale; but it's not Rafael!" Adams, feeling himself incompetent to discuss this subject, reported the result to Palgrave, who said that Reed knew nothing about it. Also this point lay beyond Adams's competence; but he noted that Reed was in the employ of the British Museum as Curator of the best — or nearly the best — collection in the world, especially of Rafaels, and that he bought for the Museum. As expert he had rejected both the Rafael and the Rembrandt at first-sight, and after his attention was recalled to the Rafael for a further opinion he rejected it again.

A week later, Adams returned for the drawing, which Mr. Reed took out of his drawer and gave him, saying with what seemed a little doubt or hesitation: "I should tell you that the paper shows a water-mark, which I find the same as that of paper used by Marc Antonio." A little taken back by this method of studying art, a method which even a poor and ignorant American might use as well as Rafael himself, Adams asked stupidly: "Then you think it genuine?" "Possibly!" replied Reed; "but much overdrawn."

Here was expert opinion after a second revise, with help of water-marks! In Adams's opinion it was alone worth another twelve shillings as education; but this was not all. Reed continued: "The lines on the back seem to be writing, which I cannot read, but if you will take it down to the manuscript-room, they will read it for you."

Adams took the sheet down to the keeper of the manuscripts and begged him to read the lines. The keeper, after a few minutes' study, very obligingly said he could not: "It is scratched with an artist's crayon, very rapidly, with many unusual abbreviations and old forms. If any one in Europe can read it, it is the old man at the table yonder, Libri! Take it to him!"

This expert broke down on the alphabet! He could not

even judge a manuscript; but Adams had no right to complain, for he had nothing to pay, not even twelve shillings, though he thought these experts worth more, at least for his education. Accordingly he carried his paper to Libri, a total stranger to him, and asked the old man, as deferentially as possible, to tell him whether the lines had any meaning. Had Adams not been an ignorant person he would have known all about Libri, but his ignorance was vast, and perhaps was for the best. Libri looked at the paper, and then looked again, and at last bade him sit down and wait. Half an hour passed before he called Adams back and showed him these lines: —

> "Or questo credo ben che una elleria
> Te offende tanto che te offese il core.
> Perche sei grande nol sei in tua volia;
> Tu vedi e gia non credi il tuo valore;
> Passate gia son tutte gelosie;
> Tu sei di sasso; non hai piu dolore."

As far as Adams could afterwards recall it, this was Libri's reading, but he added that the abbreviations were many and unusual; that the writing was very ancient; and that the word he read as "elleria" in the first line was not Italian at all.

By this time, one had got too far beyond one's depth to ask questions. If Libri could not read Italian, very clearly Adams had better not offer to help him. He took the drawing, thanked everybody, and having exhausted the experts of the British Museum, took a cab to Woolner's studio, where he showed the figure and repeated Reed's opinion. Woolner snorted: "Reed's a fool!" he said; "he knows nothing about it; there may be a rotten line or two, but the drawing's all right."

For forty years Adams kept this drawing on his mantelpiece, partly for its own interest, but largely for curiosity to see whether any critic or artist would ever stop to look at it. None ever did, unless he knew the story. Adams himself never wanted to know more about it. He refused to seek further light. He never cared to learn whether the drawing was Rafael's, or whether the verse were Rafael's, or whether even the water-mark was Rafael's. The experts — some scores of them including the British Museum, — had affirmed that the drawing was worth a certain moiety of twelve shillings. On that point, also, Adams could offer no opinion, but he was clear that his education had profited by it to that extent — his amusement even more.

Art was a superb field for education, but at every turn he met the same old figure, like a battered and illegible signpost that ought to direct him to the next station but never did. There was no next station. All the art of a thousand — or ten thousand — years had brought England to stuff which Palgrave and Woolner brayed in their mortars; derided, tore in tatters, growled at, and howled at, and treated in terms beyond literary usage. Whistler had not yet made his appearance in London, but the others did quite as well. What result could a student reach from it? Once, on returning to London, dining with Stopford Brooke, some one asked Adams what impression the Royal Academy Exhibition made on him. With a little hesitation, he suggested that it was rather a chaos, which he meant for civility; but Stopford Brooke abruptly met it by asking whether chaos were not better than death. Truly the question was worth discussion. For his own part, Adams inclined to think that neither chaos nor death was an object to him as a searcher of knowledge — neither would have vogue in America — neither would help him to a career. Both of them led him away from his objects, into an English dilettante museum of scraps, with nothing but a wall-paper to unite them in any relation of sequence. Possibly

English taste was one degree more fatal than English scholarship, but even this question was open to argument.
Adams went to the sales and bought what he was told to
buy; now a classical drawing by Rafael or Rubens; now a
water-color by Girtin or Cotman, if possible unfinished
because it was more likely to be a sketch from nature; and
he bought them not because they went together — on the
contrary, they made rather awkward spots on the wall as
they did on the mind — but because he could afford to buy
those, and not others. Ten pounds did not go far to buy a
Michael Angelo, but was a great deal of money to a private
secretary. The effect was spotty, fragmentary, feeble; and
the more so because the British mind was constructed in
that way — boasted of it, and held it to be true philosophy
as well as sound method.

What was worse, no one had a right to denounce the
English as wrong. Artistically their mind was scrappy, and
every one knew it, but perhaps thought itself, history, and
nature, were scrappy, and ought to be studied so. Turning
from British art to British literature, one met the same
dangers. The historical school was a playground of traps
and pitfalls. Fatally one fell into the sink of history —
antiquarianism. For one who nourished a natural weakness
for what was called history, the whole of British literature
in the nineteenth century was antiquarianism or anecdot-
age, for no one except Buckle had tried to link it with ideas,
and commonly Buckle was regarded as having failed.
Macaulay was the English historian. Adams had the greatest admiration for Macaulay, but he felt that any one who
should even distantly imitate Macaulay would perish in
self-contempt. One might as well imitate Shakespeare. Yet
evidently something was wrong here, for the poet and the
historian ought to have different methods, and Macaulay's
method ought to be imitable if it were sound; yet the
method was more doubtful than the style. He was a

dramatist; a painter; a poet, like Carlyle. This was the English mind, method, genius, or whatever one might call it; but one never could quite admit that the method which ended in Froude and Kinglake could be sound for America where passion and poetry were eccentricities. Both Froude and Kinglake, when one met them at dinner, were very agreeable, very intelligent; and perhaps the English method was right, and art fragmentary by essence. History, like everything else, might be a field of scraps, like the refuse about a Staffordshire iron-furnace. One felt a little natural reluctance to decline and fall like Silas Wegg on the golden dust-heap of British refuse; but if one must, one could at least expect a degree from Oxford and the respect of the Athenæum Club.

While drifting, after the war ended, many old American friends came abroad for a holiday, and among the rest, Dr. Palfrey, busy with his "History of New England." Of all the relics of childhood, Dr. Palfrey was the most sympathetic, and perhaps the more so because he, too, had wandered into the pleasant meadows of antiquarianism, and had forgotten the world in his pursuit of the New England Puritan. Although America seemed becoming more and more indifferent to the Puritan except as a slightly rococo ornament, he was only the more amusing as a study for the Monkbarns of Boston Bay, and Dr. Palfrey took him seriously, as his clerical education required. His work was rather an Apologia in the Greek sense; a justification of the ways of God to Man, or, what was much the same thing, of Puritans to other men; and the task of justification was onerous enough to require the occasional relief of a contrast or scapegoat. When Dr. Palfrey happened on the picturesque but unpuritanic figure of Captain John Smith, he felt no call to beautify Smith's picture or to defend his moral character; he became impartial and penetrating. The famous story of Pocahontas roused his latent New England scepticism. He suggested to Adams, who wanted to make a position for himself, that an article in the *North American Review* on Captain John Smith's relations with Pocahontas would attract as much attention, and probably break as much glass, as any other stone that could be thrown by a beginner. Adams could suggest nothing better. The task seemed likely to be amusing. So he planted himself in the British Museum and patiently worked over all the material he could find, until, at last, after three or four months of labor, he got it in shape and sent it to Charles Norton, who was then editing the *North American*. Mr. Norton very civilly and even kindly accepted it. The article appeared in January, 1867.

Surely, here was something to ponder over, as a step in education; something that tended to stagger a sceptic! In spite of personal wishes, intentions, and prejudices; in spite of civil wars and diplomatic education; in spite of determination to be actual, daily, and practical, Henry Adams found himself, at twenty-eight, still in English society, dragged on one side into English dilettantism, which of all dilettantism he held the most futile; and, on the other, into American antiquarianism, which of all antiquarianism he held the most foolish. This was the result of five years in London. Even then he knew it to be a false start. He had wholly lost his way. If he were ever to amount to anything, he must begin a new education, in a new place, with a new purpose.

15

Darwinism

(1867–1868)

Politics, diplomacy, law, art, and history had opened no
outlet for future energy or effort, but a man must do something, even in Portland Place, when winter is dark and
winter evenings are exceedingly long. At that moment
Darwin was convulsing society. The geological champion
of Darwin was Sir Charles Lyell, and the Lyells were intimate at the Legation. Sir Charles constantly said of Darwin, what Palgrave said of Tennyson, that the first time he
came to town, Adams should be asked to meet him, but
neither of them ever came to town, or ever cared to meet
a young American, and one could not go to them because
they were known to dislike intrusion. The only Americans
who were not allowed to intrude were the half-dozen in
the Legation. Adams was content to read Darwin, especially his "Origin of Species" and his "Voyage of the
Beagle." He was a Darwinist before the letter; a predestined follower of the tide; but he was hardly trained to
follow Darwin's evidences. Fragmentary the British mind
might be, but in those days it was doing a great deal of
work in a very un-English way, building up so many and
such vast theories on such narrow foundations as to shock
the conservative, and delight the frivolous. The atomic

theory; the correlation and conservation of energy; the mechanical theory of the universe; the kinetic theory of gases, and Darwin's Law of Natural Selection, were examples of what a young man had to take on trust. Neither he nor any one else knew enough to verify them; in his ignorance of mathematics, he was particularly helpless; but this never stood in his way. The ideas were new and seemed to lead somewhere — to some great generalization which would finish one's clamor to be educated. That a beginner should understand them all, or believe them all, no one could expect, still less exact. Henry Adams was Darwinist because it was easier than not, for his ignorance exceeded belief, and one must know something in order to contradict even such triflers as Tyndall and Huxley.

By rights, he should have been also a Marxist, but some narrow trait of the New England nature seemed to blight socialism, and he tried in vain to make himself a convert. He did the next best thing; he became a Comteist, within the limits of evolution. He was ready to become anything but quiet. As though the world had not been enough upset in his time, he was eager to see it upset more. He had his wish, but he lost his hold on the results by trying to understand them.

He never tried to understand Darwin; but he still fancied he might get the best part of Darwinism from the easier study of geology; a science which suited idle minds as well as though it were history. Every curate in England dabbled in geology and hunted for vestiges of Creation. Darwin hunted only for vestiges of Natural Selection, and Adams followed him, although he cared nothing about Selection, unless perhaps for the indirect amusement of upsetting curates. He felt, like nine men in ten, an instinctive belief in Evolution, but he felt no more concern in Natural than in unnatural Selection, though he seized with greediness the new volume on the "Antiquity of Man" which Sir Charles Lyell published in 1863 in order to support Darwin by wrecking the Garden of Eden. Sir Charles next brought out, in 1866, a new edition of his "Principles," then the highest text-book of geology; but here the Darwinian doctrine grew in stature. Natural Selection led back to Natural Evolution, and at last to Natural Uniformity. This was a vast stride. Unbroken Evolution under uniform conditions pleased every one — except curates and bishops; it was the very best substitute for religion; a safe, conservative, practical, thoroughly Common-Law deity. Such a working system for the universe suited a young man who had just helped to waste five or ten thousand million dollars and a million lives, more or less, to enforce unity and uniformity on people who objected to it; the idea was only too seductive in its perfection; it had the charm of art. Unity and Uniformity were the whole motive of philosophy, and if Darwin, like a true Englishman, preferred to back into it — to reach God *a posteriori* — rather than start from it, like Spinoza, the difference of method taught only the moral that the best way of reaching unity was to unite. Any road was good that arrived.

Life depended on it. One had been, from the first, dragged hither and thither like a French poodle on a string, following always the strongest pull, between one form of unity or centralization and another. The proof that one had acted wisely because of obeying the primordial habit of nature flattered one's self-esteem. Steady, uniform, unbroken evolution from lower to higher seemed easy. So, one day when Sir Charles came to the Legation to inquire about getting his "Principles" properly noticed in America, young Adams found nothing simpler than to suggest that he could do it himself if Sir Charles would tell him what to say. Youth risks such encounters with the universe before one succumbs to it, yet even he was surprised at Sir Charles's ready assent, and still more so at finding himself, after half an hour's conversation, sitting down to clear the minds of American geologists about the principles of their profession. This was getting on fast; Arthur Pendennis had never gone so far.

The geologists were a hardy class, not likely to be much hurt by Adams's learning, nor did he throw away much concern on their account. He undertook the task chiefly to educate, not them, but himself, and if Sir Isaac Newton had, like Sir Charles Lyell, asked him to explain for Americans his last edition of the "Principia," Adams would have jumped at the chance. Unfortunately the mere reading such works for amusement is quite a different matter from studying them for criticism. Ignorance must always begin at the beginning. Adams must inevitably have begun by asking Sir Isaac for an intelligible reason why the apple fell to the ground. He did not know enough to be satisfied with the fact. The Law of Gravitation was so-and-so, but what was Gravitation? and he would have been thrown quite off his base if Sir Isaac had answered that he did not know.

At the very outset Adams struck on Sir Charles's Glacial Theory or theories. He was ignorant enough to think that the glacial epoch looked like a chasm between him and a uniformitarian world. If the glacial period were uniformity, what was catastrophe? To him the two or three labored guesses that Sir Charles suggested or borrowed to explain glaciation were proof of nothing, and were quite unsolid as support for so immense a superstructure as geological uniformity. If one were at liberty to be as lax in science as in theology, and to assume unity from the start, one might better say so, as the Church did, and not invite attack by appearing weak in evidence. Naturally a young man, altogether ignorant, could not say this to Sir Charles Lyell or Sir Isaac Newton; but he was forced to state Sir

Charles's views, which he thought weak as hypotheses and worthless as proofs. Sir Charles himself seemed shy of them. Adams hinted his heresies in vain. At last he resorted to what he thought the bold experiment of inserting a sentence in the text, intended to provoke correction. "The introduction [by Louis Agassiz] of this new geological agent seemed at first sight inconsistent with Sir Charles's argument, obliging him to allow that causes had in fact existed on the earth capable of producing more violent geological changes than would be possible in our own day." The hint produced no effect. Sir Charles said not a word; he let the paragraph stand; and Adams never knew whether the great Uniformitarian was strict or lax in his uniformitarian creed; but he doubted.

Objections fatal to one mind are futile to another, and as far as concerned the article, the matter ended there, although the glacial epoch remained a misty region in the young man's Darwinism. Had it been the only one, he would not have fretted about it; but uniformity often worked queerly and sometimes did not work as Natural Selection at all. Finding himself at a loss for some single figure to illustrate the Law of Natural Selection, Adams asked Sir Charles for the simplest case of uniformity on record. Much to his surprise Sir Charles told him that certain forms, like *Terebratula*, appeared to be identical from the beginning to the end of geological time. Since this was altogether too much uniformity and much too little selection, Adams gave up the attempt to begin at the beginning, and tried starting at the end — himself. Taking for granted that the vertebrates would serve his purpose, he asked Sir Charles to introduce him to the first vertebrate. Infinitely to his bewilderment, Sir Charles informed him that the first vertebrate was a very respectable fish, among the earliest of all fossils, which had lived, and whose bones were still reposing, under Adams's own favorite Abbey on Wenlock Edge.

By this time, in 1867, Adams had learned to know Shropshire familiarly, and it was the part of his diplomatic education which he loved best. Like Catherine Olney in "Northanger Abbey," he yearned for nothing so keenly as to feel at home in a thirteenth-century Abbey, unless it were to haunt a fifteenth-century Prior's House, and both these joys were his at Wenlock. With companions or without, he never tired of it. Whether he rode about the Wrekin, or visited all the historical haunts from Ludlow Castle and Stokesay to Boscobel and Uriconium; or followed the Roman road or scratched in the Abbey ruins, all was amusing and carried a flavor of its own like that of the Roman Campagna; but perhaps he liked best to ramble over the Edge on a summer afternoon and look across the Marches to the mountains of Wales. The peculiar flavor of the scenery has something to do with absence of evolution; it was better marked in Egypt: it was felt wherever time-sequences became interchangeable. One's instinct abhors time. As one lay on the slope of the Edge, looking sleepily through the summer haze towards Shrewsbury or Cader Idris or Caer Caradoc or Uriconium, nothing suggested sequence. The Roman road was twin to the railroad; Uriconium was well worth Shrewsbury; Wenlock and Buildwas were far superior to Bridgnorth. The shepherds of Caractacus or Offa, or the monks of Buildwas, had they approached where he lay in the grass, would have taken him only for another and tamer variety of Welsh thief. They would have seen little to surprise them in the modern landscape unless it were the steam of a distant railway. One might mix up the terms of time as one liked, or stuff the present anywhere into the past, measuring time by Falstaff's Shrewsbury clock, without violent sense of wrong, as one could do it on the Pacific Ocean; but the triumph of all was to look south along the Edge to the abode of one's earliest ancestor and nearest relative, the ganoid fish, whose name, according to Professor Huxley, was *Pteraspis*, a cousin of the sturgeon, and whose kingdom, according to Sir Roderick Murchison, was called Siluria. Life began and ended there. Behind that horizon lay only the Cambrian, without vertebrates or any other organism except a few shell-fish. On the further verge of the Cambrian rose the crystalline rocks from which every trace of organic existence had been erased.

That here, on the Wenlock Edge of time, a young American, seeking only frivolous amusement, should find a legitimate parentage as modern as though just caught in the Severn below, astonished him as much as though he had found Darwin himself. In the scale of evolution, one vertebrate was as good as another. For anything he, or any one else, knew, nine hundred and ninety-nine parts of evolution out of a thousand lay behind or below the *Pteraspis*. To an American in search of a father, it mattered nothing whether the father breathed through lungs, or walked on fins, or on feet. Evolution of mind was altogether another matter and belonged to another science, but whether one traced descent from the shark or the wolf was immaterial even in morals. This matter had been discussed for ages without scientific result. La Fontaine and other fabulists maintained that the wolf, even in morals, stood higher than man; and in view of the late civil war, Adams had doubts of his own on the facts of moral evolution: —

> "Tout bien considéré, je te soutiens en somme,
>   Que scélérat pour scélérat,
>   Il vaut mieux être un loup qu'un homme."

It might well be! At all events, it did not enter into the problem of *Pteraspis*, for it was quite certain that no complete proof of Natural Selection had occurred back to the

time of *Pteraspis*, and that before *Pteraspis* was eternal
void. No trace of any vertebrate had been found there;
only starfish, shell-fish, polyps, or trilobites whose kindly
descendants he had often bathed with, as a child on the
shores of Quincy Bay.

That *Pteraspis* and shark were his cousins, great-uncles,
or grandfathers, in no way troubled him, but that either or
both of them should be older than evolution itself seemed
to him perplexing; nor could he at all simplify the problem
by taking the sudden back-somersault into Quincy Bay in
search of the fascinating creature he had called a horseshoe, whose huge dome of shell and sharp spur of tail had
so alarmed him as a child. In Siluria, he understood, Sir
Roderick Murchison called the horseshoe a *Limulus*,
which helped nothing. Neither in the *Limulus* nor in the
Terebratula, nor in the *Cestracion Philippi*, any more than
in the *Pteraspis*, could one conceive an ancestor, but, if one
must, the choice mattered little. Cousinship had limits but
no one knew enough to fix them. When the vertebrate
vanished in Siluria, it disappeared instantly and forever.
Neither vertebra nor scale nor print reappeared, nor any
trace of ascent or descent to a lower type. The vertebrate
began in the Ludlow shale, as complete as Adams himself
— in some respects more so — at the top of the column of
organic evolution: and geology offered no sort of proof
that he had ever been anything else. Ponder over it as he
might, Adams could see nothing in the theory of Sir
Charles but pure inference, precisely like the inference
of Paley, that, if one found a watch, one inferred a maker.
He could detect no more evolution in life since the *Pteraspis* than he could detect it in architecture since the Abbey. All he could prove was change. Coal-power alone
asserted evolution — of power — and only by violence
could be forced to assert selection of type.

All this seemed trivial to the true Darwinian, and to Sir

Charles it was mere defect in the geological record. Sir Charles labored only to heap up the evidences of evolution; to cumulate them till the mass became irresistible. With that purpose, Adams gladly studied and tried to help Sir Charles, but, behind the lesson of the day, he was conscious that, in geology as in theology, he could prove only Evolution that did not evolve; Uniformity that was not uniform; and Selection that did not select. To other Darwinians — except Darwin — Natural Selection seemed a dogma to be put in the place of the Athanasian creed; it was a form of religious hope; a promise of ultimate perfection. Adams wished no better; he warmly sympathized in the object; but when he came to ask himself what he truly thought, he felt that he had no Faith; that whenever the next new hobby should be brought out, he should surely drop off from Darwinism like a monkey from a perch; that the idea of one Form, Law, Order, or Sequence had no more value for him than the idea of none; that what he valued most was Motion, and that what attracted his mind was Change.

Psychology was to him a new study, and a dark corner of education. As he lay on Wenlock Edge, with the sheep nibbling the grass close about him as they or their betters had nibbled the grass — or whatever there was to nibble — in the Silurian kingdom of Pteraspis, he seemed to have fallen on an evolution far more wonderful than that of fishes. He did not like it; he could not account for it; and he determined to stop it. Never since the days of his *Limulus* ancestry had any of his ascendants thought thus. Their modes of thought might be many, but their thought was one. Out of his millions of millions of ancestors, back to the Cambrian mollusks, every one had probably lived and died in the illusion of Truths which did not amuse him, and which had never changed. Henry Adams was the first in an infinite series to discover and admit to himself that he really did not care whether truth was, or was not, true. He did not even care that it should be proved true, unless the process were new and amusing. He was a Darwinian for fun.

From the beginning of history, this attitude had been branded as criminal — worse than crime — sacrilege! Society punished it ferociously and justly, in self-defence. Mr. Adams, the father, looked on it as moral weakness; it annoyed him; but it did not annoy him nearly so much as it annoyed his son, who had no need to learn from Hamlet the fatal effect of the pale cast of thought on enterprises great or small. He had no notion of letting the currents of his action be turned awry by this form of conscience. To him, the current of his time was to be his current, lead where it might. He put psychology under lock and key; he insisted on maintaining his absolute standards; on aiming at ultimate Unity. The mania for handling all the sides of every question, looking into every window, and opening every door, was, as Bluebeard judiciously pointed out to his wives, fatal to their practical usefulness in society. One could not stop to chase doubts as though they were rabbits. One had no time to paint and putty the surface of Law, even though it were cracked and rotten. For the young men whose lives were cast in the generation between 1867 and 1900, Law should be Evolution from lower to higher, aggregation of the atom in the mass, concentration of multiplicity in unity, compulsion of anarchy in order; and he would force himself to follow wherever it led, though he should sacrifice five thousand millions more in money, and a million more lives.

As the path ultimately led, it sacrificed much more than this; but at the time, he thought the price he named a high one, and he could not foresee that science and society would desert him in paying it. He, at least, took his education as a Darwinian in good faith. The Church was gone, and Duty was dim, but Will should take its place, founded deeply in interest and law. This was the result of five or six years in England; a result so British as to be almost the equivalent of an Oxford degree.

Quite serious about it, he set to work at once. While confusing his ideas about geology to the apparent satisfaction of Sir Charles who left him his field-compass in token of it, Adams turned resolutely to business, and attacked the burning question of specie payments. His principles assured him that the honest way to resume payments was to restrict currency. He thought he might win a name among financiers and statesmen at home by showing how this task had been done by England, after the classical suspension of 1797–1821. Setting himself to the study of this perplexed period, he waded as well as he could through a morass of volumes, pamphlets, and debates, until he learned to his confusion that the Bank of England itself and all the best British financial writers held that restriction was a fatal mistake, and that the best treatment of a debased currency was to let it alone, as the Bank had in fact done. Time and patience were the remedies.

The shock of this discovery to his financial principles was serious; much more serious than the shock of the *Terebratula* and *Pteraspis* to his principles of geology. A mistake about Evolution was not fatal; a mistake about specie payments would destroy forever the last hope of employment in State Street. Six months of patient labor would be thrown away if he did not publish, and with it his whole scheme of making himself a position as a practical man-of-business. If he did publish, how could he tell virtuous bankers in State Street that moral and absolute principles of abstract truth, such as theirs, had nothing to do with the matter, and that they had better let it alone?

Geologists, naturally a humble and helpless class, might not revenge impertinences offered to their science; but capitalists never forgot or forgave.

With labor and caution he made one long article on British Finance in 1816, and another on the Bank Restriction of 1797–1821, and, doing both up in one package, he sent it to the *North American* for choice. He knew that two heavy, technical, financial studies thus thrown at an editor's head, would probably return to crush the author; but the audacity of youth is more sympathetic — when successful — than his ignorance. The editor accepted both.

When the post brought his letter, Adams looked at it as though he were a debtor who had begged for an extension. He read it with as much relief as the debtor, if it had brought him the loan. The letter gave the new writer literary rank. Henceforward he had the freedom of the press. These articles, following those on Pocahontas and Lyell, enrolled him on the permanent staff of the *North American Review*. Precisely what this rank was worth, no one could say; but, for fifty years the *North American Review* had been the stage coach which carried literary Bostonians to such distinction as they had achieved. Few writers had ideas which warranted thirty pages of development, but for such as thought they had, the *Review* alone offered space. An article was a small volume which required at least three months' work, and was paid, at best, five dollars a page. Not many men even in England or France could write a good thirty-page article, and practically no one in America read them; but a few score of people, mostly in search of items to steal, ran over the pages to extract an idea or a fact, which was a sort of wild game — a blue-fish or a teal — worth anywhere from fifty cents to five dollars. Newspaper writers had their eye on quarterly pickings. The circulation of the *Review* had never exceeded three or four hundred copies, and the *Review* had never paid its reasonable expenses. Yet it stood at the head of American literary periodicals; it was a source of suggestion to cheaper workers; it reached far into societies that never knew its existence; it was an organ worth playing on; and, in the fancy of Henry Adams, it led, in some indistinct future, to playing on a New York daily newspaper.

With the editor's letter under his eyes, Adams asked himself what better he could have done. On the whole, considering his helplessness, he thought he had done as well as his neighbors. No one could yet guess which of his contemporaries was most likely to play a part in the great world. A shrewd prophet in Wall Street might perhaps have set a mark on Pierpont Morgan, but hardly on the Rockefellers or William C. Whitney or Whitelaw Reid. No one would have picked out William McKinley or John Hay or Mark Hanna for great statesmen. Boston was ignorant of the careers in store for Alexander Agassiz and Henry Higginson. Phillips Brooks was unknown; Henry James was unheard; Howells was new; Richardson and La Farge were struggling for a start. Out of any score of names and reputations that should reach beyond the century, the thirty-years-old who were starting in the year 1867 could show none that was so far in advance as to warrant odds in its favor. The army men had for the most part fallen to the ranks. Had Adams foreseen the future exactly as it came, he would have been no wiser, and could have chosen no better path.

Thus it turned out that the last year in England was the pleasantest. He was already old in society, and belonged to the Silurian horizon. The Prince of Wales had come. Mr. Disraeli, Lord Stanley, and the future Lord Salisbury had thrown into the background the memories of Palmerston and Russell. Europe was moving rapidly, and the conduct of England during the American Civil War was the last thing that London liked to recall. The revolution since

1861 was nearly complete, and, for the first time in history, the American felt himself almost as strong as an Englishman. He had thirty years to wait before he should feel himself stronger. Meanwhile even a private secretary could afford to be happy. His old education was finished; his new one was not begun; he still loitered a year, feeling himself near the end of a very long, anxious, tempestuous, successful voyage, with another to follow, and a summer sea between.

He made what use he could of it. In February, 1868, he was back in Rome with his friend Milnes Gaskell. For another season he wandered on horseback over the campagna or on foot through the Rome of the middle ages, and sat once more on the steps of Ara Cœli, as had become with him almost a superstition, like the waters of the fountain of Trevi. Rome was still tragic and solemn as ever, with its mediæval society, artistic, literary, and clerical, taking itself as seriously as in the days of Byron and Shelley. The long ten years of accidental education had changed nothing for him there. He knew no more in 1868 than in 1858. He had learned nothing whatever that made Rome more intelligible to him, or made life easier to handle. The case was no better when he got back to London and went through his last season. London had become his vice. He loved his haunts, his houses, his habits, and even his hansom cabs. He loved growling like an Englishman, and going into society where he knew not a face, and cared not a straw. He lived deep into the lives and loves and disappointments of his friends. When at last he found himself back again at Liverpool, his heart wrenched by the act of parting, he moved mechanically, unstrung, but he had no more acquired education than when he first trod the steps of the Adelphi Hotel in November, 1858. He could see only one great change, and this was wholly in years. Eaton Hall no longer impressed his imagination;

even the architecture of Chester roused but a sleepy interest; he felt no sensation whatever in the atmosphere of the British peerage, but mainly an habitual dislike to most of the people who frequented their country houses; he had become English to the point of sharing their petty social divisions, their dislikes and prejudices against each other; he took England no longer with the awe of American youth, but with the habit of an old and rather worn suit of clothes. As far as he knew, this was all that Englishmen meant by social education, but in any case it was all the education he had gained from seven years in London.